Organizing
the
School
Library

A Canadian
Handbook

To   Doris Pauline Fennell

Foreword

The increasing use of modern technology is streamlining such library operations as acquisitions, cataloguing, circulation, and information retrieval. School librarians can no longer afford to work in comparative isolation from each other and from the larger library world. They must keep up with current practices in cataloguing and information retrieval so that they may make full use of services available through library networks and commercial firms that will assist with the technical and organizational aspects of providing library services.

For some time I have been concerned that there is no comprehensive up-to-date handbook available in Canada that would clearly define the changes that are taking place in librarianship and provide school librarians with both the background knowledge necessary to cope with these changes and with references to appropriate sources for a more in-depth study of these topics. I am, therefore, very pleased to see the completion of *Organizing the School Library: A Canadian Handbook*, especially at this time when the new rules for cataloguing print and non-book library materials are being implemented.

School librarians are no doubt facing a decade in which more will be expected of them in terms of involvement in planning and implementing school programs. At the same time, schools are faced with limited resources in both materials and staff. *Organizing the School Library: A Canadian Handbook* should prove of great benefit to busy school librarians and make it possible for them to organize their materials in such a way that they may take full advantage of the networks and services available. It is only in this way that school libraries can meet the challenges and demands of the 1980's as vital components of the total library world.

Doris Pauline Fennell

Education Officer,
Ontario Ministry of Education

President,
Canadian School Library
Association, 1979-80

Preface

The past two years have seen a great change in bibliographic standards and the new standards are beginning to be reflected in the work of the national libraries and commercial cataloguers, as well as in the original cataloguing done in up-to-date school libraries. There have been new tools and new rules in the fields of subject headings, classification, filing, and above all, in the basic guide to cataloguing, the *Anglo-American Cataloguing Rules*. There have also been evolutionary changes of importance to the school library in the areas of acquisitions and commercial cataloguing, in the treatment of French materials and in computerization.

We confidently offer this textbook to the school media specialist who is facing this time of transition, expecting that, as with any library tool, the user will revise it with handwritten annotations as prompted by experience and the onrush of events.

We school librarians realize more and more the advantages of tuning in to the larger library world. In cataloguing particularly, we have a great opportunity for saving time and improving service through the knowledge of how modern cataloguing networks operate and what their standards are. Today, cataloguing data is available from many sources, ready to be tapped by the aware librarian. In the small number of cases where original cataloguing is called for, it should be done in conformity with the newest standards.

Antecedents and Origins of This Work. In introducing this new book, we cannot claim that Canadian school librarians have heretofore been totally lacking in handbooks on school library organization. In many provinces, there have been useful manuals produced by departments of education, by institutions for teacher education, and by professional groups.

There are two such books with which this work has a connection, namely, *Library Handbook for Elementary Schools in Ontario*, written by Doris Pauline Fennell for the Ontario Department of Education (1967), and *Cataloguing for School Libraries*, by Margaret B. Scott and Doris P. Fennell (Pergamon of Canada, 1970).

After the lamented death of Miss Scott, her collaborator, Mrs. Fennell initiated a plan of revision and expansion of their joint work, determining that it should include, besides cataloguing, some topics from the *Library Handbook for Elementary School Libraries in Ontario*, such as circulation, and some new topics, such as acquisitions, to make it a more comprehensive guide for school library organization. She recruited the present authors to assist her and collaborated on the first draft; she is, therefore, responsible for the very existence of and, to a considerable extent, the subjects treated in, this book.

Primary Sources of This Work. Despite its admitted connection to previous works, this one is entirely new, and had to be, because the primary sources upon which it is based are all new—either totally revised, like *AACR*, or, in the case of old standbys like *DDC* and *Sears*, sufficiently revised to make previous commentaries obsolete.

The principal sources are:

ALA Filing Rules, draft edition (American Library Association, 1979: Chicago)

ALA Rules for Filing Catalog Cards, 2nd ed., edited by Pauline A. Seely (American Library Association, 1968: Chicago)

ALA Rules for Filing Catalog Cards, 2nd ed. abr., edited by Pauline A. Seely (American Library Association, 1968: Chicago)

Abridged Dewey Decimal Classification and Relative Index, 11th ed. (Forest Press, 1979: Albany, N.Y.)

Anglo-American Cataloguing Rules, 2nd ed., edited by Michael Gorman and Paul W. Winkler (American Library Association, 1978: Chicago; Canadian Library Association, 1978: Ottawa)

Canadian Subject Headings (National Library of Canada, 1979: Ottawa)

Dewey Decimal Classification and Relative Index, 19th ed. (Forest Press, 1979: Albany, N.Y.)

Haycock, Ken, and Lynne Isberg, *Sears List of Subject Headings, Canadian Companion* (H.W. Wilson, 1978: New York)

Sears List of Subject Headings, 11th ed., edited by Barbara M. Westby (H.W. Wilson, 1977: New York)

Weihs, Jean, with Shirley Lewis and Janet Macdonald, *Nonbook Materials: The Organization of Integrated Collections,* 2nd ed. (Canadian Library Association, 1979: Ottawa)

In addition to the above sources, there are many other works referred to throughout this book. These references are footnoted and cited in full at the conclusion of the appropriate chapter. General reference sources concerning cataloguing of French materials which apply mainly to Chapter XI are, for the reader's convenience, grouped at the end of that chapter.

This Work as a Reference Book on Technical Services for School Libraries.

In the following pages we hope that we have mentioned all the tools, terms and concepts in the field of technical services that a school librarian is likely to need information on. We believe we have treated each work or idea in the appropriate depth in the context of a book for school librarians.

As with any reference book, the user may find that some of the contents are beyond what is needed in everyday work. We have preferred to err on the side of inclusiveness, ensuring that for cataloguing purposes this work will not be considered superficial. All the same, compared to the primary sources, it is not the last word in profundity.

In depth of treatment, Chapters I, IX and X are not meant to be comprehensive; in places they show only one acceptable or proven procedure out of many possible ones. Chapters III, IV and VIII, on the other hand, go into considerable detail to provide rules and examples covering nearly any cataloguing and filing problems that may be encountered in a school. The justification for the different emphasis in these latter three chapters is that the rules upon which they are based have been revised so recently that they are not yet well known or accessible to many school librarians. In any case, many school librarians may be more inclined to choose what they need from a secondary source like the present work, rather than go to the primary sources.

Two chapters, V and VI, are intended as introductions to their respective subjects, subject headings and classification. The advice in those two chapters will not take the school librarian very far without the use and study of the basic texts, *DDC* and *Sears.*

Timeliness and Urgency. The years 1978 and 1979 saw the launching or the revision of more basic tools in cataloguing than any other two years we can think of. The next few years will see the implementation of the new edition of *AACR* and *DDC* by the national libraries and the processors who follow their lead. This is, therefore, a time when school librarians have to relearn cataloguing to some extent. While this book will be helpful to school librarians seeking current information on all aspects of technical services, we realize that the last word will never be said, and that obsolescence will creep in even while we are awaiting the publication of our writings.

The interpretation of some of the rules in *AACR2* and the likely implementation of them are in a state of flux at our time of writing. *AACR2* shows options, among which the choices of the major interpreters, national libraries and card catalogue suppliers are not yet known. It is apparent that the Library of Congress and the National Library of Canada will disregard some of the new rules or delay their implementation. Those school librarians who have the time and inclination to keep abreast of the decisions and deliberations may find them in the pages of the *Cataloguing Service Bulletin* (Library of Congress: Washington), and the *National Library News/Nouvelles de la bibliothèque nationale* (National Library of Canada: Ottawa), which provide the latest word in an ever-changing field.

We did not feel that we should wait until more of the smoke had cleared, but should come out with the book while the information is fresh. The urge to be timely is our excuse for weaknesses that we think we could have overcome given "world enough and time."

Intended Audience. This work will prove useful to all levels of school librarians. Beginners may use it for daily reference in the running of their libraries. The experienced may sample it to update themselves on trends, rules and terminology. Isolated school librarians may use it as an authority and reference, perhaps to reinforce their convictions in adverse or indifferent circumstances. Librarians in small public and special libraries will likely find that it meets most of their needs. The contents and examples are slanted to the Canadian user, but not to an extent which would disqualify the book for use outside Canada. Even those who depend entirely on centralized or commercial cataloguing could profit by finding here an explanation of the changes and usages which purchased cards embody.

Terminology. We have used the same terminology as our primary sources, in other words, the standard terminology of the library profession. Although we have tried to make each term clear in its context, we are also supplying a glossary. With a few frequently repeated terms, we are using the traditional, brief term in preference to the current standard one, for example, "library" and "librarian" rather than their longer modern synonyms, though we grant that the latter may sometimes be more accurate.

Acknowledgements

Although many, many persons gave us advice, encouragement and assistance, we will mention by name only the few whose support was most outstandingly timely, persistent or useful:

W.J. Oatway, Ministry of Education, Sudbury, for assistance in launching the project.

Shirley Lewis, Bramalea Public Library, for advice on our manuscript and trends in non-book cataloguing.

Jean Henderson, Teacher of Cataloguing, Elementary School Librarians' Summer Course, Toronto, 1979, for testing and criticizing Chapters V and VI.

Elizabeth Bream, Teacher-Librarian, L'Amoreaux C.I., Scarborough, Ontario, for her assistance in obtaining the photograph in Chapter IX.

Gerry Génier, Ottawa Board of Education, for comments on Chapter XI.

Jim Whalen, Public Archives of Canada, Ottawa, for editing bibliographical citations and other references.

Tom Delsey, Assistant Director (Standards), National Library of Canada, for advice on Chapter VIII, and interpretations of *AACR2*.

David Balatti, Chief, Subject Analysis Division, National Library of Canada, for advice on Chapters V and VI.

Clarisse Cardin, Chief, Office of Bibliographic Standards, National Library of Canada, for interpretations of and advance information on *AACR2*.

We gratefully acknowledge permission to include in our text the material from the sources specified:

La centrale des bibliothèques, for catalogue cards in French.

Hurtig Publishers, for Fig. 2:5.

McGraw-Hill Ryerson Limited, for Fig. 1:1.

Sears List of Subject Headings Copyright © 1977 by The H.W. Wilson Company. Material reproduced by permission of the publisher.

Sears List of Subject Headings, Canadian Companion, Copyright © 1978 by Ken Haycock and Lynne Isberg. Material reproduced by permission of the publisher.

Some of the cataloguing examples and glossary terms are quoted from *Anglo-American Cataloguing Rules*, Second Edition, by permission of the publishers and copyright holders, the American Library Association, the Canadian Library Association and the Library Association.

The *DDC* numbers and some of our glossary terms are reprinted from the unabridged 19th and Abridged 11th editions (1979) of the *DEWEY Decimal Classification and Relative Index*, by permission of Forest Press Division, Lake Placid Education Foundation, owner of copyright.

Nonbook Materials: The Organization of Integrated Collections, second edition, as one of the earliest implementations of *AACR2*, influenced the style of our examples. It also provided a definition of the term "kit" which we have quoted by permission of the author, Jean Weihs, and the publisher, the Canadian Library Association.

The section on PRECIS is reprinted, with minor editing, as graciously contributed by Audrey Taylor, Teacher-Librarian and Co-Principal Investigator, PRECIS Project, Aurora H.S., Aurora, Ont.

Chapter XI has appeared in a slightly different form in *Moccasin Telegraph*, published by the Canadian School Library Association.

Contents

Foreword vii
Preface ix
Acknowledgements xiii

I Acquisition of Library Materials
   Contents 1
   Introduction 2
   Starting a Collection 2
   Adding to the Collection 3
   Choosing Among Dealers 6
   Buying Canadian and "Buying Around" 9
   Centralized vs. Decentralized Ordering 9
   Frequency of Ordering 10
   Year-End Procedures 10
   Formats and Types of Orders 11
   Encumbering the Budget 13
   Paying Invoices 13
   Special Cases 15
   Footnotes 20

II Cataloguing Aids and Services
    Contents 23
    Alternatives to Original Cataloguing 24
    Commercial Cataloguing 24
    Cataloguing in Publication (CIP) 30
    MAchine-Readable Cataloguing (MARC) and CAN/MARC 31
    Derived Cataloguing 32
    Footnotes 32

III Main Entry Headings
     Contents 33
     Introduction 35
     Meaning of the Term "Author" 36
     Determining the Main Access Point for Works of Personal Authors and
        Corporate Bodies 37
     Choosing Headings for Persons 45
     Choosing Headings for Corporate Bodies 53
     Choosing Headings for Subordinate and Related Bodies 56
     Choosing Headings for Government Bodies and Officials 58

Main Entry Under Title 62
Uniform Titles 63
Footnotes 76

IV   Description of the Work
Contents 77
Introduction 79
Title and Statement of Responsibility Area 82
Edition Area 89
Material (or Type of Publication) Specific Details Area 90
Publication, Distribution, Etc., Area 93
Physical Description Area 97
Series Area 114
Note Area 117
Standard Number and Terms of Availability Area 119
Facsimiles, Photocopies and Other Reproductions 120
Footnotes 121

V   Subject Headings
Contents 123
Determining the Subject(s) of an Item 124
Expressing the Subject of an Item 124
Features of *Sears List of Subject Headings* and *Canadian Companion*   127
Headings Omitted From *Sears* 129
Subdividing Headings From *Sears* 130
General vs. Specific Subject Headings 133
Subject Headings for Biography 133
Subject Analytics 133
Recording Additions to and Variations From *Sears* and *Canadian
   Companion* 134
Use of *Sears* and *Canadian Companion* by the Public 135
Adapting to New Editions of *Sears* 135
Footnotes 135

VI   Classification
Contents 137
Introduction 138
Dewey Decimal Classification System 138
Relationship Between Classification and Subject Headings 140
Relationship Between Classification and Literary Form 140
Classifying an Item by *DDC* 140
Expansion of the Abridged *DDC* 142
Abbreviations of Numbers in *DDC* 142
Call Number 143
Special Subjects and Forms 147
Adapting to a New Edition of *DDC* 150
Library of Congress Classification 151
Footnotes 151

VII   Completing the Card Set
Contents 153
Card Set 154
Main Entry Card 154
Shelf-List Card 157
Added Entry Cards 162
Extension Cards 163
Typewriters and Type Styles 164
Sample Cards 166

VIII   Bibliographic Files
Contents 179
Card Catalogue 181
Common Qualities of Filing Rules 182
Rules Allowing for Hierarchy and Filer's Decisions 182
Possibilities Allowed in Manual Filing 191
Programmable, Non-Hierarchical Filing Rules 191
Choosing a Filing Code 196
References 196
Other Aids for the User 201
Filing the Shelf List 201
Keeping the Card Catalogue Up to Date 202
Other Library Catalogue Formats 203
Library Networks and Data Bases 205
Footnotes 205

IX   Processing and Shelving the Collection
Contents 207
Processing Print Materials 208
Processing Non-Book Materials 212
Preparing AV Hardware for Use 217
Considering Integration vs. Separation 218
Shelving of the Materials 220
Aids to Self-Orientation 225
Footnotes 226

X   Circulation and Upkeep
Contents 227
Introduction 228
Date Due Cards 228
Circulation Routines 228
Renewals 232
Loan Period 232
Retrieval of Library Materials 233
Reserved Items 233
Machine and Computerized Charging 234
Inventory 235

Weeding 236
Repair and Rebinding 237

XI   French Usage
    Contents 239
    Introduction 240
    Capitalization 240
    Hyphenation 243
    Abbreviation 243
    Names of Publishers, Distributors, Etc. 244
    Filing 245
    Footnotes 247
    General Reference Sources 247

Glossary 249
Abbreviations 257
Index 259

Contents I

Acquisition of Library Materials

Introduction 2
Starting a Collection 2
Adding to the Collection 3
    Selection Tools 3
    Users' Requests 4
    "Hands-On" Selection 4
    Commercial Promotion 5
    Non-Evaluative Bibliographies 5
    Files of Selections 6
Choosing Among Dealers 6
    Local Bookstores 6
    Publishers and Producers 6
    Jobbers 6
Buying Canadian and "Buying Around" 9
Centralized vs. Decentralized Ordering 9
Frequency of Ordering 10
Year-End Procedures 10
Formats and Types of Orders 11
    Multiple-Copy Order Forms 11
    Check-Lists or Lists Made by the Library 12
    Standing Orders 13
    Blanket Orders 13
Encumbering the Budget 13
Paying Invoices 13
    Purchase Orders 13
    Other Kinds of Orders 14
Special Cases 15
    Paperbacks 15
    Remainders 16
    Government Publications 16
    AV Items 16
    Free and Inexpensive Materials 17
    Periodicals 17
    Services 19
Footnotes 20

Chapter I

Acquisition of Library Materials

INTRODUCTION

Acquisition is part of the library activity known as technical services, which also includes cataloguing and processing. (See Chapters II to XI.)

Acquisition includes:

- the selection of materials
- searching bibliographic tools for full ordering data
- comparing the selections with the library catalogue and with the on-order file to forestall unwanted duplication
- establishing relations with suppliers so as to get the best service
- establishing good business procedures to account for budgeted funds.

The subject of selection is a book in itself. Although a few general principles of selection appear below, it is recommended that a more specialized book be consulted for detailed advice on how to select materials genre by genre and medium by medium.

Following selection, the library's principal aims in acquisition are: First, to obtain all the items ordered, an aim whose fulfilment depends partly on the care with which the orders are expressed and on the choice of suppliers, and, second, to fill the orders at the lowest cost. Where the second aim conflicts with the first, prefer service and fulfilment of orders to economy. There is, in fact, no economy where there is a low rate of fulfilment and much reordering to do. The time wasted in paperwork and the delay in serving customers are hidden costs.

STARTING A COLLECTION

For a new school, a basic collection should be acquired and organized before opening day. Either a school librarian may be appointed early enough to see that this is accomplished, or the centralized library service of the board can put a collection in place. Whoever is responsible should use basic book lists of an appropriate reading level and number of entries. (See below, "Selection Tools.") For example, a sound establishing collection of 5000 titles for a K-6 school could be chosen by using *Children's Catalog*,[1] *The Elementary School Library Collection: A Guide to Books and Other Media*,[2] and *Canadian Books for Young People/Livres canadiens pour la jeunesse*,[3] edited by Irma McDonough.

Expensive reference items such as encyclopaedia sets should not initially be bought all at once but should be acquired on a plan of phased acquisition over a period of years. Then the very best titles should be periodically replaced by new editions, for example, *World Book* perhaps every five years.

To start a library in an existing school, centralize books of suitable quality and condition from among those already in the school, using basic selection tools to aid your judgment. Order as many new books as the budget allows up to the number necessary to support the curriculum and to fill in weak areas of the collection.

ADDING TO THE COLLECTION

With the aims of supporting the curriculum, encouraging reading and practising thrift, the library should base selection upon:

Selection Tools

BASIC BIBLIOGRAPHIES IN BOOK FORM

These, which include some books published by H.W. Wilson, Bowker, University of Toronto Press and Peter Martin Associates, and by library and education associations like ALA and NCTE, are bibliographies that list selected titles from among the offerings of many publishers. They are the primary tools of acquisition, e.g., *Canadian Selection: Books and Periodicals for Libraries*,[4] by Edith Jarvi *et al.*, and *After Survival: A Teacher's Guide to Canadian Resources*,[5] by Paul Robinson.

REVIEWING TOOLS

For current publishing select from:

Library periodicals with evaluative annotations. The most useful are *Booklist*,[6] *School Library Journal*,[7] *Previews*,[8] *Canadian Materials*,[9] *In Review*,[10] and *Science Books and Films.*[11]

Literary magazines. Larger libraries use periodicals such as *Horn Book Magazine*,[12] *Canadian Children's Literature*,[13] *New York Times Book Review*,[14] *The School Librarian*,[15] and *Saturday Review.*[16]

Periodicals with occasional reviews. These include newspapers, teachers' periodicals, and subject periodicals, e.g., *Canadian Geographical Journal.*[17]

Users' Requests

In order to suit the library's service to the needs and preferences of the clientele and to give the customers a stake in the library through helping in collection-building, the librarian should be very sensitive to users' requests. When a request is by subject, the librarian may make selections, using the tools referred to above, or the customer may be encouraged to participate, using those same tools. Teachers whose selections by title may tend to come from a few publishers' catalogues can learn the advantages of using library tools. Students and teachers making requests should be directed, possibly by means of a form, towards giving the proper bibliographic information for ordering, though the librarian should not make it irksome to request an item. Titles that customers request should be given priority in the ordering and processing queue and routed to them when processed.

Notwithstanding a sincere aim of involving the user in selection, the librarian has to apportion the budget so that all school subjects are covered and so that the collection is as balanced as, in the librarian's judgment, it should be. Otherwise, aggressive or senior teachers, English teachers, or some other bloc may have undue influence, as often happens where collection-building is conducted in a decentralized or unprofessional way in a school.

When requests are contrary to the library's selection policy, the librarian should *consider* them anyway. In the case of a child asking for the occasional inexpensive item that is non-curricular, e.g., on golf or taxidermy, when the library has given such subjects low priority, it is probably worth making an exception for the sake of goodwill and the encouragement of reading. On the other hand, when users select in areas that the library does not want to build up, the librarian can point to a policy to avoid following the unwelcome suggestions. Such an assertion of the priorities of the library over those of the user may be necessary in the case of books on cults, pseudoscience, pop figures, or other marginal subjects, or with coffee-table and hobby books of high price and low relevance to the school.

"Hands-On" Selection

Locations for examination of material before purchase:

SCHOOL AND PUBLIC LIBRARIES

School and public libraries contain selections worth considering. Some, however, may prove to be out of print when you try to acquire them.

NON-CIRCULATING DISPLAY COLLECTIONS

These are often set up by boards of education.

BOOKSTORES AND WHOLESALERS' WAREHOUSES

Both bookstores and wholesalers' warehouses are good places for the librarian to browse and judge the appearance and, to some extent, the content of materials. As a way of exercising some personal judgment while quickly disposing of an end-of-the-year surplus, or of filling in a weak part of the collection, the shopping trip has something to recommend it, but cannot be advocated as the main method of acquisition.

The range and proportion of worthy titles in basic bibliographies and reviewing tools are greater than in a bookstore, and the reviewers and compilers whose opinions are reflected in the best selection tools tend to show more practiced and unhurried judgment than librarians throwing books into a shopping cart.

All the same, part-time librarians may have to save time by bypassing such stages in the acquisition process as regularly using the selection tools and keeping track of back orders and invoices; unqualified librarians may not even know that these stages exist. For such buyers, shopping has its place. To lessen the risk of buying unwanted duplicates, they can check the suppliers' current catalogues against their holdings before going out to shop. They can maintain a portable card file of items to ask for in the warehouse, so as to take advantage of users' requests and some previous research. Best of all, they can work from selection tools while shopping. (See also p. 15, "Paperbacks.")

Commercial Promotion

PUBLISHERS' ADVERTISEMENTS AND FLIERS

While these can be very informative and persuasive, the attention they focus on a new publication should usually be reinforced by a favourable review before a decision to purchase is made. Exceptions may be made for a very reliable author or important subject.

SALESMEN'S AND PUBLISHERS' DISPLAYS

Such displays have the desirable effect of bringing the library and publishing worlds closer together and of giving prominence to the publishers' latest offerings. Such exhibits are one of the features of library and educational conferences and professional development courses.

PUBLISHERS' CATALOGUES

These may be scanned for possible purchases. They should also be filed for reference, having value as a source of up-to-date prices, statements of publishers' discount policies, and annotations.

Non-Evaluative Bibliographies

These tell what is available and give ordering information:

BIBLIOGRAPHIES OF FORTHCOMING BOOKS

An example of bibliographies of books coming into print is *Quill & Quire*.[18] Note: *Quill & Quire* is a hybrid, containing some reviews.

NATIONAL BIBLIOGRAPHIES AND SIMILAR TOOLS

These include *Canadiana*,[19] *Books in Print*,[20] and *NICEM*[21] (National Information Centre for Educational Media).

SELECTIVE BIBLIOGRAPHIES AND MATERIALS LISTS

Other sources for further bibliographical references include books, public libraries, etc.

Files of Selections

Some titles are ordered immediately when chosen because there is money in the budget, and an immediate need for them. Other selections are noted, and slips are made for them, but the slips are marked or separately filed so that they will be recognizable as entries for second-choice items. The titles may be of the highest literary merit, but on a subject adequately represented in the library, or of less-than-top quality, though on a subject important in the school. In either case, the file can be reviewed if cancellations or reallocation of funds allow for more ordering than expected, or if an area of need is discovered and worthy publications have to be located and ordered quickly. (See also p. 12, "Filing in the On-Order File.")

CHOOSING AMONG DEALERS

Local Bookstores

Buying items from the stock of a store accessible to the librarian in person or by a local telephone call is the speediest way of getting them. Giving some business to local suppliers is a desirable gesture of community support. Bookstores, however, tend to provide only a limited number of the services that libraries expect. For instance, they do not usually offer top discount or processing. They usually do not have a comprehensive stock, including the slow-selling items that make up a part of the library's needs. While bookstores may attempt to procure whatever they do not stock when it is ordered, there is neither time nor price advantage to the library in letting them do so.

Publishers and Producers

Publishers and producers vary greatly as suppliers. Sometimes the publisher is the only source, for instance, H.W. Wilson, many associations, local publishers of books in small quantities, and many AV manufacturers. On the other hand, some publishers will not sell direct, or discourage orders by not giving the discounts that are available elsewhere. A few give top discounts, and services such as processing. On the average, publishers give quicker and more complete fulfilment of orders for their own books than jobbers do, but their discount is usually lower. When a jobber declares a book out of print, it may still be worth trying the publisher, who may have some copies left.

Jobbers

As a type of dealer, jobbers tend to provide the best combination of service, price and speedy fulfilment in the library business, because they have the most complete stock and the best-developed systems. By patronizing a good jobber, a library can reduce the number of business transactions it must make, with their attendant administrative costs. Since there are great variations among jobbers, the librarian, library consultant or purchasing agent should be looking for the best combination of the following services:

DISCOUNT

Typically, there are three degrees of discount:

None. When the publisher or producer gives 0 to 10% discount to a jobber, the library can expect no discount.

Short. The library can expect a 5 to 20% discount on textbooks and technical books.

Trade. The library can expect 20 to 40% off on bookstore-type books. Sometimes a premium may be charged, for instance, for finding an out-of-print or foreign book. Discount also varies according to the amount bought cumulatively; try to avoid having the jobber vary it according to the size of each order. A good jobber is consistent and predictable in passing on discounts in proportion as received.

A high discount with many cancellations is characteristic of a jobber who favours high-discount, easy-to-obtain items at the expense of service and a high rate of fulfilment of orders. Many discounters in Canada in recent years have gone out of business after winning contracts by underbidding the competition, leaving their client libraries with unspent money and no books.

Sometimes a better discount can be negotiated if a library or system can demonstrate that it pays its bills promptly, buys mostly trade books, buys multiple copies or makes few complaints.

FULFILMENT OF ORDERS

Unfilled orders deprive the users of needed material and necessitate costly reordering. The librarian needs to learn what items it is unreasonable to expect the jobber to supply and order these separately.

SPEED OF RESPONSE

Jobbers with a large proportion of processed books in stock can best help the library to minimize the time between choosing an item and providing it on the shelf.

CATALOGUING AND PROCESSING

This should be carried out according to the library's code and tradition. (See also p. 24, "Selecting a Commercial Cataloguing Service.") Jobbers should heed specifications like "Process one copy only"; "Do not cover paperbacks"; "Library binding where available."

OTHER SERVICES

Approval and return privileges. Experienced librarians do not avail themselves of these very often, except for items that call for preview. (See p. 16, "AV Items.")

Provision of useful catalogues, bibliographies and order forms. Some jobbers excel in the buying guides they give away, which are especially welcome if they are objective, annotated, and multi-media.

Rectification of errors. There should be a quick and guaranteed procedure for handling complaints.

Reporting. Standard codes should be used in invoicing, shipping, and any other notifications.

McGRAW-HILL RYERSON LIMITED

330 PROGRESS AVENUE, SCARBOROUGH, ONTARIO M1P 2Z5
TELEX 02-21661
416-293-1911

D.U.N.S. 20-151-6572

SOLD TO / VENDU À
MINISTRY OF EDUCATION
A.D. VENUGOPAL, SUPT. OF BUS.
1349 LASALLE BLVD.
SUDBURY, ONT.   P3A 1Z5

SHIP TO / EXPÉDIER À

CUSTOMER ORDER NO. NUMÉRO DE COMMANDE DU CLIENT	CUSTOMER ORDER NO. NUMÉRO DE COMMANDE DU CLIENT	NUMÉRO DE COMMANDE DU CLIENT
3 26 79	3 26 79	PAGE 1

BACK ORDER REPORT - THIS IS NOT AN INVOICE.
AVIS DE COMMANDE EN SOUFFRANCE - CECI N'EST PAS UNE FACTURE

QUANT.	ISBN	AUTHOR AND TITLE · AUTEUR ET TITRE	DATE MO·MOIS DAY·JOUR YEAR·ANNÉE	CUSTOMER NUMBER	CODE	EXPECTED AVAILABLE DATE DATE DE DISPONIBILITÉ ATTENDUE
1	0705936-0	SOLOMON COMPLETE ASIAN COOKBOOK	APR 03/79	00000 000 0 NO.	08	
	0757219			6 19.25035	CODE DE COMM EN SOUFF OS	MAY 13/79

BACK ORDER CODES

OS · OUT OF STOCK, WILL BE SHIPPED WHEN AVAILABLE
IP · IN PRESS, WILL SHIP WHEN PUBLISHED.
NOP · NOT OUR PUBLICATION.
NCR · NO CANADIAN RIGHTS.
UID · UNABLE TO IDENTIFY · ORDER CANCELLED.
OSI · OUT OF STOCK INDEFINITELY · ORDER CANCELLED
NYC · NEXT YEAR'S COPYRIGHT · WILL SHIP NEXT YEAR
NFR · NO FOREIGN RIGHTS
RFR · RESTRICTED FOREIGN RIGHTS
OP · OUT OF PRINT
PC · PUBLICATION CANCELLED
PD · PUBLICATION DELAYED · ORDER CANCELLED
SB · SUBSTITUTE IS AVAILABLE
RES · SALE RESTRICTED TO INSTRUCTORS

CODES DE COMMANDE EN SOUFFRANCE

OS · NON DISPONIBLE · SERA LIVRÉ QUAND DISPONIBLE.
IP · SOUS PRESSE · SERA EXPÉDIÉ APRÈS PUBLICATION.
NOP · PAS NOTRE PUBLICATION.
NCR · AUCUN DROIT CANADIEN.
UID · IMPOSSIBLE D'IDENTIFIER · COMMANDE ANNULÉE.
OSI · STOCK INDÉFINIMENT ÉPUISÉ · COMMANDE ANNULÉE.
NYC · COPYRIGHT DE L'ANNÉE PROCHAINE
NFR · SANS DROITS D'AUTEUR À L'ÉTRANGER
RFR · DROITS D'AUTEUR À L'ÉTRANGER LIMITÉS
OP · ÉDITION ÉPUISÉE
PC · PUBLICATION CONTREMANDÉE
PD · PUBLICATION DIFFÉRÉE · COMMANDE ANNULÉE.
SB · SUBSTITUT EN VENTE
RES · VENTE RESTREINTE AUX PROFESSEURS

NOTE !
EXPECTED AVAILABLE DATE IS OUR BEST ESTIMATE
OF AVAILABILITY, NOT A PROMISE OF DELIVERY.

AVIS !
DATE DE DISPONIBILITÉ ATTENDUE N'EST QUE NOTRE
ESTIMATION, ET NON PAS UNE PROMESSE DE LIVRAISON.

CUSTOMER'S COPY COPIE DU CLIENT

FORM NO. 82-100

Fig. 1:1   Publisher's or jobber's report

Not misusing "OP" (out of print). Some suppliers tend to take the easy way out by using "OP" when they could obtain the item with a little more time and effort.

Librarians may well patronize several jobbers so as to take advantage of the strengths of each. No one jobber is an ideal source of materials in all languages or for all levels of audience.

BUYING CANADIAN AND "BUYING AROUND"

Needless to say, one should buy in-print Canadian books in Canada and Canadian editions of Canadian books when they are also published elsewhere. There is some question about the propriety of buying remaindered foreign editions of in-print Canadian titles in Canadian bookstores.

There is much argument in Canada about the purchase of foreign books from other than Canadian sources, or "buying around," as the Canadian agents and jobbers call it. Foreign prices tend to be inflated by some Canadian agents who convert the foreign price to Canadian dollars in what often seems an arbitrary way and then add commissions. To their credit, they are saving the librarian the time and work of importing. Some of the agents earn the loyalty of the Canadian librarians by devoting some of the profits from their imports to the publication of marginal or money-losing Canadian titles.

On the other hand, some Canadian agents and jobbers are remiss in recognizing and stocking new foreign publications. Their lack of service drives more librarians into "buying around" than dissatisfaction over price. One should give the Canadian agents or jobbers as much of one's business as possible, balking only at unreasonable mark-ups and their repeated failure to supply items which they should be expected to import.

Use the *Canadian Publishers Directory*[22] and the monthly revision of it in *Quill & Quire* to determine what foreign publishers are represented in Canada and by whom. It is the guide to where to order if orders are being placed directly with publishers or agents of foreign publishers. On orders to Canadian jobbers, give the name of the original publisher, with the name of the agent shown parenthetically or omitted.

CENTRALIZED VS. DECENTRALIZED ORDERING

Where acquisition is centralized within a system, as in a board processing centre, there are advantages:

- More tools may be available than at the school level, including a master bibliographic record which, when built up, can serve both for acquisition and cataloguing.
- There may be more experienced leadership.
- There may be economies of mass production.

- There may be more reason to claim discounts for multiple copies and larger quantities.

Where acquisition is done at the school level, there are these advantages:

- There is economy in direct contact between each school and the supplier rather than in collating orders centrally and unpacking and rerouting books.
- There is more likelihood of speedy acquisition where there are fewer middlemen.

A school board can partly centralize acquisitions by having a resource staff who provide lists and displays, give advice and bibliographic information, and establish basic or model collections.

✓ FREQUENCY OF ORDERING

It is advantageous to phase acquisition around the calendar because:

- Many books will go out of print if not bought when first seen in the selection tools.
- Small publishers need a quick return on their inventory in order to stay in business and to publish more, which they cannot do if librarians do not buy new books promptly.
- It makes for better use of staff and for more security to have a phased intake resulting from frequent orders, rather than to get most of a year's shipments close together.
- Regular accessions add novelty and interest to the collection.
- Users' requests can be satisfied promptly.
- The librarian can take advantage of the interest in new books generated by TV, bookstore displays, ads and movies.

The librarian should have an arrangement that permits payment from petty cash or confirmation order so that the time of acquisition can be cut to a minimum for the small number of cases that justify utmost speed. A helpful jobber will heed book orders marked "Rush" and will handle and ship such orders the quickest, if not the cheapest, way.

YEAR-END PROCEDURES

As the budget year wanes, the librarian may take steps to prevent underspending because of cancellations, or overspending because of inflation and unexpectedly complete fulfilment of orders. A helpful jobber will observe a ceiling set by the buyer, and will also substitute from a list of second-choice items when out-of-stock first-choice items cannot be supplied. (See p. 6, "Files of Selections.")

The closer it is to the end of the budget year, the more one's business should go to the quickest supplier. The library can make it easier for the school or board's business department by ordering fewer items, and only such as are likely to be in stock, in the last month or two of the fiscal year. In some jurisdictions, arrangements may be made to carry over unspent funds from one year to supplement the budget in the next year, but usually not. If not, specify "No back orders" or "Delivery required by Nov. 30" on orders placed late. To deal with shorts at the end of the year, cancel and reorder in the new year, or leave on order and pay by petty cash or confirmation as received.

It is usual to specify a time for cancellation, either "No back orders," or 60, 90 or 120 days. At the end of the specified time, the supplier should have either supplied the item or reported on it.

FORMATS AND TYPES OF ORDERS

Multiple-Copy Order Forms

These are standard. They come with varying numbers of sheets. A library requires one copy for its on-order file and one to send to the dealer. Other copies may be required by the purchasing department or may be used to notify customers.

Fig. 1:2 Multiple-copy order form

FILLING IN THE FORM

If the multiple-copy forms are serially numbered, their numbers can serve as purchase order numbers corresponding to the entries on them.

The amount of data to be included on the form will vary. A librarian or technician should realize when abbreviations and omissions are allowable and when extra data, e.g., the address of a small or obscure publisher, must be added if the desired item is to be found by the dealer. If a clerk is to type the order form, the librarian should mark or annotate the selection tool, the review or the request form so that the right amount of data will be entered on the slip. A clerk may even have to be shown which space on the order form matches each area in the bibliographical record, e.g., which is the author and which is the publisher.

Some forms have a box for typing information in brief to show what person or review prompted the order, e.g., Q Q D 78 (*Quill & Quire*, Dec. 1978). Such data will subsequently help trace the source in cases of doubt or error.

Cataloguing instructions, e.g., "Do not process"; "Catalogue one copy only," may be typed on each form. In addition, a covering specification form, usually supplied by the processor, can be included with batches of orders. (See also p. 24, "Selecting a Commercial Cataloguing Service.")

The ISBN should be included. Most large dealers now arrange their stock by ISBN. Orders that include it are more quickly matched up with the stock and filled than orders that the dealer must first add the ISBN to.

Unless the number of orders to be sent at one time is very few, the dealer's copies may be sorted into batches such as:

Process and catalogue
Do not process
Paperbacks
Do not apply plastic jacket
Rush
Second-choice items (See also p. 6, "Files of Selections," and p. 10, "Year-End Procedures.")

The bottom slip from the multiple copies is on heavy stock. It is the library's copy for the on-order file. On it may be written special information, the publisher's reports, special instructions about the wishes of the person requesting the title, and reorder information. If catalogue cards are ordered separate from the book, and arrive before it, they may be filed, attached by an elastic to the on-order slip for safe keeping.

FILING IN THE ON-ORDER FILE

The on-order file is often sorted by main entry, but arrangement by title may be more convenient in a small library. The main entry may be difficult to determine from a review or request before receipt of the item, and the title *is* the main entry for many of those items that are the hardest to search. The title is less likely to be lost in the file than an author which, as a heading, may not be the same on the filed slip as on the entry being searched. More than one slip, cross-referenced, may be made for an item if it will facilitate searching and cut down on unwanted duplicates and slips astray in the on-order file.

NOTATIONS ON THE FORM

When the item arrives, write "received" on the on-order slip, and any accession data needed on the item. Then leave the slip in the file until the shelf-list card is filed in the shelf list to represent the item. Remove the on-order slip, which may be disposed of, or used as a notice that the item is available to be borrowed.

Check-Lists or Lists Made by the Library

These may be a supplement to order slips. They may be covered by multiple-copy order forms reading "Books (etc.) as per attached list" and filed in the on-order file.

Since items on lists are hard to keep track of individually, use lists only when careful checking from files is not necessary or possible:

- When the items are too inexpensive or ephemeral to justify filing records of them in the on-order file, or, eventually perhaps, in the library catalogue.
- When they are part of the founding collection of a library and therefore not likely to duplicate any existing holdings or orders.
- When they are distinct enough to be kept in mind as special cases not requiring filed records.
- When they are likely to be all in stock and shipped together without back orders or cancellations to complicate payment.

Standing Orders

To avoid having to remember and place individual orders for year-books and books being consecutively published in a series, the library may have a standing order with the jobber or publisher and thus receive the books automatically. The invoices may be covered by confirmation orders or petty cash.

Blanket Orders

A publisher or jobber may be empowered to supply items according to a library profile or general specification, rather than by title, e.g., all new Canadian children's books in paperback, or all publications of library organizations dealing with school libraries. Blanket-order arrangements usually permit returns for credit of unwanted items received.

ENCUMBERING THE BUDGET

Each order includes an estimate of cost which is added to a running total that is provisionally deducted from the amount of the library budget. The deduction is called an encumbrance. If an order is received, the exact cost is deducted in place of the estimate; if the order is cancelled wholly or in part, the budget is disencumbered to the extent of the estimated cost of the items cancelled. Many boards have the budgets and encumbrances computerized; they can automatically hold orders that threaten to push encumbrances beyond the budgeted amount and can let the library know its financial standing regularly or on request. Even if this record can be called upon, the library should keep its own in case of errors or uncertainties.

PAYING INVOICES

Purchase Orders

If, as is usual, invoices are sent to the board's business office, the library will send in the corresponding packing slips, signed, dated and marked "received." If the invoice is sent to the library it should be passed along, signed if it is the only enclosure with the shipment. If there is no packing slip, send a substitute such as the letterhead label of the parcel with a list of the contents and their purchase-order numbers, or whatever will verify the invoice.

Since the librarian needs to keep a tally of expenditures, to compare prices with quotations and estimates, and to copy them with the other accession data from the packing slip into the books and from there to the shelf-list cards, the prices ought to be readable on the packing slip, not obscured by dots. Otherwise, the librarian must wait for or secure a copy of the invoice to see what the prices were, before and after discount.

If each book is on a separate purchase-order slip, it should be possible to pay for books individually as received. Even if books are ordered by list and the order is only partly filled, it is better to pay for what has been received rather than hold the invoice for payment until all back orders are received, if ever. The business office should keep a file of paid invoices with a record of payment, such as a copy of its cheques or money orders. By such routines, the board should avoid non-payment, double payment, or paying for items ordered but not received or received but not ordered.

For wrong title supplied, too many copies, defective or damaged copies, establish a routine with the supplier for redress. Returns should be accompanied by a copy of the purchase order and invoice so that credit or replacement will follow. When the cost involved is trivial, the library might as well absorb the loss and reorder.

Estimates of the cost of handling a purchase order vary, but are always being revised upward and amount to many dollars. Where purchase orders are not required by board policy and not justified by the size of the order, payment may be made in one of the following ways.

Other Kinds of Orders

CONFIRMATION ORDERS

Confirmation orders are written to cover material received without a previous purchase order. There should be allowance for enough of these to cover purchases made by telephone, by letter, and personal shopping. Such orders allow flexibility in acquisitions so that urgently needed and ephemeral materials can be bought without the delay inherent in making purchase orders. By confirmations the library can also take advantage of unforeseen opportunities, for instance, when a teacher acquires books for the library at a sale or conference. Confirmations can be routinely used to cover the accession of items on standing order or items for which purchase orders were written that are no longer in effect because of the lapse of time.

Confirmation orders tend to cover a greater proportion of careless choices and duplications than purchase orders. They should not be written against the budget of the library to legitimize *faits accomplis* that are not in its best interest.

Subscription. Reference books, series and reprints are often available at a special price for payment in advance of publication or of regular sale. Since the amounts involved are often sizeable, purchase orders are usually necessary. (See also p. 17, "Periodicals.")

Deposit accounts. A requisition can be made for cash to be deposited with a supplier against future orders. Transactions with suppliers of pamphlets and government publications are often handled best by letter and prepayment, without purchase orders or invoices.

Money with order. Orders for inexpensive items are more cheaply and expeditiously handled by letter with a money order or cheque enclosed, than by purchase order and invoice or confirmation. If the amount, possibly including postage, is not known in advance, a blank cheque with a specified limit can even be enclosed.

Petty cash. This could be raised by the library or requisitioned, and used for small purchases, as mentioned just above.

SPECIAL CASES

Paperbacks

QUALITY PAPERBACKS

Order these like hardbound books.

NEWS-STAND PAPERBACKS

Acquisition of news-stand paperbacks requires varying strategies:

News-stand. Buy them at the local news-stand as they become available; since they tend to be ephemeral, there may not be another opportunity. Pay by confirmation order or petty cash.

Wholesaler. Patronize the local paperback wholesaler, who is usually also a magazine distributor. Most wholesalers have a permanent educational department where librarians and their helpers — teachers, students, technicians or volunteers — are welcome to browse. Additional selections may be made elsewhere in the warehouse, among the paperbacks destined for quick turnover in retail outlets, but this stock may be hard to browse without help from the wholesaler's staff.

Some wholesalers offer educational paperbacks in check-lists and in catalogues, facilitating mail orders and purchase orders.

Publisher. Order titles unavailable elsewhere from the publisher. Since the profit on paperbacks is low, the publishers usually give instructions on ways to make it worth their while to supply a title. They often require prepayment at list price plus a handling charge. If it is worth the trouble of ordering single titles, it is usually worth ordering several copies at once.

Book jobber. Send multiple-copy order forms for desired paperbacks to a jobber, if it is known to give good service on paperbacks as well as hardbacks. Do not, however, expect the same rate of fulfilment or discount as on hardbacks.

Remainders

These are usually found by serendipity rather than premeditation. Many bookstores, e.g., Coles, feature them, along with a similar class of book, the low-cost reprint. In subjects such as art and history, and genres such as fiction and biography, a librarian may get some good buys by watching for remainders.

The field of bargains is not completely unorganized. There *is* a publication, *Best Buys in Print*,[23] and some dealers who specialize in remainders have catalogues and fliers showing their current bargains, sometimes even available with catalogue cards.

Government Publications

These may be ordered from the catalogues and check-lists of the issuing bodies, which the library may sign up for or subscribe to if interested. The governments and agencies often expect the customer to have a deposit account or to make payment with order. Some government publications, of course, are free. There is often a stock number that must be quoted to ensure shipment of the right document.

There are no Canadian federal government bookstores; Canadian federal publications are sold in the larger cities by designated private bookstores. Federal publications may also be ordered direct from Supply and Services Canada. Free publications must usually be ordered direct from the federal issuing agency, e.g., department. There are a few provincial government bookstores in this country and some commercial bookstores that selectively handle provincial publications.

Many university and large public libraries are depositories for government publications, receiving them free in return for making them available for inspection by the public. The school librarian can do hands-on selection at such depository libraries.

Canadian federal publications are catalogued comprehensively in *Canadiana* and *Canadian Government Publications*[24] and listed selectively in some library periodicals, such as *Canadian Materials*. Provincial government publications are catalogued in *Canadiana* and in the check-lists and catalogues issued by the provinces.

American government publications, which are, overall, far too numerous to be kept up with by a school librarian, can be sampled by using the selective lists in *Wilson Library Bulletin*,[25] *Booklist*, *Selected U.S. Government Publications*,[26] and in many books which are guides to or bibliographies of these publications.

AV Items

Buy these, like books, after reading favourable reviews. Where reviews are lacking or unreliable and the cost forbids snap judgment, obtain them on approval for preview. For 16 mm film, which is the most costly medium, previewing is standard. On the other hand, phonograph records, which are at the other end of the cost scale and easy to find reviews of, are never previewed (auditioned). Their vulnerability also makes auditioning undesirable, so much so that no one should buy records from a supplier who permits auditioning.

Where the manufacturer's standard can be relied upon or the material must be chosen because it is all that is available on an important subject, buy without previewing, reserving the right to return the occasional item that is disappointing technically or artistically.

Free and Inexpensive Materials

These may be solicited by subject, e.g., travel posters from embassies, or by title, derived from tools such as the *Educators Guide Series*,[27] the *Vertical File Index*,[28] or *1001 Valuable Things You Can Get Free in Canada*,[29] by Harriet Hart Saalheimer. The orders can be prepared by volunteers, or by students for practice in letter-writing. Wherever appropriate, enclose self-addressed envelopes or labels, stamps or international postal coupons, or whatever may increase the rate of return on the mailing. To distinguish incoming mail containing free material from more urgent mail, specify a notation on the package such as "Attention: Free materials," or a code.

Materials may be obtained by exchange with neighbouring schools which need what you want to deaccession. The National Book Exchange, Ottawa, is a good source of discoveries and desiderata in periodicals and books, available for the cost of shipping.

Periodicals

Subscriptions should be undertaken after some deliberation. A subscription is a commitment to continuity and costs something to discontinue after the library has gone to the expense of setting up a Kardex record or periodical record card, and back file and has aroused an expectation in its customers.

There is always a place in the collection for non-subscription copies of magazines bought off the rack for their individual interest, as duplicates of subscription copies, or as trial copies bought before subscribing. Trial copies may also be solicited from the publishers.

Some subscriptions are placed individually, directly with the publisher, because that is the only way they are available, or because they are tentative and, therefore, are easier to cancel if they are on a separate purchase order.

It is most convenient to have the bulk of the library's subscriptions on one purchase order from one jobber, with synchronized dates of renewal. The jobber supplies a print-out for annual review several months in advance of renewal time and the library makes additions and deletions. Then the invoice is prepaid, though there may be subsequent adjustments to be invoiced or credited.

Some periodicals have an invariable date of renewal and cannot be synchronized; the jobber may invoice these separately or make some other arrangement between publisher and library. While it is seldom worth the

TITLE **Teacher**

FREQUENCY **Monthly**   DAY DUE

PUBLISHER OR AGENT **Macmillan Professional Magazines, Inc.**   SUBSCRIP. DATE **Jan.**

ADDRESS **77 Bedford St., Stamford, CT 06901**   NOS. PER VOL. **Sept. to May**

BOUND   VOLS. PER YEAR **9**

PREPARED   IN BINDERY   TITLE PAGE

INDEX

YEAR	SER.	VOL.	JAN.	FEB.	MAR.	APR.	MAY	JUNE	JULY	AUG.	SEPT.	OCT.	NOV.	DEC.	T.P.	I.
1972			✓	✓	✓		✓				✓	✓	✓	✓		
1973			✓	✓	✓	✓	✓				✓	✓	✓	✓		
1974			✓	✓	✓		✓				✓	✓	✓	✓		
1975			✓	✓	✓	✓	✓				✓	✓	✓	✓		
1976			✓	✓	✓	✓	✓				✓	✓	✓	✓		
1977			✓	✓	✓	✓	✓				✓	✓	✓	✓		
1978			✓	✓	✓	✓	✓				✓	✓	✓	✓		
1979			✓	✓	✓	✓	✓				✓	✓	✓	✓		

Continues: Grade teacher

INC.   TITLE

Teacher

JAN	FEB	MAR	APR	MAY	JUN	JUL	AUG	SEP	OCT	NOV	DEC
X	X	X	X	X				X	X	X	X

This magazine   Bimonthly

JAN	FEB	MAR	APR	MAY	JUN	JUL	AUG	SEP	OCT	NOV	DEC

Time   Weekly

JAN	FEB	MAR	APR	MAY	JUN	JUL	AUG	SEP	OCT	NOV	DEC

Today's education

JAN	FEB	MAR	APR	MAY	JUN	JUL	AUG	SEP	OCT	NOV	DEC
X	X	X	X	X				X	X	X	X

Today's health   Subscription discontinued

JAN	FEB	MAR	APR	MAY	JUN	JUL	AUG	SEP	OCT	NOV	DEC
X	X	X	X					X	X	X	X

Top of the news

JAN	FEB	MAR	APR	MAY	JUN	JUL	AUG	SEP	OCT	NOV	DEC
X					X					X	

Toronto life

JAN	FEB	MAR	APR	MAY	JUN	JUL	AUG	SEP	OCT	NOV	DEC
X	X	X	X	X	X	X	X	X	X	X	X

LOWE-MARTIN CO. LTD. 1106-58

Fig. 1:3 Visible index file

trouble, the library may cancel a subscription and ask for credit before it is expired; jobbers and publishers can usually oblige. The jobber can be expected to handle claims.

Since many periodicals have obscure publishers and titles that apply to many publications, e.g., *Focus, Crucible,* it saves trouble to supply the publisher's address.

A board office may collate the orders from many schools into one grand order and thereby supposedly gain advantages. On the other hand, one school may divide its orders among jobbers to assure better service; for instance, it might require Asian periodicals and subscribe to them through a specialist agency.

Check the periodical record cards regularly to make sure that the library is receiving everything to which it has subscribed to. Determine whether any missing title is still being published and, if so, claim the missing issues or claim credit for them from your subscription agency or the publisher. Important missing issues may perhaps be purchased at a news-stand, from the publisher (though back issues of popular periodicals usually go out of print immediately) or from a dealer specializing in back issues. Microform copies are often obtainable.

TITLE	CANADIAN CONSUMER									FREQUENCY bi-monthly				
NOS. PER VOL.			VOLS. PER YEAR			VOL. BEGIN			TITLE PAGE					
VOLS. BOUND								INDEX CARR MCLEAN NO. 28-144						
Year	Vol.	Jan.	Feb.	Mar.	Apr.	May	June	July	Aug.	Sept.	Oct.	Nov.	Dec.	T.P.
1978			✓		✓		✓		✓		✓		✓	
1979			✓		✓		✓		✓		✓		✓	
1980			✓		✓									

Fig. 1:4 Periodical record card

Services

LOOSE-LEAF SERVICES

Some of these are reference services for students available by subscription, e.g., *Canadian News Facts,*[30] *Facts on File,*[31] or as single purchases, e.g., vertical files in hard copy or microform. Others are professional, e.g., *Library Technology Reports.*[32]

ENTREPRENEURIAL SERVICES

Free-lance librarians often sell selection aids and bibliographies along with consultant services, e.g., NuBook Cards. Some companies provide these free, e.g., *New Paperbacks for Young Adults*.[33]

COMPUTER SEARCHES

School libraries may avail themselves of the computer capacity of larger libraries for:

Selective dissemination of information (SDI).   Some libraries will regularly provide bibliographies on subjects searched by terms specified by the user. The terms make up a user profile. The number of terms partly determines the cost. One example is CAN/SDI from the National Library of Canada.

Professional reference service.   Some institutions can access their own or distant data bases in order to handle reference problems sent to them by smaller or less specialized libraries. For instance, the ERIC data base in California is searched by Canadian libraries which have computer access as well as reference librarians with the ability to express users' queries in terms that will lead to an efficient transaction and a useful answer. The answer is typically a bibliography on a TV screen or on paper. It will contain citations for research reports, articles and books; in addition abstracts may be printed out. Finally, the publications themselves may be provided selectively in hard copy or microform, the cost varying according to the time required, the quantity of terms, and the number of cited documents bought.

Large public libraries can undertake difficult reference searches on behalf of the teachers or students in school libraries, but may well have a policy of cost recovery if computer time and long-distance charges are involved.

FOOTNOTES

[1]*Children's Catalog*, 13th ed. (H.W. Wilson, 1976: New York).

[2]*The Elementary School Library Collection: A Guide to Books and Other Media*, 12th ed. (Bro-Dart Foundation, 1979: Newark, N.J.).

[3]*Canadian Books for Young People/Livres canadiens pour la jeunesse* (University of Toronto Press, 1978: Toronto).

[4]*Canadian Selection: Books and Periodicals for Libraries* (University of Toronto Press, 1978: Toronto).

[5]Robinson, Paul, *After Survival: A Teacher's Guide to Canadian Resources* (Peter Martin Associates, 1977: Toronto).

[6]*Booklist* (American Library Association: Chicago).

[7]*School Library Journal* (Bowker: New York).

[8]*Previews* (Bowker: New York).

[9]*Canadian Materials* (Canadian Library Association: Ottawa).

[10]*In Review* (Ontario, Libraries and Community Information Branch: Toronto).

[11]*Science Books and Films* (American Association for the Advancement of Science: Washington, D.C.).

[12]*Horn Book Magazine* (Horn Book Inc.: Boston).

[13]*Canadian Children's Literature* (Canadian Children's Press: Guelph).

[14]*New York Times Book Review* (New York Times: New York).

[15]*The School Librarian* (School Library Association: Oxford).

[16]*Saturday Review* (Saturday Review Inc.: New York).

[17]*Canadian Geographical Journal* (Royal Canadian Geographical Society: Ottawa).

[18]*Quill & Quire* (Greey de Pencier: Toronto).

[19]*Canadiana* (National Library of Canada: Ottawa).

[20]*Books in Print* (Bowker: New York).

[21]*NICEM* (University of Southern California: Los Angeles).

[22]*Canadian Publishers Directory* (Quill & Quire: Toronto).

[23]*Best Buys in Print* (Pierian Press: Ann Arbor, Mich.).

[24]*Canadian Government Publications* (Supply and Services Canada: Ottawa).

[25]*Wilson Library Bulletin* (H.W. Wilson: New York).

[26]*Selected U.S. Government Publications* (Superintendent of Documents: Washington, D.C.).

[27]*Educators Guide Series* (Educators Progress Service: Randolph, Wis.).

[28]*Vertical File Index* (H.W. Wilson: New York).

[29]Saalheimer, Harriet Hart, *1001 Valuable Things You Can Get Free in Canada* (Pagurian, 1978: Toronto).

[30]*Canadian News Facts* (Marpep: Toronto).

[31]*Facts on File* (Facts on File: New York).

[32]*Library Technology Reports* (American Library Association: Chicago).

[33]*New Paperbacks for Young Adults* (Metro Toronto News: Toronto).

Contents II

Cataloguing Aids and Services

Alternatives to Original Cataloguing 24
Commercial Cataloguing 24
    Selecting a Commercial Cataloguing Service 24
    Backlog 25
    Cards From Institutional Suppliers 25
    Adapting Commercial Catalogue Cards 27
Cataloguing in Publication (CIP) 30
MAchine-Readable Cataloguing (MARC) and CAN/MARC 31
Derived Cataloguing 32
Footnotes 32

Chapter II

Cataloguing Aids and Services

ALTERNATIVES TO ORIGINAL CATALOGUING

Although all school librarians need to know the most important rules of cataloguing and how to apply them in searching and reference work, they do not need to be expert cataloguers and should not spend a large part of their time cataloguing. Even in the largest libraries, only a fraction of the librarians specialize in cataloguing, and not many of these do original cataloguing. Large libraries rely on cataloguing shared with other libraries, and use one another's cards and printed catalogues as sources of copy, i.e., data. Teacher-librarians should do likewise, taking advantage of Cataloguing in Publication (CIP), the cataloguing of other libraries, and commercial cataloguing. Although some school boards provide centralized processing for their school libraries, it is probably simplest and cheapest in the long run to buy fully processed materials, or, at least, catalogue cards.

COMMERCIAL CATALOGUING

Selecting a Commercial Cataloguing Service

Since the cost and quality of cataloguing/processing services vary, the librarian should shop around. Some processors will cater to individual preferences, but there may be extra costs involved. Although a large school system may find it worthwhile to make elaborate specifications to the processors, in general the librarian can take it for granted that commercial processing firms conform to standard practice, while allowing for some preferences on the part of the user. Inquire about the availability of such options as the following:

- Classification: *Dewey Decimal Classification* (abridged ed.; unabridged ed.)
- Call number for easy books (E or other)
- Call number for fiction (F, Fic, FIC)
- Call letters (Number of letters of name; lower or upper case; cuttering)
- Call number for individual biography (B, 92, 921, or left blank to give the librarian the option of classifying by subject or by form)
- Designation of biographee and author of biography, i.e., number of letters of biographee's surname; some or none of author's letters
- Limit to the length of call number
- Position of call number on cards
- Special numbers for Canadian literature
- Subject headings used: *Sears List of Subject Headings*, and *Canadian Companion*; LC without JUVENILE LITERA-TURE subdivision and with *Canadian Subject Headings*
- Annotations
- Number of cards in a set and the availability of extra cards
- Varying processing of multiple copies. (Try to avoid wasting money on duplicate card sets.)
- Location of book pocket
- Omission of plastic cover for books without dust-jackets
- Location of spine label
- Binding of paperbacks
- Supplying of library bindings where available

Backlog

Where there are uncatalogued materials on hand, the librarian may be able to buy card sets or complete kits containing catalogue cards, book pockets, spine labels, and borrower's cards. Some processors will undertake to catalogue all of a library's backlog, but the service costs more than cataloguing at the time of purchase. Where there are many old books and AV items in a library's cataloguing arrears, it may be a waste of time to catalogue them.

Cards From Institutional Suppliers

LIBRARY OF CONGRESS

The Library of Congress has been selling its printed cards since 1901. A school library can avail itself of the inexpensive card service by starting an account and obtaining order slips, which will include the library's preprinted name.

Each slip has a blank space for the LC card number; this is found on the verso of the title page of books from the U.S. and sometimes from other countries, in CIP and in reference books such as *NUC*[1] (National Union Catalog), *Books in Print*,[2] *NICEM*[3] (National Information Centre for Educational Media), and in such library periodicals as *Publisher's Weekly*,[4] *Booklist*,[5] and *Library Journal*.[6]

> Library of Congress Cataloging in Publication Data
>
> Raskin, Ellen.   The Westing Game.
>
> SUMMARY: The mysterious death of an eccentric millionaire brings together an unlikely assortment of heirs who must uncover the circumstances of his death before they can claim their inheritance.
> [1. Mystery and detective stories]   I. Title.
> PZ7.R181We [Fic] 77-18866 ISBN: 0-525-42320-6

Fig. 2:1   LC card number, i.e., 77-18866

Cards are available for vast numbers of films, records and other hard-to-catalogue media. Even if no card number can be found, the cards may still be ordered by such bibliographic information as may be at hand; if available, they will be sold for the regular card price plus a small searching charge. The cards are sold in sets of eight.

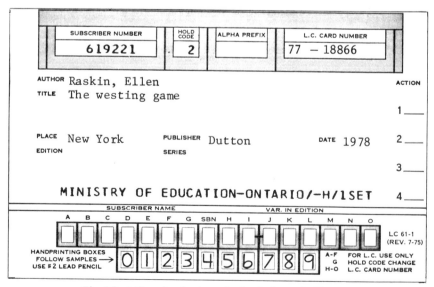

Fig. 2:2   LC card order form for book shown in Fig. 2:1

The needs of the Library of Congress being different from those of a school, LC cards sometimes require adapting. They contain much detail, as required at the third level of cataloguing. (See p. 79, "Levels of Description.") Some of the tracings may be deleted, if considered dispensible in a school, or made compatible with *Sears*. Call numbers and headings must be typed on by the buyer. The LC card service is not without problems of non-supply and mistakes in shipping and cataloguing. All the same, the service can be a useful supplement to other kinds of purchased cataloguing.

LC cards are not as difficult to integrate with other cards as non-users may think. Dewey numbers are usually shown as well as LC; for children's books, alternative, simple subject headings are shown along with LC subjects, through the LC Annotated Card (AC) program. Today cataloguing is growing more standardized; since much of it is based on LC cataloguing and MARC format, cards from all sources tend to resemble LC's. (See p. 31, "Machine-Readable Cataloguing (MARC) and CAN/MARC.")

CANADIAN NETWORKS

Many universities and other libraries in Canada have formed networks which use cataloguing information supplied by various national libraries as well as original input from the member libraries using MARC format. This data may be accessed by computer terminal or in print form. A high school library may want to sample the cataloguing services of the networks and to obtain hard-to-get cards by working through a present subscriber, such as a university or public library. For ordinary school library items, cards are still quite a bit cheaper if bought from a jobber.

Canadian examples of such networks are: UTLAS, UNICAT/TELECAT, the British Columbia Union Catalogue Project, AAU/BNA in the Atlantic Provinces and a service from the Saskatchewan Provincial Library.

LA CENTRALE DES BIBLIOTHÈQUES

This is an agency of the Ministère de l'Éducation du Québec. The cataloguing and reviewing tools of the Centrale show a CB card order number, like an LC card number; the CB number is sometimes printed in books and AV items published in Québec. Cards may also be ordered by title without the CB number, with an additional searching charge. French titles not yet catalogued will be done at the user's request provided they are current.

Adapting Commercial Catalogue Cards

Although in a small library the work of the processing company should generally be acceptable as received, some adaptations are necessary, or desirable if time permits. If data on a card must be revised, the old data may be removed by eraser, correction fluid, a stick-on label, or by the stroke of a pencil. Revised information is then put in to replace what has been deleted.

Instances where commercial catalogue cards may be adapted:
- Any with outright mistakes in cataloguing, or typographical or spelling errors should be corrected.
- Information in open entries may be completed in pencil to reflect the current state of the library's holdings. To save time, the main cards may be left as they are and a note such as "For current holdings see shelves," or "Library has: Current edition" may be added instead.
- If the supplier leaves the space for the call number blank and shows options at the bottom of the cards, the librarian is expected to choose a number that is compatible with ones in the collection. For example, the biography of an opera singer may be classed 782.1, 921 or B, depending on the library's practice.
- If the cards are supplied with an open date after the author's name, the date should be stroked out, unless the library is ready to take the responsibility of closing the date on each card when the author dies.
- Subject headings in non-Canadian spelling should be adapted to the extent necessary to conform to the library's practice. (See also p. 128, "Spellings Used in Headings.")
- Non-Canadian subject headings may be replaced with Canadian ones, e.g., HOCKEY for ICE HOCKEY. (See p. 125 for various authorities.)
- When the cards supplied describe the work in hand approximately but such details as publisher or paging apply to another edition, make such modifications as will match the description to the item.
- When the call number supplied will result in an item's being shelved apart from others among which it would be more useful to put it, change the call number to the one habitually used.
- If cuttering or some other unusual form of call letters is supplied, adapt it to conform to the library's practice. (See also p. 147, "Cuttering.")
- When the new number for a subject, different from the one the library has been using, is indicative of better classifying or of the use of a new edition of *DDC*, retain it. Old items in the collection can be reclassified to conform to this preferred number as time permits. (See also p. 150, "Adapting to a New Edition of *DDC*.")
- When new cards show subject headings that have been introduced or changed in such authorities as *Sears*, retain the new headings, as they probably reflect an adaptation to the advance of knowledge. Corresponding old headings in the collection can be updated as time permits. "See also" references can temporarily direct users to the new and

```
793.735     Anno, Mitsumasa, 1926-
A615c             Château de cartes / Mitsumasa Anno ; adaptation fran-
Ann           çaise Sophie Barbaroux. -- Paris : L'Ecole des Loisirs,
              c1974.
                  27 p. : ill. en coul. ; 27 cm.

                  ISBN 2-211-02844-6 Cart. : $5,75



                  1. Devinettes et énigmes - Albums.   I. Titre.


              793.735                              CB : 77-19860 E
              A615c                                (5)
                                                       E*3
```

Fig. 2:3   Commercial card with cuttering changed to call letters

preferred headings until the headings for the old materials have been changed. (See also p. 135, "Adapting to New Editions of *Sears*.")

• When a call number has a greater or lesser number of digits than desired, it may occasionally be worthwhile to adjust the number by adding or deleting as provided for in *DDC*.

• When subject headings or subject tracings have more or fewer subject subdivisions than desired, remove or add subdivisions to match the other entries in the library catalogue.

• When there are headings and tracings for cards that will not be filed, cross out the unwanted tracings, e.g., when the librarian thinks that there are too many cards and tracings for subjects, series or joint authors.

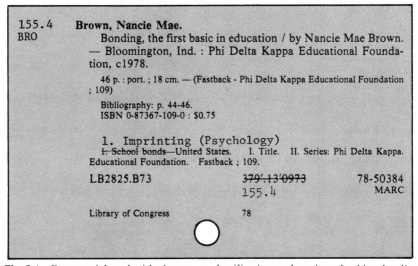

Fig. 2:4   Commercial card with changes to classification and tracing of subject heading

- If additional cards, such as subject or analytical added entries, are made to meet the library's special needs, tracings are added to the commercially supplied shelf-list card so that it will show all added entries.

CATALOGUING IN PUBLICATION (CIP)

CIP is a program which provides the major cataloguing information about an item somewhere in the work itself. CIP requires a high degree of cooperation between the publishers and the major cataloguing agency of a country, such as the National Library of Canada or the Library of Congress. Using galley proofs and/or front matter sent in by the publishers, the cataloguing agency or the libraries which assist it prepares an abbreviated bibliographic record. This information is returned to the publisher and is usually printed on the verso of the title page.

The entry for a book published in North America would consist of the following, if and when appropriate:

- Main entry. CIP provides the statement "Main entry under title" when appropriate so that the user will be able to identify items entered under title rather than author.
- Title
- Series statement, including ISSN for monographic series
- Bibliographical notes, including reprint information and contents notes
- ISBN
- LC subject headings
  — LC headings in square brackets are from LC Annotated Card (AC) series
  — Canadian CIP uses *Canadian Subject Headings* and *Répertoire de vedettes-matière,*[7] to supplement LC subject headings. Subject headings unique to *Canadian Subject Headings* are identified by an asterisk, e.g., METIS—CANADA*
- Added entries
- LC classification number
- Dewey Decimal classification number
- LC card number or *Canadiana*[8] entry serial number; the latter is preceded by a "C"
- Binding statement, if available

By providing the data elements which require the most expertise to determine and which are the least likely to change during the publication process, CIP should reduce cataloguing time and costs, and should help to get materials on the shelves quickly.

Canadian Cataloguing in Publication Data

Freeman, Minnie Aodla.
Life among the Qallunaat

ISBN 0-88830-164-2

1. Freeman, Minnie Aodla.   2. Eskimos –
Canada – Biography   I. Title.
E99.E7F74   971'.004'97   C78-002128-2

Fig. 2:5   CIP found in a book

CIP may have to be adapted to the library's practice; here the tracing "Inuit"
replaces "Eskimos":

```
971.      Freeman, Minnie Aodla.
00497        Life among the Qallunaat / Minnie Aodla
FRE       Freeman. -- Edmonton : Hurtig Publishers,
          c1978.
             217 p. ; 23 cm.
             ISBN 0-88830-164-2  :  $9.95.



          1. Freeman, Minnie Aodla.   2. Inuit--
          Canada--Biography.   I. Title.
```

Fig. 2:6   Catalogue card developed from above CIP of book

MACHINE-READABLE CATALOGUING (MARC) AND CAN/MARC

MARC is a cataloguing format developed by the Library of Congress. MARC
organizes bibliographic information so that data may be identified and
manipulated by computer.

Since 1973, the National Library of Canada has developed several Canadian
MARC formats, such as those for monographs and serials, based upon and
compatible with LC MARC formats. Canadian MARC (CAN/MARC) differs
slightly from other MARC formats in that it does contain some extra fields
and subfields which are deemed necessary for Canadian requirements, and
which provide bilingual access points for authors, series and subjects.

Machine-readable records for all material published by Canadians, in
Canada, or about Canada, are created at the National Library using an
internal processing format based on CAN/MARC. These records are then
converted to the CAN/MARC communication format and used to make a

variety of products including the national bibliography, i.e., *Canadiana* and the CAN/MARC tapes.

In addition, the National Library converts foreign MARC records to the CAN/MARC communication format. Thus both Canadian and foreign cataloguing records are available to libraries and library networks across Canada in a single format, CAN/MARC, for applications as varied as acquisitions, cataloguing, and information retrieval.

DERIVED CATALOGUING

When there is no recourse but for the librarian to do original cataloguing, data for the purpose may often be derived or adapted from such sources as CIP, *Children's Catalog*,[9] *Junior High School Library Catalog*,[10] *Senior High School Library Catalog*,[11] *Booklist, Canadiana*, or *The Elementary School Library Collection: A Guide to Books and Other Media*,[12] along with catalogues from various jobbers and from public libraries.

FOOTNOTES

[1] *NUC* (Edwards: Ann Arbor, Mich.; Library of Congress: Washington, D.C.).

[2] *Books in Print* (Bowker: New York).

[3] *NICEM* (University of Southern California: Los Angeles).

[4] *Publishers' Weekly* (Bowker: New York).

[5] *Booklist* (American Library Association: Chicago).

[6] *Library Journal* (Bowker: New York).

[7] *Répertoire de vedettes-matière*, 8e éd. (Université Laval, Bibliothèque, Section de l'analyse documentaire, 1976: Québec).

[8] *Canadiana* (National Library of Canada: Ottawa).

[9] *Children's Catalog*, 13th ed. (H.W. Wilson, 1976: New York).

[10] *Junior High School Library Catalog*, 4th ed. (H.W. Wilson, 1980: New York).

[11] *Senior High School Library Catalog*, 11th ed. (H.W. Wilson, 1977: New York).

[12] *The Elementary School Library Collection: A Guide to Books and Other Media*, 12th ed. (Bro-Dart Foundation, 1979: Newark, N.J.).

Contents III

Main Entry Headings

Introduction 35
  Access Points to a Work 35
  Sources of Information 35
Meaning of the Term "Author" 36
  Determining What is a Personal Author 36
  Determining What is a Corporate Body 36
  Determining What is a Subordinate Body 36
Determining the Main Access Point for Works of Personal Authors and
Corporate Bodies 37
  Works of One Author or Corporate Body 37
  Works of Unknown, Uncertain, or Unnamed Authorship 38
  Works of Shared Responsibility 39
  Works and Collections Produced Under Editorial Direction 40
  Works of Mixed Responsibility — Modifications of Other Works ... 41
  Works of Mixed Responsibility — New Works 45
  Related Works 45
Choosing Headings for Persons 45
  Form of Name 45
  Entry Element 47
Choosing Headings for Corporate Bodies 53
  Form of Name 53
  Corporate Body Entries 54
Choosing Headings for Subordinate and Related Bodies 56
  Names Entered Subordinately 56
  Names Entered Directly 57
  Direct or Indirect Subheadings 58
Choosing Headings for Government Bodies and Officials 58
  Names Entered Subordinately 58
  Names Entered Directly 60
  Direct or Indirect Subheadings 60
  Special Subheadings 61
  Two or More Governmental Jurisdictions With Same Name 61
  Place Names Unlikely to be Confused 62
Main Entry Under Title 62
  Form of Heading 62
  Entry Under Title 63
Uniform Titles 63
  Form of Uniform Title 64
  Determining Uniform Titles 65

34

    Additions to Uniform Titles 66
    Parts of Works 67
    Two Works Issued Together 68
    Collective Titles 68
    Special Rules for Law, Sacred Scriptures and Music 70
Footnotes 76

√

Chapter III

Main Entry Headings

INTRODUCTION

Access Points to a Work

In order to see if a library has something on a particular topic, an inquirer usually checks the catalogue via one or more access points or headings. The search might be by subject (very often in schools), by title, or by the name of a person or corporate body.

This chapter outlines the rules for, first, determining the main access point for a work, and then, choosing the form and the entry point, i.e., the first word in the heading, for it. Usually this main access point or main entry heading is the name of a person or a corporate body, but it may also be the title of a work. Whichever it is, the main entry heading appears in every reference to the work, on every card in a card set, and in every bibliographic citation. It is not enough to achieve consistency in establishing and using main entry headings within one library and its catalogues. Increasingly, cataloguing is shared, and standards are being imposed to ensure that different cataloguers establish the same main entry heading, given the same item to catalogue. This identity of decision will be facilitated by the appearance of the second edition of *Anglo-American Cataloguing Rules* (*AACR2*) upon which this chapter is based.

Information about establishing access through the subject may be found in Chapter V. Information about making cards for subject and other access points, including added entries, may be found in Chapter VII.

Sources of Information

Whenever possible, the information needed for the main entry heading should be taken from the chief source of information, e.g., the title page of a book and its verso, the introductory frames of visual materials, the labels on sound recordings, or the equivalent. If this source is ambiguous or insufficient, information may be derived from other parts of the item, such as the flyleaf of a book, or a record jacket cover. Use square brackets in the main entry heading to indicate information not taken from the chief source of information.

MEANING OF THE TERM "AUTHOR"

Determining What is a Personal Author

The term "personal author" is used here to denote the person chiefly responsible for the intellectual or artistic content of a work. This would include writers, composers, cartographers, artists, and compilers of bibliographies. In some cases, performers are treated as the authors of sound recordings, video tapes, etc. (See p. 44, "Sound Recordings, Video Recordings, Etc.")

Determining What is a Corporate Body

The term "corporate body" is used here to denote an organization or a group of persons with a particular name that acts or may act as an entity. This includes associations, institutions, business firms, non-profit organizations, governments, governmental agencies, projects and programs, religious organizations, local churches, conferences, events such as athletic contests and exhibitions, and vessels such as ships and spacecraft.

A work is entered under a corporate-body main-entry heading *only* if it falls into one or more of the following categories. The five categories take precedence over any personal author(s) or editor(s) named:

- works of an administrative nature dealing with the corporate body itself, its internal policies, procedures and/or operations, or its resources, e.g., inventories and catalogues
- certain legal items and governmental works, e.g., laws
- works expressing the collective thought of the corporate body, e.g., reports of committees and commissions
- works expressing the collective activity of a conference, expedition, or an event, e.g., proceedings of a conference, or the report of an expedition, or event; the corporate name is used only if it is prominently displayed on the item
- works such as sound recordings, films and video recordings which result from the collective activity of a performing group

If the work does not fall into any of the above categories, treat it as if no corporate body were involved. An added entry may be made for the corporate body if deemed necessary. (See p. 162, "Name Added Entry Card.")

Determining What is a Subordinate Body

The term "subordinate body" is used here to denote a body which is an integral part of a larger corporate body within which the subordinate body holds a lower position in the hierarchy. Depending on the name of the subordinate body, the work may be entered either under the name of the subordinate body, i.e., entered directly, or under the name of the parent corporate body, i.e., entered indirectly, with the name of the subordinate body as a subheading:

Canadian School Library Association.
Entered directly.

Canadian Library Association.   Committee on Publications.
The committee is entered as a subheading, i.e., entered indirectly.

In both cases, the work must fall into one or more of the required categories for works of corporate bodies (p. 36). (See p. 53 for instructions on choosing the headings for corporate bodies.)

DETERMINING THE MAIN ACCESS POINT FOR WORKS OF PERSONAL AUTHORS AND CORPORATE BODIES

Works of One Author or Corporate Body

GENERAL RULE

Enter a work under the name of the author, or enter it under the corporate body if it falls into those categories set out above. For example:

A pattern of history / by Arthur R.M. Lower
This book would have its main entry under the heading for Lower.

Colombo's Canadian quotations
Main entry under the heading for Colombo.

A room-to-room guide to the National Gallery / by Michael Levey
Main entry under the heading for the gallery. This catalogue represents the resources of the gallery. Therefore, the heading for the gallery would take precedence over the personal author (as indicated on p. 36, "Determining What is a Corporate Body").

Dada, Surrealism, and their heritage / by William S. Rubin. --
New York : Museum of Modern Art
This is a catalogue of a loan exhibition held at the museum. The main entry would therefore be under the heading for Rubin.

Selected poems of John Keats
Main entry under the heading for Keats.

WORK ATTRIBUTED TO A FICTITIOUS OR ERRONEOUS PERSON OR CORPORATE BODY

Enter the work under the actual personal author or corporate body, if known. If not known, enter it under the title. Make an added entry under the name of the person or corporate body to whom authorship is attributed only if the author is a real person or body:

The hums of Pooh / by Winnie the Pooh
Since this was written by A.A. Milne, make a main entry under the heading for Milne. No added entry is needed.

Works of Unknown, Uncertain, or Unnamed Authorship

WORK OF UNKNOWN AUTHORSHIP OR BY A BODY THAT LACKS A NAME

Enter the work under title as the main entry:

The Canadian home cook book / compiled by ladies of Toronto
    and chief cities and towns in Canada
Since the body lacks a name, the main entry is under title.

The Penguin book of Canadian folk songs / selected and
    edited by Edith Fowke
Main entry is under title. (See p. 40, "Works and Collections Produced Under Editorial Direction.")

Go ask Alice / by Anonymous
Main entry is under title.

WORK OF UNCERTAIN AUTHORSHIP

A work controversially attributed to more than one personal author or body. Enter the work under the title as the main entry. If attributed authorship information is found either in the edition or in reference sources, make added entries for the persons or corporate bodies of attributed authorship, if their claims are strong enough.

A work attributed in reference sources to a probable author. Enter the work under the heading for the person. Make an added entry under title.
    The two paragraphs above usually apply more often to cases found in art and music rather than in literature.

WORK WITH UNKNOWN PERSONAL AUTHOR OR CORPORATE BODY AND AUTHORSHIP INDICATED BY A COMMON NOUN OR PHRASE

Enter the work under the common noun or phrase. Make an added entry under title:

/ by a surgeon
Name of author is unknown. Main entry under the common noun, i.e., Surgeon.

/ by the author of ...
Name of author is unknown. Main entry under the phrase, i.e., "Author of . . .".

WORK WITH AUTHORSHIP INDICATED BY A NON-ALPHABETIC AND OR NON-NUMERIC DEVICE

Enter the work under the title as the main entry. An added entry under the device is not necessary:

˘ ˘ ˘, Comtesse de
Main entry under the title.

Works of Shared Responsibility

Shared responsibility refers to two or more people, or two or more corporate bodies, or a combination of the two, collaborating and performing the same kind of activity to produce a work. It does not apply to works produced under editorial direction. (See p. 40 for guidelines to such works.)

WORK OF TWO OR THREE PERSONS AND OR CORPORATE BODIES

Enter the work under the name of the person or body most prominently displayed, or if no indication is given, under the one named first. Make an added entry under the headings for the other person or body involved, to a maximum of two, if the user of the catalogue is likely to search for this access point:

The basement tapes / Bob Dylan and the Band
Main entry under the heading for Dylan; added entry under the heading for the Band.

The humanities and the library ... / by Lester Asheim and Associates
Main entry under the heading for Asheim.

Billie Jean / by Billie Jean King with Kim Chapin
Main entry under the heading for King; added entry under the heading for Chapin.

WORK OF FOUR OR MORE PERSONS AND OR CORPORATE BODIES

Enter the work under title. Make an added entry under the heading for the first person or corporate body named if the user of the catalogue is likely to search for this access point:

```
Elements of geography : physical and cultural / Vernon
   C. Finch ... [et al.]
```
On the title page, the authors are listed as: Vernon C. Finch, Glenn T. Trewartha, Arthur H. Robinson, Edwin H. Hammon. Main entry under title; added entry under the heading for Finch.

Works and Collections Produced Under Editorial Direction

This includes collections and works consisting of extracts or contributions by different persons or bodies. It does not apply to works of a corporate body (as described on p. 36) or to papers or proceedings of a named conference.

WORK WITH A COLLECTIVE TITLE

Enter the work under title. Make an added entry heading for each editor or compiler/editor, to a maximum of three, if named prominently, and if the user of the catalogue is likely to search for this access point. If there are more than three editors or compilers/editors, make an added entry under the heading for the principal one or the one named first:

```
The Oxford book of Canadian verse : in English and French /
   chosen and with an introduction by A.J.M. Smith
```
Main entry under title; added entry under the heading for Smith.

Work composed of two or three independent works. Make a name-title analytic for each work in the collection if the user of the catalogue is likely to search for the item on its own:

```
Classic Irish drama / introduced by W.A. Armstrong
```
Contents: The Countess Cathleen/W.B. Yeats; The Playboy of the Western World/J.M. Synge; Cock-A-Doodle Dandy/Sean O'Casey. Main entry under title; name title analytics under the headings for Yeats, Synge and O'Casey.

Work with many contributions or independent works but only two or three contributors. Make a name analytic (or name-title analytic when appropriate) under the heading for each contributor:

```
Regency poets : Byron, Shelley, Keats / compiled by C.R. Bull
```
Main entry under title; name analytics under the headings for Byron, Shelley, Keats, and if considered useful, Bull.

WORK WITHOUT A COLLECTIVE TITLE

Enter under the heading appropriate for the first work. Make name-title analytics for other works, and added entries for editors/compilers as described above. For example:

Our intellectual strength and weakness / by John George
Bourinot. English-Canadian literature / by Thomas Guthrie
Marquis. French-Canadian literature / by Camille Roy
*Main entry under the heading for Bourinot; name-title analytics under the
headings for Marquis and Roy.*

Works of Mixed Responsibility — Modifications of Other Works

The term "mixed responsibility" refers to different persons or bodies
performing different kinds of activity in the creation of a work, e.g., writing,
illustrating, arranging, translating, adapting.

Modifications of other works may be either minor ones, such as updatings,
abridgements, revisions, rearrangements, etc., or major ones, where the
original has been substantially changed in nature, scope, or medium.

TEXTS — MINOR MODIFICATIONS

Works that have been illustrated, revised in a minor way, enlarged, updated,
abridged, condensed, translated, etc., or have a biographer/critic as editor,
compiler, etc., are entered under the heading appropriate to the original work.
Make an added entry for illustrator, reviser, etc., if the user of the catalogue is
likely to search for the access point:

Arabian nights / by Andrew Lang ; illustrated by William
Dempster
*Main entry under the heading for Lang; added entry under the heading for
Dempster.*

Anatomy of the human body / by Henry Gray -- 25th ed. /
edited by Charles Mayo Goss
*Main entry under the heading for Gray; added entry under the heading for
Goss.*

The letters of Frederick Philip Grove / edited with an introd.
and notes by Desmond Pacey
*Main entry under the heading for Grove; added entry under the heading for
Pacey. (If much critical/biographical material has been added to a work, then
see "Texts — Major Modifications," below.)*

Homer / Gabriel Germain : translated by Richard Howard
*Main entry under heading for Germain; added entry under heading for
Howard.*

TEXTS — MAJOR MODIFICATIONS

Works that paraphrase, rewrite, adapt for a different audience, or differ in
literary form from the original, as in the case of a novelization or dramatiza-
tion, are entered under the heading for the adapter. If the adapter is unknown,
enter the work under its title. Make a name-title added entry for the original
work:

Adventures of Tom Sawyer / by Mark Twain ; rewritten for
young readers by Felix Sutton
*Main entry under the heading for Sutton; name-title added entry under the
heading for Twain.*

Works that have major revisions which are indicated in the chief source of
information are entered under the reviser. Make a name-title added entry
under the heading for the original, if the user of the catalogue is likely to
search by this access point.

Works that interweave the work of one writer with considerable
biographical/critical material by another person are entered under the
biographer/critic:

Life and letters of Mrs. Jason Lee ... / by Theressa Gay
*Main entry under the heading for Gay; added entry under the heading for Lee.
(If the biographer/critic adds little to the original writer's work, see "Texts—
Minor Modifications," p. 41.)*

ART WORKS — REPRODUCTIONS

Works that are reproductions, including photographs, photomechanical
copies, or models of a sculpture, are entered under the heading for the
original work. For instance, in the case of a plaster reproduction of Le
penseur, by Rodin, the main entry would be made under the heading for
Rodin.

Works that consist of reproductions of one artist's work without any
accompanying text are entered under the heading for the artist.

Works that consist of reproductions of one artist's work with a text about
the artist or the works reproduced will be entered under the heading for the
author of the text if the chief source of information clearly indicates authorship; otherwise, enter under the heading for the artist. When in doubt, enter
under the heading for the artist. If entering under the author, make an added
entry heading for the artist. If entering under the heading for the artist, make
an added entry heading for the author, should the user of the catalogue be
likely to search for this access point.

ART WORKS — ADAPTATIONS

Works that are adaptations from one medium of the graphic arts to another
are entered under the heading for the adapter. If the name of the adapter is not
known, enter the work under its title. Make a name-title added entry for the
original work:

Children crying forfeits / engr. by C. Turner from an
original painting by Joshua Reynolds
*Main entry under the heading for Turner; name-title added entry under the
heading for Reynolds.*

MUSICAL WORKS — ARRANGEMENTS, TRANSCRIPTIONS, ETC.

Arrangements, transcriptions, etc., include works in which music for one medium of performance has been rewritten for another.

Works of one composer that have been arranged or transcribed are entered under the heading for the composer. Make an added entry under the heading for the arranger or transcriber only if the user of the catalogue is likely to search for the item under this access point:

John Philip Sousa's The Stars and Stripes forever /
transcribed for piano by Vladimir Horowitz
Main entry under the heading for Sousa; added entry under the heading for Horowitz.

MUSICAL WORKS — ADAPTATIONS

Adaptations include works which are a distinctly altered version of another work, e.g., a free transcription, a paraphrase of a work or of the general style of a composer, or a rhapsody or variations on a theme.

Works that have been adapted are entered under the heading for the adapter. If the adapter is not known, then enter under the title. If the work is related to the title of another work, or to the music of another composer, make a title-added entry for the former and a name added entry for the latter.

Since the difference between arrangements and adaptations may be hard to distinguish, treat doubtful cases by the rule for arrangements. (See section immediately above.)

MUSICAL WORKS — WITH WORDS

Works such as musical comedies, operas, songs, and ballets with scenarios are entered under the heading for the composer. Make an added entry for the writer of the words, e.g., poem, libretto, or scenario, and for the composer of the instrumental accompaniment or the additional parts, if the user of the catalogue is likely to search for the access point. If the words are based on another text, e.g., novel, make a name-title added entry under the original:

Candide : comic operetta based on Voltaire's satire /
music by Leonard Bernstein ; lyrics by Richard Wilbur ;
book by Lillian Hellman
Main entry under the heading for Bernstein; added entries under the headings for Wilbur and Hellman; name-title added entry under the heading for Voltaire.

Works of one writer set to music by two or more composers are entered as a collection. Make a name added entry under the heading for the writer:

```
Songs from Shakespeare's tragedies : a collection of
   songs for concert or dramatic use / edited from
   contemporary sources by Frederick Sternfeld
```
Main entry under title; name added entry under the heading for Shakespeare.

SOUND RECORDINGS, VIDEO RECORDINGS, ETC.

Single work. Enter under the heading appropriate for the work. For instance, a novel, an abridgement of a book or a musical work presented on a sound recording would be entered under the heading for its author or its composer. Make added entries for the principal performers, e.g., readers, singers, orchestras, to a maximum of three, if the user of the catalogue is likely to search for these access points. If there are more than three principal performers, then make an added entry only for the first one named:

```
The little prince [sound recording] / by Antoine de Saint-
Exupéry   Read by Peter Ustinov.
```
Main entry under the heading for Saint-Exupéry; added entry under the heading for Ustinov.

```
Water music / by George Frideric Handel   This version is played by
the Academy of St. Martin-in-the-Fields.
```
Main entry under the heading for Handel; added entry for the Academy.

Two or more works by the same person or group. Enter under the heading appropriate to these works. For instance, songs of one composer sung or performed by another person would be entered under the heading for the composer. Make added entries for the principal performers, e.g., readers, singers, orchestras, to a maximum of three, if the user of the catalogue is likely to search for the item under these access points. If there are more than three principal performers, then make an added entry only for the first named:

```
Any day now : songs of Bob Dylan   Sung by Joan Baez.
```
Main entry under the heading for Dylan; added entry under the heading for Baez.

Works by different persons with three or fewer principal performers. Enter under the heading for the person or group represented as the principal performer. When there are two or three principal performers, enter the work under the first one named. Make an added entry for each performer if the user of the catalogue is likely to search for the item under this access point.

Work by different persons with more than three principal performers, or no principal performers. Enter the work under the title. If the work does not have a collective title, refer to p. 40.

Works of Mixed Responsibility — New Works

Works of a collaborative nature between an artist and a writer are entered under the heading for the first one named or the one whose name is given greater prominence by the wording or in the layout. Make an added entry for the one not named in the main entry heading if the user is likely to search the card catalogue for the item under this access point:

Cartoons / by E.W. Kemble ; limericks by G. Mayo
Main entry under the heading for Kemble; added entry under the heading for Mayo.

   Goodby baby & amen : a saraband for the sixties / David Bailey and Peter Evans *Photographs by Bailey, text by Evans.*
Main entry under the heading for Bailey; added entry under the heading for Evans.

Related Works

The term "related works" denotes a relationship between the item to be catalogued and another work. This type of work includes continuations, sequels, supplements, indexes, concordances, screen-plays and collections of extracts from serials.

   Related works are entered under the heading appropriate to the related work itself according to the above rules in this chapter. Make an added entry for the work to which it is related:

   Sears list of subject headings, Canadian companion / compiled by Ken Haycock and Lynne Isberg
Main entry under Haycock; added entry for Isberg, and for the work to which the Companion *is related, namely,* Sears List of Subject Headings.

CHOOSING HEADINGS FOR PERSONS

Form of Name

GENERAL RULES

- Choose the form of name by which the person is commonly known. Most often this is the real name, but it may be a pseudonym, set of initials, title of nobility, etc.
- Choose the same form of name for main entry headings and name added entry headings.
- Follow the form of punctuation as illustrated in the examples below.
- Omit terms of address, title of position or office, initials of academic degrees, initials denoting memberships in an organization, etc.:

Rev., Captain, Jr., Ph.D., F.R.C.M.
For exceptions to this rule, see pp. 51 and 53, "Entry Element." Titles of honour and nobility are retained: see p. 50, "Title Names."

- If an author shows a preference for a nickname, initials, etc., it is not necessary to regularize the name.
- When in doubt, consult a standard English-language reference source for guidance, e.g., *Webster's Biographical Dictionary*.
- Many librarians keep an authority file of the more complicated headings for names that have been established for their catalogue.

CHOICE AMONG DIFFERENT NAMES

- Choose the form of name that appears most frequently in a person's works if the person is known by more than one name. If this cannot be determined, then choose the name that appears most frequently in reference sources, or the person's latest name.
- Choose the latest form of a name if the person has changed it, unless there is reason to believe that an earlier form of name is likely to persist.

CHOICE AMONG DIFFERENT FORMS OF THE SAME NAME

If a choice needs to be made among various forms of a person's name, the librarian should consider making references as required to assist the user of the catalogue in finding the chosen form. (See p. 196, "References.")
- Choose the degree of fullness of a name that is most commonly found. If this cannot be determined, then choose the latest form of the name or the fullest form:

A.E. Housman   *not Alfred Edward Housman*
Form with initials is the most common form of his name.

- Choose the English form of the name for a person entered under a given name, a Roman of classical times, and a person whose given name is written in non-roman script:

Nicholas II   *not Nicolai II*

Virgil   *not Publius Vergilius Maro*

Maimonides   *not Moses ben Maimon*

- Choose the romanized form of a person's name if it is in a language written in a non-roman script, and if it has become well established in English-language reference sources. The Library of Congress and other large libraries prefer to romanize according to transliteration tables, but their policy is in a state of flux.

Yevgeny Yevtushenko   *(Form in English language reference sources.) Not Evgenyi Evtushenko, the preferred form of the Library of Congress*

Moshe Dayan   *not Mosheh Dayan*
Modern Jewish and Yiddish names should be in the form that is currently in use in English-language writing in Israel.

Entry Element

The term "entry element" refers to the first word of the main entry heading for persons, or of a name added entry.

SIMPLE SURNAMES

Enter under the surname or term that functions as a surname followed by forenames and/or initials:

Lightfoot, Gordon.

Pratt, E.J.

Ali, Muhammad.
The element "Ali" functions as a surname.

Additions to distinguish between names. If headings for two or more persons known by their surnames and initials are the same, add the fuller form of their names in brackets after the headings:

Lawrence, D.H. (Daniel Henry)

Lawrence, D.H. (David Herbert)

If headings for two or more persons consist of the same surname and forename(s) add dates or parts of dates as known, to distinguish among them:

Smith, John, b. 1814.   *Year of death unknown.*

Smith, John, 1832–1898.   *Years of birth and death.*

Smith, John, 1924–   .   *Still living.*

Abbreviations:

    b., born — used only when year of birth known
    d., died — used only when year of death known
    ca., circa — year approximate, i.e., ca. 1905
    1854? — authorities differ; 1854 probable

COMPOUND SURNAMES

The term "compound surname" means a surname consisting of two or more proper names. Such names sometimes include hyphens, conjunctions or prepositions. Make a name reference from the element of the compound surname which is not used as the entry element.

With no hyphens, conjunctions, or prepositions. Enter under the element of the compound surname which the person prefers, or which is given in standard reference sources:

Lloyd George, David.
Name reference may be made from George, David Lloyd.

Hungry Wolf, Adolf.
Name reference may be made from Wolf, Adolf Hungry.

Married women with surnames consisting of a maiden name and husband's surname, without a hyphen. Enter under the husband's surname unless a standard reference source indicates otherwise. Check there for non-English names:

Browning, Elizabeth Barrett.
Name reference might be made from Barrett Browning, Elizabeth, or Barrett, Elizabeth.

Hyphenated surnames. Enter under the first element of the compound name:

Chaput-Rolland, Solange.
Name reference may be made from Rolland, Solange Chaput-.

Surname uncertain. If the person's name in English has the appearance of a compound surname, check in a standard reference source. Unless treated as a compound surname there, enter under the last part of the name:

Adams, John Crawford.

SURNAMES WITH PREFIXES

English surnames with prefixes. Enter under the prefix:

De la Mare, Walter.

Van Doren, Carl.

French surnames with prefixes consisting of an article, or of a contraction of an article and a preposition (le, la, les, du, des). Enter under the prefix:

Des Branges, Charles-Marc.

(See also p. 246 for rules for filing French proper names.)

French surnames with prefixes consisting of a preposition, or a preposition followed by an article. Enter under the part of the name following the preposition:

La Fontaine, Jean de.
Name references may be made from De la Fontaine, Jean, and Fontaine, Jean de la.

Other foreign names with prefixes. Consult a standard reference source for the accepted form of the name. Make a name reference if the entry element is not the prefix:

Van der Post, Laurens.

Beethoven, Ludwig van.
Name reference may be made from Van Beethoven, Ludwig.

PSEUDONYMS

The entry element for a pseudonym is decided upon in the same way as for a real name.

One pseudonym. Enter a work by an author who uses a pseudonym under the pseudonym as it appears in the work. Make a name reference from the person's real name only if the users of the catalogue are likely to search for this access point:

Twain, Mark.
Name reference may be made from Clemens, Samuel Langhorne.

One predominant pseudonym out of several, or real name and one or more pseudonyms. Enter under the predominant name found in the person's own work, in critical works, or in reference sources. Make name references from other names or pseudonyms, if the user of the catalogue is likely to search for these access points:

Gardner, Erle Stanley.
Name references may be made from Fair, A.A., and Kenny, Charles J.

No predominant name out of several. Enter a work under the name appearing in it. Make name references to link this name with other pseudonyms and the real name as necessary:

Creasey, John.   *Real name.*
Name references may be made to and from his pseudonyms as necessary: Ashe,
Gordon; Halliday, Michael; Marric, J.J.; Morton, Anthony; York, Jeremy.

Person known by title of nobility. Enter under the proper name in the title of
nobility followed by forename, surname, and terms of rank in the vernacular,
in that order. Make a name reference from the person's surname only if it is
different from the proper name in the title of nobility, and the users of the
catalogue are likely to search for this access point:

Beaverbrook,	Maxwell	Aitken,	Baron.
proper name in	*forename*	*surname*	*rank*
title of nobility			

In the above example the surname differs from the proper name in the title of
nobility and therefore a name reference may be made from it, i.e.: Aitken,
Maxwell. See Beaverbrook, Maxwell Aitken, Baron.

Byron,	George Gordon	Byron,	Baron.
proper name in	*forenames*	*surname*	*rank*
title of nobility			

In the above example, the surname and the proper name in the title of nobility
are the same. Do not confuse the title of address, e.g., "Lord Byron," with the
title of honour, "Lord" (see "British Titles of Honour," below).

Titled person generally identified by surname rather than title. Enter under
surname. Add the title after the forename(s) only if it commonly appears with
the name in the person's work, or in reference sources:

Buchan, John.
Title, "Baron Tweedsmuir," is not used in the majority of his works.

British titles of honour: Sir, Dame, Lord, Lady. Add these terms if they appear
with the rest of the name in the person's work, or in reference sources:

Churchill, Sir Winston Leonard Spencer.

Roberts, Sir Charles G.D. Roberts.

but

Christie, Agatha.
Her title of honour, "Dame," is not used in her works.

Although *AACR2* shows the title of honour or address in a position before
the forenames, some libraries, to facilitate machine filing, are placing the
titles of honour and address at the end of the main entry, e.g., Churchill,

Winston Leonard Spencer, Sir. In this book, the example of *AACR2* is followed.

GIVEN NAMES ONLY

Enter a heading for a person known by a given name only, including sovereigns, popes, saints, under the given name followed by a word or phrase denoting place of origin, rank, position, or title of honour. In some cases, there may be two groups of words or phrases. Make a name reference if the user of the catalogue is likely to search for an item under a variant form of the name:

Leonardo, da Vinci.
Phrase indicates place of origin. Name reference from Vinci, Leonardo da.

Joan, of Arc, Saint.

John Paul II, Pope.

Angelico, fra.

More, Sir Thomas, Saint.

Elizabeth II, Queen of Great Britain.
AACR2 *shows "Queen of the United Kingdom," but most libraries are not following that form.*

Philip, Prince, consort of Elizabeth II, Queen of
   Great Britain.

Frederick II, King of Prussia. *not Frederick, the Great*

GIVEN NAMES WITH EPITHETS OR BYNAMES

Enter under the given names:

Thomas, Aquinas, Saint.
Name reference from Aquinas, Thomas, Saint.

Omar Khayyam.
Name reference from Khayyam, Omar.

SURNAMES ONLY, WITH TITLE OF ADDRESS

Enter a real or plausible surname accompanied not by a forename but by a term such as Dr., Mr., Rev., under the surname followed by the title of address:

Seuss, Dr.

Moses, Grandma.

Gaskell, Mrs.

For a phrase consisting of something other than the real or plausible name, see also below, "Unusual Names."

CLASSICAL NAMES

One name. Enter under the English form of the name:

Homer.

Plato.

With surname and forename. Enter under the English form of the name, surname first followed by forename. If in doubt, consult a standard reference source:

Cicero, Marcus Tullius.

UNUSUAL NAMES

Phrase consisting of forename with another word or words. Enter under the forename followed by the other word(s):

Richard, Poor.
Name reference may be made from Poor Richard.

Initials, letters, or numerals. Enter in the same order as given, including any typographical devices:

H.D.
A reference may be made from D., H. to the form used.

Non-alphabetic and non-numeric devices. Enter under the title. Do not make an added entry under the device:

··· _ _ _ ···   *"SOS" in Morse Code.*
If this device appeared as the name of the person responsible for an item, the item would be entered under the title.

Phrase, common noun, or adjective in place of a name. Enter under the common noun or adjective, omitting any initial articles unless required for grammatical reasons:

Heartbroken.   *Wording on item "by heartbroken."*

Survivor.   *Wording on item "A Survivor."*

Physician.   *Wording on item "by a physician."*

Phrase naming another work. Enter under the phrase in the order as given in the work omitting any initial articles unless required for grammatical reasons. If "by the Author of . . ." appeared on an item, the main entry heading would be "Author of . . .". If appropriate, make a reference from the title of the quoted work in this form: title, "author of."

Phrase consisting of something other than the real or plausible name. Enter under the name as it is on the item. Make a name reference from the other part of the name:

Bureaucrat X. *Name reference from X, Bureaucrat.*

Mr. Fixit. *Name reference from Fixit, Mr.*

Mother Goose. *Name reference from Goose, Mother.*

For a real or plausible surname only, with title of address, see p. 51.

If the phrase has the appearance of a forename and a surname, enter under the pseudo-surname. Make a name reference from the phrase as it appears on the item:

Other, A.N.
Name reference from A.N. Other.

If the name does not convey the idea of a person, add a suitable designation in parentheses after the name:

Taj Mahal (Musician)

CHOOSING HEADINGS FOR CORPORATE BODIES

To be considered the work of a corporate body, an item must fall into one of the five categories outlined on p. 36, "Determining What is a Corporate Body."

Form of Name

GENERAL RULES

- Choose the name by which the corporate body is predominantly known, unless the rules require entering it as a subordinate body (see p. 56) or entering it under the name of a government (see p. 58).
- Choose the name of the corporate body from the item itself whenever possible. If this is not possible, then determine it from materials written about the corporate body.
- Choose the form of name including initials, periods, etc., that the corporate body uses predominantly on items issued by it:

AFL-CIO.
Used as predominant name by the corporate body.

- No spaces are left between a period and the following initial:

H.W. Wilson.

- No spaces are left between the letters of an initialism written without periods:

IBM.

- Omit any initial articles unless required for grammatical purposes, and omit initial abbreviations for ships' names, such as S.S., U.S.S., H.M.S. and H.M.C.S.
- Omit adjectival terms of incorporation, e.g., Inc., Incorporated, Limited, etc., unless without the term the corporate name would be unrecognizable:

Bell Canada.
Omit unnecessary terms of incorporation.

Films Incorporated.
Firm would be unrecognizable without the term of incorporation.

- Capitalization follows the rules for the language in which the corporate body's name is transcribed.
- Choose the same form of name for main entry headings and name added entry headings.

CHOICE AMONG DIFFERENT NAMES

Choose the latest form of a corporate body's name if it has changed. Make name references between earlier and later names in both directions.

CHOICE AMONG DIFFERENT FORMS OF THE SAME NAME

- Choose the form of the name in the official language of the corporate body.
- Choose the English form of the name if the corporate body has several official languages, and one of them is English.

Corporate Body Entries

ORDER OF NAMES

Enter the name of the corporate body in the order in which it is found:

Art Gallery of Ontario.

Canadian Library Association.

Montreal Museum of Fine Arts.

Queen's University.

Royal Ontario Museum.

Unicef.

United Nations.
Full name is predominantly used by the corporate body. Make name reference from the initials.

University of Alberta.

Vancouver Art Gallery.

Westminster Abbey.
Conventional name is predominantly used.

NAMES THAT DO NOT CONVEY THE IDEA OF CORPORATE BODY

Enter under the name and add a general designation in parentheses, such as (Spacecraft), (Fraternal order), (Firm), (Association):

France (Ship)
Great Speckled Bird (Folk band)

TWO OR MORE CORPORATE BODIES WITH THE SAME NAME

Add a specific local jurisdiction in parentheses after the name of each corporate body to distinguish between them:

Queen's University (Kingston)
The Library of Congress and some other large libraries have decided to use the form (Kingston, Ontario) to allow for maximum differentiation of place names.

Queen's University (Belfast)

RELIGIOUS ORDERS AND SOCIETIES

Enter under the conventional form of the name by which the members are known in English:

Jesuits.

CONFERENCES, CONVENTIONS, MEETINGS, ETC.

Enter under the specific name of the conference, etc., followed in parentheses by one or more of the following elements as appropriate in the order and with the punctuation given below:
Name of conference (its ordinal number : year : location). For example:

```
Couchiching Conference (45th : 1976 : Geneva Park, Ont.)
```

EXHIBITIONS, FAIRS, FESTIVALS, ETC.

Enter under the specific name of the exhibition, etc., followed in parentheses by one or more of the following elements as appropriate in the order and with the punctuation given below:
Name of exhibition (its ordinal number : year : location). For example:

```
Canadian National Exhibition (102nd : 1980 : Toronto)

Expo 67 (Montréal)
```

CHOOSING HEADINGS FOR SUBORDINATE AND RELATED BODIES

As outlined on p. 36, "Determining What is a Subordinate Body," there are two possible ways to enter a subordinate body depending on its name. It may be entered directly, under its own name, in which case all the above rules for corporate bodies would apply. Or, it may be entered subordinately, as a subheading of the name of the parent body.

Names Entered Subordinately

This section describes the types of names of subordinate or related bodies which are entered subordinately. If a name falls into any one of the following five types, then it is entered as a subheading. Do not repeat the name of the higher body in noun form in the subheading unless it is necessary to prevent distortion.

NAMES WITH TERMS THAT BY DEFINITION IMPLY THAT THE BODY IS PART OF ANOTHER

These would include terms such as "department," "division," "section," "branch":

```
University of Toronto. Department of Fine Arts.
```

NAMES WITH TERMS NORMALLY IMPLYING ADMINISTRATIVE SUBORDINATION

These would include terms such as "committee" and "commission," but only if the name of the higher body is needed for its identification. For choice of heading follow the example for government bodies with names of agencies with terms normally implying administrative subordination shown on p. 58.

NAMES THAT HAVE BEEN OR MIGHT BE USED BY OTHER PARENT BODIES FOR THEIR
SUBORDINATE BODIES

These would include names of a general nature such as "Class of 1980," which
might be used by various universities, or "Friends of the Library," which
might pertain to various libraries:

Bell Telephone Laboratories. Technical Information Library.

University of Calgary. Alumni Association.

NAMES OF UNIVERSITY FACULTIES, SCHOOLS, COLLEGES, INSTITUTES, LABORATORIES, ETC.,
WHICH INDICATE ONLY THE FIELD OF STUDY

These would include names of particular faculties, schools, etc., which
do not include the name of the university itself, such as School of Pharmacy.
For example:

University of Western Ontario.   Faculty of Dental Science.

but

Harvard Law School.
The name of the school includes the name of the parent body, but not in full.

NAMES THAT INCLUDE THE ENTIRE NAME OF THE PARENT BODY

Isolate the entire name of the parent body from the name of the subordinate
part. If the name of the subordinate part does not include the name of the
parent body, then enter it as a subheading:

Yale University. Library.
*The name "Yale University Library" is analyzed as parent body—Yale
University; subordinate body—Library.*

Canadian Library Association. Conference (34th : 1979 : Ottawa)
*The name "34th Annual Conference of the Canadian Library Association" is
analyzed as parent body—Canadian Library Association; subordinate part—
34th Annual Conference.*

Names Entered Directly

If a subordinate or related body is named prominently in the item to be
catalogued, and the name does not fall into any of the types outlined
immediately above, then the subordinate or related body is entered directly
under its own name. Make a name reference from the subordinate or related
body as if it were entered as a subheading:

Henrietta Harvey Library.
Name reference from Memorial University of Newfoundland. Henrietta Harvey Library.

Direct or Indirect Subheadings

If a subordinate body, as described on pp. 56 to 57, has several intervening elements of the hierarchy between it and the top of the hierarchy, it is entered under the lowest element above it that is entered under its own name. For choice of heading follow the example for government bodies shown on p. 60.

CHOOSING HEADINGS FOR GOVERNMENT BODIES AND OFFICIALS

Names Entered Subordinately

If the name of a government agency falls into one of the following 10 categories, then it is entered as a subheading of the heading for the government. Do not repeat the name or abbreviation of the name of the government in noun form unless it is necessary to prevent distortion.

NAMES WITH TERMS THAT BY DEFINITION IMPLY A BODY IS PART OF ANOTHER SUBORDINATION

This would include terms such as "department," "division," "section," "branch," etc.:

Ottawa. Department of Community Development.

NAMES OF AGENCIES WITH TERMS NORMALLY IMPLYING ADMINISTRATIVE SUBORDINATION

This would include terms such as "commission," "committee," etc., but only if the name of the government is necessary to identify the agency:

Canada. Royal Commission on Bilingualism and Biculturalism.

but

Royal Commission on Higher Education in New Brunswick.
Name of commission includes the name of the government.

NAMES OF AGENCIES THAT HAVE BEEN OR MIGHT BE USED BY OTHER GOVERNMENTS FOR THEIR AGENCIES

Use only if the name of the government is necessary to identify the agency.

Illinois. Environmental Protection Agency.

United States. Environmental Protection Agency.

NAMES OF AGENCIES THAT ARE MINISTRIES OR SIMILAR MAJOR EXECUTIVE AGENCIES WHICH
HAVE NO AGENCIES ABOVE THEM

Their position is defined by official publications of the government.

Canada. Agriculture Canada.
*The second "Canada" cannot be omitted because the results of omission
would create a distortion.*

United States. National Aeronautics and Space Administration.

LEGISLATIVE BODIES

Great Britain. Parliament.

United States. Congress.

COURTS

Canada. Supreme Court.

Ontario. High Court of Justice.

PRINCIPAL ARMED SERVICES

Canada. Canadian Armed Forces.

United States. Army.

CHIEFS OF STATE AND HEADS OF GOVERNMENT

Winnipeg. Mayor.

Alberta. Premier.

Canada. Prime Minister.

Great Britain. Sovereign.
Some libraries use "United Kingdom."

EMBASSIES, CONSULATES, ETC.

Canada. Embassy (U.S.)
The Canadian embassy in the U.S.

Great Britain. Consulate (New York)
The heading shows the city where the consulate is located.

```
Canada. Delegation to the United Nations.
```

Names Entered Directly

If a government body is prominently named on the item to be catalogued, and the name does not fall into any of the above types, then the government body is entered directly under its own name. Make a name reference from the government body as if it were entered as a subheading:

```
Canadian National Railways.
```
Refer from Canada. Canadian National Railways.

```
Canadian Broadcasting Corporation.
```

```
National Film Board of Canada.
```

```
Ontario Hydro.
```

```
Public Archives of Canada.
```

When in doubt about the names of Canadian government bodies, consult the appropriate section of *Canadiana.*

Direct or Indirect Subheadings

A government body, as described on pp. 58 to 60, is entered subordinately to the heading for the government unless the name of the agency has been, or is likely to be, used by another agency entered under the heading for the same government. In that case, put in the name of the lowest intervening element in the hierarchy that will distinguish between the agencies:

```
Great Britain. Department of Employment. Solicitor's Office.
```
Hierarchy: Great Britain.
       Department of Employment.
       Solicitor's Office.

The department's name cannot be omitted here since the name "Solicitor's Office" might be used by other governmental bodies, and also entered under the heading "Great Britain." Then the governmental bodies could not be distinguished.

but

```
Ontario. Heritage Administration Branch.
```
Hierarchy: Ontario.
       Ministry of Culture and Recreation.
       Heritage Administration Branch.

Since there is (or will likely be) only one Heritage Administration Branch in the Ontario Government, the name of the intervening element is omitted. The name of the ministry is inserted in its hierarchical position if a name reference is made from the full hierarchy to the branch.

Special Subheadings

LEGISLATIVE BODIES

In a legislature that has more than one chamber, the chamber is entered as a subheading to the heading for the legislature as on p. 59, "Legislative Bodies." For example:

Canada. Parliament. Senate.

United States. Congress. House.
"House of Representatives" is shown in AACR2, *but this book follows the Library of Congress in using "House."*

Committees and other subordinate units are entered under the subheadings of the legislative, or particular chamber, as appropriate:

United States. Congress. Joint Committee on the Library.

ARMED FORCES

Military units, component branches, etc., are entered as a subheading of the heading for the principal service as on p. 59, "Principal Armed Services." For example:

United States. Army. General Staff.

Great Britain. Royal Navy. Sea Cadet Corps.

If the component branch, etc., contains the name of the principal service, it is entered as a subheading to the name of the government:

United States. Army Map Service.

Two or More Governmental Jurisdictions With Same Name

Add distinguishing information as necessary in parentheses after the name of the governmental jurisdiction:

Québec (Québec)   *i.e., Quebec City.*
AACR2 *recommends the use of the English form of geographical names. It does, however, use the forms "Québec" and "Montréal."*

Québec (Province)
New York (N.Y.)   *i.e., New York City.*
New York (State)
London (Ont.)
AACR2 *abbreviates the names of the provinces of Canada and of the states of the U.S.*

London (England)
AACR2 *does not abbreviate "England," "Ireland," and "Scotland."*
Berlin (Germany : West)
Berlin (Germany : East)
Georgia (U.S.)
Georgia (Soviet Union)
AACR2 *uses "Union of Soviet Socialist Republics," but the Library of Congress and the National Library of Canada prefer "Soviet Union."*

The practice of the national libraries is not totally consistent with the rules in *AACR2. AACR2* itself shows some options. While forms of main entry headings for places are being reconsidered and adapted to suit national preferences, some inconsistency just has to be lived with.

Place Names Unlikely to be Confused

Where confusion of names is not likely, the place name may stand alone:

Charlottetown
AACR2, *however, shows the abbreviated name of the next higher jurisdiction after the names of cities, e.g., "Charlottetown (P.E.I.)."*

Manitoba
With the names of states and provinces of several countries, among them Canada, Australia and the U.S., AACR2 allows the option of omitting the name of the next larger jurisdiction. This option agrees with the present practice of the Library of Congress and the National Library of Canada.

MAIN ENTRY UNDER TITLE

Form of Heading

PUNCTUATION AND SPACING

The title as main entry begins a paragraph at the first indention on the fourth line down. The second and subsequent lines of the first paragraph begin at the second indention. This form of margin is known as a "hanging indention." (See p. 157.)

The spacing and punctuation of the title main entry is the same as for the title element in the title and statement of responsibility area. (See p. 83, "Introduction.")

CAPITALIZATION

Capitalization is the same as for title element of the title and statement of responsibility area with one exception. If the first word of the title main entry is an article, then the second word is capitalized:

A Dictionary of Canadianisms
Title main entry.

Entry Under Title

A work is entered under its title only if it falls into one of the categories below (see also p. 65, "Determining Uniform Titles").

WORK OF UNKNOWN AUTHORSHIP OR BY A BODY THAT LACKS A NAME

Go ask Alice
This work has been ascribed to "Anonymous."

WORK OF FOUR OR MORE PERSONS AND/OR CORPORATE BODIES

Make an added entry under the heading for the first person or body if the user of the catalogue is likely to search for the item in this way:

Texas country / Willie Nelson, Freddy Fender, Asleep at the
   Wheel, Bob Wills and his Texas Playboys
This is a sound disc set. An added entry may go under the heading for Nelson.

WORKS AND COLLECTIONS PRODUCED UNDER EDITORIAL DIRECTION

Both works with and without collective titles are entered under title, and added entries made, as detailed on pp. 40 to 41, "Works and Collections Produced Under Editorial Direction."

WORKS EMANATING FROM CORPORATE BODIES WHICH DO NOT FALL INTO CATEGORIES OUTLINED ABOVE (P. 36, "DETERMINING WHAT IS A CORPORATE BODY") AND WHICH DO NOT HAVE A PERSONAL AUTHOR

SACRED SCRIPTURE OF A RELIGIOUS GROUP

The whole work or part of the work is entered under a uniform title. Make an added entry under the name of any person associated with the work. (See p. 71, "Sacred Scriptures.")

UNIFORM TITLES

A uniform title is one way of bringing together in the catalogue all editions, translations, etc., of a work which may have various titles.

The need to use uniform titles will vary greatly from catalogue to catalogue, and will partly depend on how well the work is known, how may different versions the library has, and whether the work was originally in another language.

Form of Uniform Title

A uniform title is enclosed in square brackets, and is placed between the main entry heading and the title proper. Both the uniform title and title proper begin on new lines at the second indention.

If the work is entered under title, then the uniform title will become the heading. It is optional in this case whether to put the uniform title in square brackets. In the examples shown throughout the remainder of this chapter, the square brackets have been omitted when a uniform title is the main entry heading.

The elements of a uniform title are separated by *a period and a space*. The period comes *immediately* after the last letter of the preceding element.

CAPITALIZATION

Individual uniform titles are capitalized as in the title and statement of responsibility area, or as title main entry headings.

Collective uniform titles, have only the first word capitalized:

[Short stories]

For any additions to uniform titles, both individual and collective, capitalize the first word and other words according to the rules of the language involved. For example:

[Poems. Selections]

For music, put in lower case words and abbreviations which indicate medium of performance, accompanying serial numbers, opus or thematic index number, and words accompanying statement of keys:

[Trios, piano, strings, no. 2, op. 66, C minor]

When such words are proper names or abbreviations of them, they are, naturally, capitalized:

[..., K. 370]
K stands for Köchel, the thematic indexer of Mozart.

[..., English horn]

Determining Uniform Titles

INDIVIDUAL TITLES—WORKS CREATED AFTER 1500

Create the uniform title in the original language of the work and from its best known name in common usage. Include any initial articles except when the uniform title is the main entry heading. Then leave the initial articles in only if required for reasons of grammar.

```
Shakespeare, William.
   [Hamlet]
   The tragicall historie of Hamlet, Prince of Denmarke ...
```

```
Whitaker's almanack.
   An almanack for the year of Our Lord ...
```
In this example the uniform title as main entry heading is not put in square brackets, exercising the option mentioned on p. 64, "Punctuation and Position."

Works published simultaneously in the same language under two different titles would have the uniform title of the work published in the home country of the library doing the cataloguing. If the work is not published in the home country, use as the uniform title the title of the first edition received.

```
Herriot, James.
   [All creatures great and small]
   If only they could talk ...
```
This Canadian library received All Creatures Great and Small *before receiving the same work in the British editions, entitled,* If Only They Could Talk *and* It Shouldn't Happen to a Vet.

INDIVIDUAL TITLES—WORKS CREATED BEFORE 1501

Create the uniform title in its original language as it is found in modern reference sources. If these sources are inconclusive, then use the title of modern, then early, editions of the work, in that order. Initial articles are omitted in main entry headings unless required for grammatical purposes:

```
Beowulf.
   The song of Beowulf / edited by ...
```
Uniform title as main entry heading.

```
Bryson, Bernarda.
   [Gilgamesh]
   Gilgamesh : man's first story ...
```

For classical and Byzantine Greek works, use a well-established English title. If an English title is not available, preference should be given to the Latin title over the Greek title, if both exist.

```
Virgil.
   [Aeneid]
```
English used, not Latin form, "Aeneis."

For anonymous works that are written neither in Greek nor in a Roman script, use an established English title if there is one:

```
Arabian nights
```

```
I ching
```

Additions to Uniform Titles

Uniform titles used as main entry headings may be similar or identical to another title or the heading of a person. In order to distinguish between them, add a word, phrase, or designation in parentheses after the uniform title:

```
Genesis (Rock group)
```

```
Genesis (Book of the Bible)
```
Used only as a reference.

Works in one language. Add the name of the language of the work being catalogued if it differs from the language of the original. It is separated from the uniform title by *a period and a space*. For example:

```
Dumas, Alexandre.
   [Les trois mousquetaires. English]
   The three musketeers ...
```
An English translation of a French novel. The Library of Congress omits all initial articles to facilitate automated filing.

Works in two languages. If one language is the original language, name it second. If neither language is the original, name the languages in alphabetic order of their names in English, e.g., English, French, German, Spanish, etc.

```
Camões, Luis de.
   [Os lusiadas. English, Portuguese]
   The Lusiads ...
```
Original language was Portuguese.

Works in three or more languages. Use the term "Polyglot" when the original work itself is in one language but the item in hand consists of the work in three or more languages. If the original is in three or more languages, list the languages as outlined in the previous paragraph. For example:

United States.
   [The Declaration of Independence. Polyglot]
   The Declaration of Independence of the United States,
in ten languages ...

General material designations (GMD's) are added after any distinguishing or language designations at the end of the uniform title, if the library exercises the option of using them:

Brunhoff, Jean de.
   [Les aventures de Babar. English. Sound recording.]
   The story of Babar, the elephant ...
Option of using GMD is exercised.

Mother Goose. Sound recording.
   Songs of Mother Goose ...
Option of using the GMD is exercised, as well as the option of omitting square brackets from the uniform title when it is a main entry heading.

Some of the national libraries are deliberating on the possibility of putting the GMD after the title proper rather than the uniform title.

Parts of Works

The following is an alternative to analytics and general references as ways of making headings for parts of works.

SINGLE PARTS

If the work to be catalogued has a title of its own, and is part of a larger work, make a uniform title out of the title of the part. Make a "see" reference or a general reference from the work as a whole with the subheading and number, if there is one, of the part:

Le Guin, Ursula K.
   [The tombs of Atuan]   *Uniform title of the part.*
   The Earthsea trilogy ...
"See" reference may be made from Le Guin, Ursula K. The Earthsea trilogy. The tombs of Atuan.

SEVERAL PARTS

Consecutively numbered parts. These are shown by a designation in the singular as a subheading of the title of the whole work followed by the inclusive numbers of the parts:

```
Virgil.
   [Aeneid. Books 1-6]
   The first six books of Virgil's Aeneid ...
```

Two unnumbered or non-consecutive parts. Use a uniform title for the first part and a name title added entry for the second for these:

```
Dante Alighieri.
   [Purgatorio. English]
   The version of Purgatory and Paradise ...
```
A name title added entry may be made for Dante Alighieri. Paradiso. English.

Three or more unnumbered or non-consecutive parts. Indicate these in the uniform title by the term "Selections":

```
Gibbon, Edward.
   [The history of the decline and fall of the Roman Empire.
Selections]
```

```
Dickens, Charles.
   [Sketches by Boz. German. Selections]
   Londoner Skizzen von Boz ...
```

Two Works Issued Together

The following is an alternative to analytics and general references as a way of making headings for two works issued together with a collective title. If the two works issued together have a personal or corporate body main entry heading and a collective title for the work that covers both, use the title of the first work as a uniform title. A name title added entry is made using the uniform title of the second:

```
Dickens, Charles.
   [Hard times]
   Dickens' new stories ...
```
This book contains Hard times *and* Pictures from Italy. *An added entry may be made for Dickens, Charles.* Pictures from Italy.

Collective Titles

COMPLETE WORKS

The collective title "Works" will bring together all items that are, or purport to be, the complete works of one person or body:

```
Shakespeare, William.
   [Works]
   The complete works of William Shakespeare ...
```

Use the collective title "Selections" for items of three or more works by one person:

```
Lamb, Charles.
  [Selections]
  Wit and wisdom of Charles Lamb ...
```

```
Morris, William.
  [Selections]
  Selected writings and designs ...
```

WORKS IN A SINGLE FORM

The following terms are used to indicate the complete, or purportedly complete, works of one person in a particular form: Correspondence; Essays; Novels; Plays; Poems; Prose works; Short stories; Speeches; others as appropriate, e.g., Posters. For example:

```
Shakespeare, William.
  [Plays]
  Collected plays of ...
```

If the item consists of three or more but not of all the works of one person in a particular form, add the term "Selections":

```
Conrad, Joseph.
  [Novels. Selections]
  Selected novels of ...
```

```
Shakespeare, William.
  [Plays. Selections]
  Four comedies ...
```

TRANSLATIONS

The names of languages when different from the language of the original work are added to the collective titles as outlined on p. 66, "Language Designations." If the term "Selections" is added to the collective title, the name of the language goes before it:

```
Shakespeare, William.
  [Works. Spanish]
  Obras completas de ...
```

```
Maupassant, Guy de.
  [Short stories. English. Selections]
  Mademoiselle Fifi and other stories ...
```

STORIES WITH MANY VERSIONS; CYCLES OF EARLY LEGENDS, POEMS, ETC.

If the versions or cycles are identified by a distinctive title, the uniform title is created from the generally accepted title. (See p. 65, "Individual Titles—Works Created Before 1501.")

If the versions or cycles are identified by a descriptive phrase only, e.g., Grail legends, or have no distinctive title, the main entry is entered under the title proper. (See p. 40, "Works and Collections Produced Under Editorial Direction.")

Special Rules for Law, Sacred Scriptures and Music

MODERN LAWS

Collections. Use the term "Laws, etc." as the uniform title for complete or partial collections of laws. Do not use for law collections on a particular subject:

```
Ontario.
  [Laws, etc.]
  Statutes of the Province of Ontario ...

Boston.
  [Laws, etc.]
  The revised ordinances of 1961 of the city of Boston ...
```

Collections of laws on a particular subject. Use as the uniform title the citation title or the standard accepted abbreviated title of the subject compilation, if it has one. If not, create one by omitting any introductory phrases and/or statements of responsibility that are part of the title proper if grammatically possible, and any initial articles if not grammatically necessary:

```
California.
  [Agricultural code]
  West's California agricultural code ...
```
Omit statement of responsibility, i.e., surname "West's."

Single laws, etc. Use in order of preference one of the following as the uniform title:

official short title or citation title

unofficial short title or citation title used in legal literature

official title of the enactment

any official designation, e.g., number or date

For example:

Ontario.
  [Education Act (1974)]
Date is added to distinguish among many Education Acts.

SACRED SCRIPTURES

Uniform title. A sacred scripture is entered under its commonly used name in English language reference sources:

Bible.

Koran.

Talmud.

Bible. Testaments, books, chapters and verses. The names of these may be added as required.

Bible. O.T.

Bible. N.T. Revelation.

Bible. N.T. Corinthians, 1st.
Numbered book.

Bible. O.T. Ecclesiastes III, 1-8.
Chapter in roman, verses in arabic, numerals.

  Groups of books:

Bible. O.T. Chronicles.

Bible. N.T. Gospels.

Bible. O.T. Pentateuch.

Single selections. A selection commonly known by its own name is entered under that name as a uniform title. Make a reference from the form of the title as shown above:

Ten commandments.
Reference may be made from Bible. O.T. Exodus XX, 2-17, and Bible. O.T. Deuteronomy V, 6-21.

Two selections. The following is an alternative to analytics and added entries to provide headings for two selections. If the item may be expressed with two uniform titles, enter the work under the uniform title for the first part. Make an added entry under the uniform title for the second part.

Other selections. Enter under the most specific Bible heading, then add language, version, "Selections," and year of publications, in that order:

```
Bible. English. Revised Standard. Selections.
   1968.
   Daily readings from the Revised Standard Version ...
```

Particular version. After the designation "Bible" or parts of the Bible add language, version, and year of publication, in that order. (See example above.)

Other sacred scriptures. Use an equivalent format to the one in the above section on the Bible, and make any additions in accordance with the rules outlined on pp. 66 to 68. For example:

```
Talmud. English. Selections.
   The Babylonian Talmud in selection / edited ...
```

```
Koran. Sūrat al-Baqarah.
```
One of the chapters of the Koran. Reference may be made from Koran. al-Sūrah II.

```
Vedas. Atharvaveda.
```
One of the collections of Vedas.

```
Upanishads. English.
```

MUSIC

Establishing uniform titles for music is not a responsibility suited to the generalist school librarian, since it presupposes a knowledge of music beyond that which the average librarian can boast of, as well as some facility in Italian, German, French and the other languages of the classics and popular music. Wherever possible, follow the instructions in Chapter II, especially on p. 25, "Library of Congress," and use the copy prepared by experts. When unable to create an original uniform title, one could take the title from the *Schwann Record and Tape Guide*,[1] available at little cost in most record stores.

Determining the uniform title of a composition. This is the original title in the original language:

```
[La fille du régiment]   not The daughter of the regiment
```

The title does not include the medium of performance, the opus and serial number and other numbers that are not integral:

[Les trois cloches]
In this title, the number is integral.

[Concertos ...]
From "Concertos, no. 3," where the number is a serial number, not integral.

[Concerto, clarinet]
Medium, clarinet, is not part of the title. Medium and number, when not integral, may be added to the title after a comma and a space.

Works can have as uniform title the name of a form of music or type of composition. This is expressed in the English plural form, unless a composer wrote only one as in the example of the clarinet concerto above. The English term may be a borrowing from another language, e.g., *divertimenti, bagatelles.* If there is a choice between established English and non-English forms, use the English, e.g., concertos, not *concerti*:

Chopin, Frédéric.
  [Etudes]   *Uniform title.*
  Butterfly étude ...   *Title on sheet music.*

Medium of performance. The medium is given if the title is a generic term, such as "Concertos," "Sonatas," "Fugues":

Mozart, Wolfgang Amadeus.
  [Quintets, string quartet, clarinet, K. 581, A major]
  Mozart's clarinet quintet ...

The medium of performance is not stated if it goes without saying:

Beethoven, Ludwig van.
  [Symphonies, no. 6, op. 68, F major]
  Pastoral symphony ...
The medium, orchestra, is implicit.

If the medium is changeable or contrary to expectations, it is added to the uniform title:

[Waltzes, men's voices]

[Mass, jazz band]

If the performers are various, list the participants by medium after the type of composition, separating each element with *a comma and a space*:

[Motet, soprano, baritone, organ, orchestra]

Levels of voices are listed from highest to lowest, then keyboard instruments, then other accompaniments. There are conventional terms for most standard groupings, e.g., string quartet, which means two violins, a viola and a cello. Use the standard English form of the name of instruments and performers when a non-English form is not the established one:

Established and preferred English form:

> bass, not basso
> violin, not violino

Foreign form established in English:

> mezzo-soprano
> celesta

Some of the most common standard terms for medium of performance are:

orchestra	brasses	women's voices
string orchestra	winds	piano
band	strings	piano (2)
woodwinds	mixed voices	

Numbers and keys. If the title is a generic name, add the serial number (e.g., Symphonies, no. 40), opus number or thematic index number (e.g., K. 420), and key signature (e.g., B major) in that order. Each element is separated by *a comma and a space.* Even an identifying date or place may be added in parentheses if necessary to distinguish the work from all others:

Uniform title.

```
Mozart, Wolfgang Amadeus.
   [Symphonies, no. 41, K. 551, C major. Sound recording]
   Symphony no. 41 in C, K. 551, "Jupiter" ...
```
Title proper of a record. Option is exercised to use the GMD.

Works with the same title. If two works have the same title which is not a generic term add a medium designator, if convenient, or make up a distinguishing comment and add it in parentheses:

```
[Boléro, orchestra]
```
French spelling of Ravel's work.

```
[Bolero, flamenco guitar]
```
Spanish spelling.

```
[Goyescas (Opera)]
```

```
[Goyescas (Piano work)]
```

Arrangements. For arrangements add the abbreviation "arr." It is separated from the preceding element by *a semi-colon and a space.*

```
[Blue Danube waltz; arr.]
```

Librettos and song texts. Librettos and song texts are entered under the name of the composer of the music for them, the uniform title being that of the musical work with the subheadings libretto, for operas, etc., or text(s), for songs:

```
Puccini, Giacomo.
   [Tosca. Libretto. English and Italian]
```

The texts, such as librettos, *can* have a language designation to show whether the work is in the original or in translation but need not, if it is seldom translated:

```
Verdi, Giuseppe.
   [Requiem]
```
No language designator because version is in the original Latin.

```
Lehár, Franz.
   [Die lustige Witwe. French]
   La veuve joyeuse ...
```
Language designator shown because the work is done as often in translation as in the original.

Parts of a work. Enter under the uniform title for the whole work, followed by the title of the part:

```
Fauré, Gabriel.
   [Requiem. Dies irae]
```
Make a "see" reference from the composer and the title of the part, if useful, i.e., Fauré, Gabriel. Dies irae.

If there are several selections, give the uniform title for the first part and make an added entry for the other parts if useful:

```
Donizetti, Gaetano.
   [Lucia di Lammermoor. Ardon gl'incensi (Mad scene)]
   Bridal chorus, sextet and mad scene from Lucia ...
```
Added entry for one selection, i.e., Mad scene.

Two works published together. Make a uniform title for the first and an added entry for the second, as shown immediately above.

Mozart, Wolfgang Amadeus.
  [Symphonies, no. 41, K. 551, C major. Videorecording]
  Mozart's Jupiter and Haydn's Surprise symphonies ...
*Added entry is made for Haydn, Joseph. Symphonies, no. 94 . . . Option is
exercised to use the GMD.*

General terms. There are broad terms for types of composition that may be
given as uniform title for complete works or groupings of works. The term
"Works" alone denotes the total works, or *oeuvre* of a composer. The term
"Selections" alone stands for a collection in different media and forms. Other
typical general terms are:

[Chamber music]
[Choral music]
[Instrumental music]
[Keyboard music]
[Vocal music]
[String quartet music]
[Concertos]
[Operas]
[Waltzes]

   The subheading "Selections" may be used with the terms listed above if
appropriate. It is preceded by *a period and a space*:

Rossini, Gioacchino.
  [Operas. Selections]
  Montserrat Caballé sings Rossini rarities ...
Option to use the GMD is not exercised.

FOOTNOTES

[1]*Schwann Record and Tape Guide* (W. Schwann Inc.: Boston).

Contents IV

Description of the Work

Introduction 79
  Levels of Description 79
  Sources of Information 80
  Framework for Description 80
  General Notes on Punctuation 82
Title and Statement of Responsibility Area 82
  Introduction 82
  Title Proper 84
  General Material Designation — Optional Addition 86
  Parallel Title 87
  Other Title Information 87
  Statement of Responsibility 87
Edition Area 89
  Introduction 89
  Edition Statement 90
  Statement of Responsibility Relating to the Edition 90
Material (or Type of Publication) Specific Details Area 90
  Introduction 91
  Cartographic Materials 91
  Serials 92
Publication, Distribution, Etc., Area 93
  Introduction 93
  Place of Publication, Distribution, Etc. 94
  Name of Publisher, Distributor, Etc. 95
  Date of Publication, Distribution, Etc. 96
Physical Description Area 97
  Introduction 97
  Extent of Item 98
  Other Physical Details 101
  Dimensions 107
  Items Made Up of Several Types of Material 111
Series Area 114
  Introduction 114
  Title Proper of Series 115
  Parallel Titles of Series 115
  Other Title Information of Series 115
  Statements of Responsibility Relating to Series 115
  International Standard Serial Number 115
  Numbering Within Series 115

Subseries 116
More Than One Series Statement 116
Note Area 117
Introduction 117
Form of Notes 117
Standard Number and Terms of Availability Area 119
Introduction 119
Standard Number 120
Terms of Availability — Optional Addition 120
Facsimiles, Photocopies and Other Reproductions 120
Footnotes 121

∨

Chapter IV

Description of the Work

INTRODUCTION

Levels of Description

After making a decision about the main entry heading, the librarian's next task is to describe the item. Since the amount of description necessary varies according to the purposes of the catalogue and the needs and sophistication of the users, the second edition of the *Anglo-American Cataloguing Rules* (*AACR2*) allows for three levels of description.

The first level supplies a minimum amount of information about an item, and many elementary school librarians may find it sufficient for describing the new items in their collection. The second level includes all the information from the first level, plus more opportunities for detailed cataloguing. Larger school libraries should consider cataloguing at the second level, as many jobbers supplying cards to schools have opted for it. Only the largest and most specialized libraries would require the amount of information given at the third level.

In this chapter, both the first and second levels will be described. Throughout the chapter, levels covered are indicated by ① and ②. It is up to the librarian in each school to decide which level to use.

```
946.086    Toland, John.                                    ①
HIT            Adolph Hitler. -- Doubleday, 1976.
TOL            2 v.
```

Book catalogued at first level of description. This book club edition has no ISBN, which would normally be included.

```
946.086    Toland, John.
HIT             Adolph Hitler / by John Toland. -- New          ②
TOL             York : Doubleday, 1976.
                2 v. : ill., maps, tables ; 22 cm.
```

Same book catalogued at second level of description.

It is permissible to catalogue one type of material, e.g., books, at the second level while cataloguing another type, e.g., filmstrips, at the first level. As well, the librarian may opt for Level 1 and add some elements or areas from Level 2 to provide more detail for the user.

AACR2 also provides for optional additions to any level of description. Several of these will be shown and labelled as optional in this chapter. Again the librarian will have to decide which options to use, and for future reference, should make a note about the decision beside the appropriate place in this book. More detailed information about cataloguing non-book materials may be found in *Nonbook Materials: The Organization of Integrated Collections.*

Sources of Information

Whenever possible, the information needed to describe an item should be taken from the part of the item itself which is the chief source of information. This might be a title page and its verso, the introductory frames of a filmstrip, the labels on a sound recording, or the equivalent. If this source is ambiguous or insufficient, information may be derived from other parts of the item, such as the flyleaf of a book or a record jacket cover.

Enclose in square brackets any information not taken from the chief source of information. Exceptions include:

> Physical description which is based on the examination of the work as a whole, e.g., realia
> The note area
> The standard number and terms of availability area

Framework for Description

The description of the item being catalogued is set in an international framework known as the General International Standard Bibliographic Description (ISBD(G)). This framework sets out the order of the areas, the order of the elements within each area, and the punctuation within and between elements and areas.

Once found, the information is arranged in the sequence shown in Table 1, column 1. This table also shows the elements that are included at the first and second level of cataloguing.

TABLE I

Areas in *AACR2*	Traditional (pre-*AACR2*) Terms	May Include	First Level of Description	Second Level of Description
Title and statement of responsibility area	Title and author statement	Title, general material designation, subtitle, author . . .	Title proper, first statement of responsibility, if different from the main entry heading or if there is a title main entry	Title proper, GMD, parallel title, other title information, first statement of responsibility, each subsequent statement of responsibility
Edition area	Edition statement	Edition statement, editor . . .	Edition statement	Edition statement, first statement of responsibility relating to the edition
Material (or type of publication) specific details area.	No equivalent	Scale or projection of a map, numbering of volumes of a serial . . .	Material (or type of publication) specific details	Material (or type of publication) specific details
Publication, distribution, etc., area	Imprint (including place and date of publication)	Place of publication, publisher, date . . .	First publisher, etc., date of publication, etc.	First place of publication, etc., first publisher, etc., date of publication, etc.
Physical description area	Collation	Paging, volumes, frames . . ., specific material designation, illustrations, dimensions . . .	Extent of item	Extent of item, other physical details, dimensions
Series area	Series statement	Series statement		Title proper of series, statement of responsibility relating to series, ISSN of series, numbering within the series. Title of subseries, ISSN of subseries, numbering within subseries
Note area	Notes	Notes	Note(s)	Note(s)
Standard number and terms of availability area	No equivalent	ISBN, price . . .	Standard number	Standard number

General Notes on Punctuation

In this book, punctuation and spacing within and between the areas is quite arbitrary in comparison with the punctuation traditionally used on catalogue cards. Details for punctuating each area are given later in this chapter.

In punctuating according to these guidelines, the librarian will have to cope with punctuation marks integral to the description, in such elements as author's name or dimensions of the work. When an element or area ends with an abbreviation that ends with a period, do not put in another period merely to comply with the formal punctuation as shown here. On the other hand, double punctuation is not to be avoided in other instances, where the integral punctuation is followed by the formal punctuation:

```
Who should play God? : the artificial creation
of life and what it means for the future of the
human race
```
Double punctuation necessary.

AACR2, being concerned with cataloguing in many formats besides that of the catalogue card, is less explicit about paragraphing and end punctuation than *this* book is. Although *AACR2* does not specify a period at the end of each paragraph, for example, after the main entry heading or a note, many authorities and suppliers of catalogue cards punctuate the ends of paragraphs on a card with the period. This practice of ending each paragraph with a full stop is followed in the examples in this book, except that a period is not put in when the paragraph ends with a square bracket or a closing parenthesis, e.g., after the series area.

TITLE AND STATEMENT OF RESPONSIBILITY AREA

Introduction

LEVELS OF DESCRIPTION

At the first level of description, this area includes at least the following elements:
> Title proper
> First statement of responsibility, if different from the main entry
>> heading or if there is a title main entry

For the second level of description, this area includes at least the following elements:
> Title proper
> General material designation
> Parallel title
> Other title information
> First statement of responsibility
> Each subsequent statement of responsibility

Not all elements of this area will necessarily be present for every item to be catalogued.

For the first level of description, punctuation of title and statement of responsibility area, and spacing between the elements, are:

> Title proper / first statement of responsibility, if different from the main entry heading or if there is a title main entry
>
> ①

The second level of description:

> Title proper [general material designation] = parallel title : other title information / first statement of responsibility ; each subsequent statement of responsibility
>
> ②

If an element is not present, then the punctuation preceding that element is also omitted. For instance, if there is no general material designation (GMD) and there is a parallel title, then the illustration of the second level of description would be:

title proper = parallel title

If there is no parallel title and no other title information, the illustration of the second level of description would be:

title proper [GMD] / first statement of responsibility

If some second-level elements are added as options to a description at the first level, then the punctuation and spacing that precede them should be added as well.

Title not as main entry heading. The first word in the title proper, alternative title, parallel, or quoted title is capitalized, but not the first word of other title information. Other words within this area are not capitalized, except for proper nouns and adjectives derived from them, important words in the names of corporate bodies, government bodies, and names of historical and legal documents, titles of nobility, of address, and of honour, the Bible and its parts:

A field guide to snow crystals
First word capitalized.

```
Twelfth night, or, What you will
```
First word of alternative title capitalized.

```
Catlands = Pays des chats
```
Parallel title; first word of parallel title capitalized.

```
Masonic imagery in The magic flute
```
First word of quoted title capitalized.

```
Colony to nation : a history of Canada
```
Proper noun, "Canada," capitalized; first word of other title information, i.e., "a history of Canada," not capitalized.

```
Colombo's Book of marvels
```
Special case. Part of the title is itself a form of title.

If a title proper is in two or more parts, naming parts which are supplementary to, or a section of, the item, and not grammatically linked with the title proper, capitalize the first word of the second and any other parts:

```
Henry IV. Part I.
```

Title as main entry heading. All the rules in the section immediately above apply. As well, the second word in the title must be capitalized if the first word is an article:

```
The Best modern Canadian short stories
```

Title Proper   ① ②

TRANSCRIPTION

Transcribe the title as it appears on the item. Do not alter wording, order, or spelling. It may be necessary to change internal punctuation, spacing and capitalization, in analogy to the examples below:

```
The complete jogger
```

```
Heather McKay's Complete book of squash
```

```
   "Dangerous foreigners" : European immigrant workers
and labour radicalism in Canada, 1896-1932
```
Retain quotation marks as given.

```
Music from Fiddler on the roof
```

```
La fête polonaise
```
Diacritical marks and French usage in capitalization retained.

```
Shakespeare's comedies
```

```
G.B.S.
```
No spaces between letters or initials followed by periods.

```
ALA rules for filing catalog cards
```
No spaces between initials or letters without periods.

```
What's a friend?
```
Retain closing punctuation as given.

```
1066 and all that
```
Numbers retained as in chief source of information.

ALTERNATIVE TITLE

Follow the first part of the title with *a comma, a space, "or," a space* and the alternative title. The first word of the alternative title is capitalized:

```
Mazel and Shlimazel, or, The milk of a lioness
```

NO TITLE PROPER

Devise a brief title and enclose in square brackets:

```
[Map of the moon]
```

```
[Photograph of Albert Einstein]
```

TITLE WITH A SUPPLEMENT OR SECTION

If the title and its supplementary part(s) are not grammatically linked in the source of information, record the main title first, followed by *a period and a space.* Then record the name(s) of the supplementary part(s):

```
Advanced calculus. Teacher's handbook
```

```
Henry IV. Part II
```

COLLECTIVE TITLE WITH TITLES OF INDIVIDUAL WORKS

Use the collective title as the title proper and put the titles of the individual works in a contents note. (See p. 118, "Contents Note.")

TWO OR MORE PARTS WITHOUT A COLLECTIVE TITLE

By same person(s) or body (bodies). Transcribe the titles in the order given. Follow the first title by *a space, a semi-colon, a space, "and," a space* and the second title. The first word of the second title is capitalized:

```
The doors of perception ; and, Heaven and hell
```

By different person(s) or body (bodies). Transcribe in the order as given the title information and statement of responsibility for the first work. Then do the same for other titles. If a GMD is used, it goes at the end of the final title and statement of responsibility element:

```
Peter and the wolf / Prokofiev ; narrated by Mia
Farrow.  The young person's guide to the orchestra /
Britten ; narrated by André Previn ; London Symphony
Orchestra conducted by André Previn [sound recording]
```

General Material Designation ② — Optional Addition ①

Librarians will need to make a decision about the use of GMD's. It is recommended that they be used for all non-book materials at both the first and second levels of cataloguing and then their omission would imply that the title belonged to a book or periodical. In this chapter, GMD's are used for non-book materials and omitted in the case of books and periodicals.

The following are GMD's that are standard in North America:

For cartographic materials—map; globe.

For graphics—art original; chart; filmstrip; flash card; picture; slide; technical drawing; transparency.

For objects—diorama; game; microscope slide; model; realia.

Others—kit; machine-readable data file; manuscript; microform; motion picture; music; sound recording; text; videorecording.

Of course some of these GMD's may never be needed in a school library.

After choosing the appropriate GMD from the above list for the item to be catalogued, place it in square brackets one space after the title proper. Put it in lower case and in the singular.

Choose the GMD for the medium, not for the content reproduced. If the reproduction of a book is on a microfilm, the GMD "microform" is chosen. If the item is a map on a transparency, the GMD "transparency" is chosen:

```
Songs of the Polka dot door [sound recording]
```

```
Mary of Mile 18 [filmstrip]
```

For items by different persons or bodies with no collective title, the GMD is placed at the end of the area in order to indicate that all titles are in the same medium:

```
The great big enormous turnip / Alexei Tolstoy ; with
pictures by Helen Oxenbury.  The three poor tailors /
Victor G. Ambrus [filmstrip]
```

Parallel title   ②

Add parallel titles in the order as given on the item. Each is separated by *a space, an "equals" sign (=) and another space*:

```
Canterbury tales = Tales of Caunterbury

Log house [motion picture] = Cabane de rondins
```

Other Title Information   ②

ON ITEM

Transcribe other title information, including what was called in *AACR1* the "subtitle," as given. This element follows the title proper or the parallel title to which it pertains. It is preceded by *a space, a colon and a space*:

```
E.P. Taylor : a horseman and his horses

    Hello Dolly! [sound recording] : original motion
picture soundtrack

    "Dangerous foreigners" : European immigrant workers
and labour radicalism in Canada, 1896-1932
```

FOR CLARIFICATION

If the title proper requires some explanation, add the explanation like any other title information. Since it does not appear on the item itself, this explanatory information goes in square brackets:

```
Keats [sound recording] : [selections]
```

Statement of Responsibility   ① ②

The first level of cataloguing requires a statement of responsibility only if it is different from the main entry heading or if there is a title main entry.

TRANSCRIPTION

Transcribe the statement of responsibility as given, i.e., if an author is represented on the title page or other chief source of information by initials, surname or some other incomplete name, transcribe the name exactly as found; it need not be the same as the name used as main entry heading. Include titles of persons if the title is grammatically necessary, if the omission would leave only a person's given name or surname, if the title is necessary to identify the person, or if the title is of nobility or a British title of honour, e.g., Sir, Dame, Lord, Lady. If necessary, a word or short phrase may be added in square brackets to clarify the relationship between the item and the person or body named. This area is preceded by *a space, a stroke (/) and a space*.

NO STATEMENT OF RESPONSIBILITY

If a statement of responsibility does not appear prominently on the item to be catalogued, do not make one.

ONE STATEMENT OF RESPONSIBILITY

Three or fewer persons or bodies:

Pride and prejudice / Jane Austen

Green eggs and ham / by Dr. Seuss

Magic of myth & legend / edited, with notes and questions by Beulah Swayze

19th century developments in art [kit] / author-consultant-narrator, Grose Evans

The Scarlet Pimpernel / by the Baroness Orczy
"Scarlet Pimpernel" is capitalized because it is an epithet standing for a person's name.

The great ideas of Plato / [selected by] Eugene Freeman and David Appel

Metric for geographers : selected tables and data / compiled by Colin Vincent

The Canadian home cook book / compiled by ladies of Toronto and chief cities and towns in Canada

Four or more persons or bodies. Transcribe the name of the first person or body responsible as given, and indicate the omission of the others with *an ellipsis and "[et al.]"*:

A New history of Canada / by Richard Howard ... [et al.]
See p. 63, "Main Entry Under Title" for explanation of capital "n" in "New."

TWO OR MORE STATEMENTS OF RESPONSIBILITY

Transcribe the statements of responsibility as given. However, if the order or layout is ambiguous, transcribe the statement in the order that makes the most sense. Statements of responsibility are separated from each other by *a space, a semi-colon, and a space*:

Joy of cooking / Irma S. Rombauer [and] Marion Rombauer Becker ; illustrated by Ginnie Hofmann and Ikki Matsumoto

Punctuation [filmstrip] / consultant, Edward F. Meaning ; artist, Clyde V. Strohsahl

EDITION AREA

Introduction

For the first level of description, this area includes at least the following elements:

Edition statement

For the second level of description this area includes at least:

Edition statement
First statement of responsibility relating to the edition

Not all elements within this area or the area itself may be present for every item to be catalogued. For example, in the case of many first editions, there is no edition statement.

PUNCTUATION AND SPACING

For the first and second levels of description, the punctuation and spacing that precede the edition area and that are found between the elements are:

. — Edition statement   ①

. — Edition statement / first statement of responsibility relating to the edition   ②

If an element is not present, omit the punctuation preceding that element. If the edition area is omitted because it is not necessary for the description of the item, then move on to the next required area.

The edition area is preceded by *a period, a space, a dash (—) and a space.* The period comes *immediately* after the last letter in the title and statement of responsibility area.

CAPITALIZATION

If the edition area begins with a word or an abbreviation, capitalize it:

. -- New ed.

. -- Rev. and enl. ed.

Edition Statement   ① ②

Transcribe the edition statement as it appears on the item, except that standard abbreviations and numerals may be used in place of words:

Source of information states: "Second edition"
Transcription: `. -- 2nd ed.`

Source of information states: "New revised edition"
Transcription: `. -- New rev. ed.`

Other typical edition statements:

`. -- 1st illustrated ed.`
Quoted from the work.

`. -- Draft`

`. -- Draft ed.`

`. -- Facsim. ed.`

Statement of Responsibility Relating to the Edition   ②

WITH AN EDITION STATEMENT

If a statement of responsibility relates to one or more editions but not to all editions, it follows the edition statement. This statement of responsibility is preceded by *a space, a stroke (/) and a space*:

`. -- 3rd ed. / with maps redrawn by J. Owens`

`  Macmillan dictionary of Canadian biography / edited`
`by W. Stewart Wallace. -- 4th ed. / rev., enl.`
`and updated by W.A. McKay`

WITHOUT AN EDITION STATEMENT

If there is no edition statement (often with first editions) go on to the next area.

EDITION STATEMENT IN QUESTION

If there is a question as to whether the statement of responsibility relates to all editions, put such a statement in the title and statement of responsibility area, i.e., not in the statement of responsibility relating to the edition.

MATERIAL (OR TYPE OF PUBLICATION) SPECIFIC DETAILS AREA

This area appears in the cataloguing of serials and cartographic materials only.

Introduction

For both the first and second levels of description this area includes at least:
Material (or type of publication) specific details

Punctuation and spacing preceding this area are as follows:

. — Material (or type of publication) specific details

① ②

If the area is omitted because it is not necessary for the description of the item, then move on to the next required area.

This area is preceded by *a period, a space, a dash (—) and a space.* The period comes *immediately* after the last letter in the preceding area.

If the material (or type of publication) specific details area begins with a word or an abbreviation, capitalize it:

`. -- Scale 1:500,000`

`. -- Vol. 1`

Cartographic Materials   ① ②

Standard abbreviations and numerals may be used in this mathematical data area.

Scale is always given in this area even if it has already appeared as part of the title proper or other title information:

Information as ratio. Representative fractions are expressed as a ratio and preceded by the word "Scale":

`. -- Scale 1:63,360`
Ratios with colons do not include spaces before or after colon.

`. -- Scale ca. 1:63,360`
Scale computed from bar graph, grid, or by comparison with a map of known scale.

`. -- Scale 1:15,000--1:25,000`
Scale within the item varies.

. -- Scale 1:744,080. Vertical scale ca. 1:96,000
Vertical scale goes after horizontal scale.

In other forms. In some situations, other terms may replace ratio:

. -- Scale indeterminable

. -- Scale varies

. -- Scales vary
Use if there are more than three scales on a multi-part item.

. -- Not drawn to scale
Use if no scale appears on such items as maps of imaginary places, bird's-eye views, etc.

. -- Vertical exaggeration 1:5
Three-dimensional item or model.

STATEMENT OF PROJECTION

Give the statement of projection if it can be found on the item. Precede this element with *a space, a semi-colon and a space*:

. -- Scale 1:1,500,000 ; Conical orthomorphic proj.

Serials ① ②

Standard abbreviations and numerals may be used in this numeric and/or alphabetic, chronological, or other designation area for serials.

NUMERIC AND/OR ALPHABETIC DESIGNATION

Use the numeric and/or alphabetic designation of the first issue of a serial as given in it. Follow with a hyphen and four spaces to leave room for a closing designation. If there are two elements in this designation, they are separated by *a comma and a space* and the second word is not capitalized:

. -- Vol. 1, no. 1–

CHRONOLOGICAL DESIGNATION

If the first issue of a serial is identified by a chronological designation, use it and follow it with a hyphen and four spaces to leave room for a closing year:

Ontario government publications. -- 1972–

If the first issue of a serial has both, give numbering before chronological designation. Enclose the latter in parentheses preceded by a space and followed by a hyphen and four spaces:

```
Owl. -- No. 1 (Apr./May 1976)-
```

```
Flare. -- Vol. 1, no. 1 (Sept. 1979)-
```

PUBLICATION, DISTRIBUTION, ETC., AREA

In *AACR1,* this area was called "imprint."

Introduction

LEVELS OF DESCRIPTION

For the first level of description, this area includes at least:
  First publisher, etc. (The term "etc." stands for manufacturer,
    distributor, or some such equivalent of publisher.)
  Date of publication, etc.
For the second level of description, this area includes at least:
  First place of publication, etc.
  First publisher, etc.
  Date of publication, etc.

PUNCTUATION AND SPACING

For the first level of description, punctuation and spacing that precede this area and that are found between the elements are:

> . — First publisher, etc., date of publication, etc.   ①

The second level of description:

> . — First place of publication, etc. : first publisher, etc., date of publication, etc.   ②

This area is preceded by *a period, a space, a dash (—) and a space.* The period comes *immediately* after the last letter in the preceding area.

Since this area is the last in its paragraph, it is closed with a period unless a bracket follows the date.

Proper nouns and names of publishers, distributors, issuers, etc., in full or abbreviated form are capitalized as shown in a standard reference source, e.g., *Books in Print*,[1] *Canadian Publishers Directory*.[2]

Capitalize the first word of each element even if it is not part of the name of a place, publisher, distributor, etc., except "s.n." (*sine nomine*—without name) and "s.l." (*sine loco*—no place). These abbreviations are transcribed in lower case when no publisher or distributor's name, or place of publication is found:

. -- Clarke, Irwin   ①

. -- Vancouver : Douglas & McIntyre   ②

   . -- Toronto : Published in association with the
Pulp and Paper Institute of Canada by University of   ②
Toronto Press

. -- [s.n.]   ①

. -- [s.l. : s.n.]   ②

Place of Publication, Distribution, Etc.   ②

Record the first named place, and also the first named place that is in the home country or that is given prominence by the layout. The second place is preceded by *a space, a semi-colon and a space*. For instance, if the following places had been given in the chief source of information: London; New York; Sydney; Toronto; Vancouver, someone cataloguing in Canada would show only the first place, London, and the first Canadian place, Toronto. For example:

. -- London ; Toronto

Add the name of the country, province, state, etc., to the name of a place, when necessary for complete identification and to distinguish it from other places with the same name:

. -- London [Ont.]
Ontario does not appear on chief source of information.

. -- Carbondale, Ill.
City and state appear on chief source of information.

NO PLACE GIVEN

Use s.l. (*sine loco*—no place):

. -- [s.l.]

Name of Publisher, Distributor, Etc. ① ②

For first-level description, this element begins the area and would be preceded by *a period, a space, a dash (—) and a space* where a period follows *immediately* after the last letter of the preceding area.

For second-level description, this element is preceded by *a space, a colon and a space* following the place of publication.

FORM OF NAME

Give the name of the publisher, distributor, etc., in the shortest possible form to be understood and differentiated from other publishers, distributors, etc.:

. -- McGraw ①   *not McGraw-Hill Ryerson*

. -- CLA   ①   *not Canadian Library Association*

. -- W.H. Allen ①   *not Allen*

. -- Allen & Unwin ①   *not Allen*

. -- Supt. of Docs ①   *U.S. Superintendent of Documents*

. -- G.P.O. ① *Government Printing Office*

. -- Personality Posters ①

. -- Learning Corp. of America ①

. -- Modern Learning Aids ①

. -- Walt Disney Productions ①

. -- New York : RCA ②

. -- London : Royal Geographical Society ②

. -- London ; Toronto : Visual Publications ②

FUNCTION (OTHER THAN SOLELY PUBLISHING)

Include words or phrases which indicate function (other than solely publishing) performed by a person or body:

: Distributed by McClelland and Stewart

: Printed for CLA by the Morriss Print. Co.

REPEATED NAME

If the name of the publisher, distributor, etc., appears in a recognizable form in the title and statement of responsibility area or the main entry heading, repeat it in this element in a shortened form:

Winnipeg : The Gallery, 1977
Winnipeg Art Gallery shortened to The Gallery

TWO OR MORE AGENCIES

If two or more agencies are given as performing the same function, include both in this element. They are separated by *a space, a colon and a space*:

    Toronto : McClelland and Stewart : World Crafts Council

NO PUBLISHER, DISTRIBUTOR, ETC., GIVEN

Use s.n. (*sine nomine*—no name):

. -- [s.n.] ①

. -- New York : [s.n.] ②

Date of Publication, Distribution, Etc. ① ②

This element must be transcribed in numbers. It is preceded by *a comma and a space*. The comma follows *immediately* after the name of the publisher, distributor, etc.

FORM OF DATE

The date of publication, distribution, etc., if given, is the date to use. Give it in arabic numerals for the edition being catalogued:

. -- Penguin, 1979. ①

. -- Santa Ana, Calif. : Doubleday Multimedia, 1973. ②

UNKNOWN DATE OF PUBLICATION, DISTRIBUTION, ETC.

Use copyright date, or, if it is not present, the date of manufacture (indicated as such):

, c1980.

, 1976 printing.

Option: Add the latest copyright date after the date of publication, distribution, etc., if the copyright date is different:

, 1974, c1972.

If no dates can be assigned, give an approximate date of publication:

, [1972?]   *Probable date.*

, [197-]   *Decade certain.*

, [197-?]   *Probable decade.*

, [ca. 1960]   *Approximate date.*

TWO OR MORE DATES ON A MULTI-PART ITEM

Give the earliest and latest dates:

, 1968–1973.

INCOMPLETE MULTI-PART ITEM

Give the earliest date and follow it with a hyphen, four spaces and a period to leave room for a closing year:

, 1978–   .

Option: Fill in the latest date when the item is complete.

PHYSICAL DESCRIPTION AREA

In *AACR1*, this area was known as the "collation."

Introduction

LEVELS OF DESCRIPTION

For the first level of description, this area includes at least:
    Extent of item.
For the second level of description, this area includes at least:
    Extent of item
    Other physical details
    Dimensions

PUNCTUATION AND SPACING

This area begins a new paragraph at the second indention. Punctuation and spacing that are found between the elements of the physical description area for the first level of description are as follows:

Extent of item	①

The second level:

Extent of item : other physical details ; dimensions	②

CAPITALIZATION

All words in this area are lower case, except trade names and certain technical terms. For example:

3M Talking Slide

Extent of Item   ① ②

This element includes the number of physical units in arabic numerals and a specific material designation.

SPECIFIC MATERIAL DESIGNATIONS

These are a breakdown of the GMD's. Unlike the GMD's, they are not put in square brackets. In this element, the item to be catalogued can be described using specific terms for each type of medium. While unique material designations may sometimes have to be devised, or found in the full lists in *AACR2*, the librarian will usually find a suitable one in the following abridged list:

For cartographic materials—aerial chart; atlas (used if "text" is given as the GMD); bird's-eye view *or* map view; block diagram; celestial globe; chart; globe (for globes other than celestial globes); hydrographic chart; imaginative map; map; map profile; map section; photo mosaic; plan; relief model; remote-sensing image; topographic drawing.
For graphic materials—art original; art print; art reproduction; chart; filmslip; filmstrip (when appropriate, "cartridge" or "reel" may be added, e.g., filmstrip cartridge); flash card; flip chart; photograph; picture; postcard; poster; slide; stereograph (when appropriate, "reel" may be added, e.g., stereograph reel); study print; technical drawing; transparency; wall chart.
For microforms—aperture card; microfiche; microfilm (when appropriate, "cartridge," "cassette," or "reel" may be added, e.g., microfilm reel); micro-opaque.

Option: If the GMD "microform" is used, the prefix "micro" may be dropped from the above terms. This option is not exercised in the examples in this chapter.

For motion pictures and video recordings—film cartridge; film cassette; film loop; film reel; videocartridge; videocassette; video disc; video reel.

Option: If the GMD "motion picture" or "videorecording" is used, the term "film" or the prefix "video" may be dropped from all of the above except the last. This option is not exercised in the examples in this chapter.

For music—score; choir book (or other appropriate specific terms); v. of music; p. of music; leaves of music.

For sound recordings — sound cartridge, sound cassette, sound disc, sound tape reel, sound track (*sic*) (when appropriate, "reel," "cassette," etc., may be added, e.g., sound track film cassette).

Option: If the GMD "sound recording" is used, the word "sound" may be dropped from all of the above terms except the last. This option is not exercised in the examples in this chapter.

For three-dimensional artifacts and realia—diorama; exhibit; game; microscope slide; mock-up; model; other specific terms for realia given as concisely as possible.

BOOKS, PAMPHLETS, AND PRINTED SHEETS

Single volume. Record the last numbered page in each sequence in the volume following the last number with the abbreviation "p." for page(s) or "v." for volume(s), or with a term such as *sheet, portfolio,* or *broadside.* Leave a space between the last or only number and the letter or word after it:

42 p.

xvi, 125 p.
Commas separate more than one sequence of pages.

1 broadside

Single small volume—without pagination. If a small volume is printed without pagination, count the number of pages and put the number in square brackets:

[59] p.

Single large volume—without pagination. If a large volume is printed without pagination, estimate the number of pages. Precede this estimated number by "ca." without square brackets.

ca. 545 p.

Single volume—complicated pagination. If the volume has complicated or irregular paging, use "1 v." followed by an appropriate term in parentheses. Leave a space before the opening parenthesis:

```
1 v. (various pagings)
```

```
1 v. (loose-leaf)
```
For publications designed to receive additions.

Two or more volumes. If the item is more than one physical volume, give the number:

```
4 v.
```

```
6 v. in 3
```
Six bibliographical volumes found in three physical volumes.

Leaves or pages of plates. The number of leaves (page plus its verso) or pages of plates is put after the number of volumes or pagination, separated by *a comma and a space*:

```
vi, 176 p., 32 p. of plates
```

```
1 v., [12] leaves of plates
```

Multi-part item. If the term "volumes" is not appropriate, choose one of the following: parts; pamphlets; pieces; case(s); portfolio(s).

NON-BOOK ITEMS

Single media—one or many parts. Record the number of physical units being catalogued, followed by the specific material designation, from p. 98. For example:

```
2 sound discs
```

```
1 hand puppet
```
Specific name made up, as allowed with three-dimensional artifacts and realia.

```
1 microfiche
```

```
2 stereograph reels (Viewmaster)
```
A trade name or technical information is added in the physical description area only if the use of the item is conditional upon this information. Otherwise it is in the note area.

Option: If the GMD "filmstrip" is used, the specific material designation is not repeated. Instead, the number of frames alone is given:

```
42 fr.
```

In order to complete the extent of item element, and, where applicable, the number of components, give the name(s) of component parts, and/or the playing time in parentheses. The following examples offer guidelines:

2 sound discs (90 min.)
Give duration in minutes, to the next minute up, for works five minutes long or over.

1 film loop (3 min., 25 sec.)
Give duration in minutes and seconds for works less than five minutes long.

1 videocassette (Beta L-750, X-2 mode) (ca. 180 min.)
Give approximate time if no indication appears on the item, its container, etc.

1 filmstrip (40 fr.)

1 filmstrip (42 fr., 4 title fr.)
Filmstrip with frames numbered separately.

39 fr.
The option has been exercised not to repeat the GMD "filmstrip" in the physical description area.

1 microfiche (150 fr.)

4 transparencies (8 attached overlays each)

2 filmstrips (ca. 50 fr. each)
Approximate number of frames.

2 transparencies (20 overlays)
Total when numbered consecutively.

1 score (2 v.)

1 jigsaw puzzle (500 pieces)

   1 game (2 players' manuals, board, cards, role cards, 2 dice)
Give number and names when applicable.

1 diorama (various pieces)
"Various pieces" used when pieces cannot be ascertained or named concisely.
Option: Give further details in the note section.

Single media—incomplete multi-part item. In this situation, give the specific material designation alone, preceded by three spaces, so that the number may be completed later:

slides

Other Physical Details ②
This element consists of details of physical description other than extent or dimensions. It is preceded by *a space, a colon and a space*. The elements are separated by commas.

This element includes illustrative matter found in the item, on lining papers, and in pockets inside the cover.

Illustrations of general type. Use the term "ill." to cover illustrative matter which is not of a particular type or when only some of it belongs to a particular type. Illustrated title pages and minor illustrations, e.g., decorations, may be disregarded. Tables are not considered to be illustrations.

274 p. : ill.

Illustrations of a particular type. These include charts, coats of arms, facsimiles, forms, geneological tables, maps, music, plans, portraits, samples. These types of illustrations, if considered important in a work, are designated in this element by the terms above, or by their abbreviation. If more than one term applies to the various illustrations, they are listed in the order shown above in this paragraph:

149 p. : maps
Consists of maps.

149 p. : ill., map
Illustrative matter consists of general illustrations and a map.

149 p. : charts, port.
Illustrative matter consists of charts and a portrait.

Coloured illustrations. If all illustrations of a general or particular type are in two or more colours, the abbreviation "col." is used before ill. or some more specific synonym. If only some of the illustrations are coloured, then *a space and "(some col.)"* appears after the general or particular term:

: col. ill.
All general illustrative matter is coloured.

: ill., col. maps, ports. (some col.)
All maps are coloured but only some of the portraits.

: ill. (some col.), plans
Some of the general illustrative matter is coloured.

Number of illustrations. Specify the number of illustrations only if that detail seems important and if the number can be easily ascertained, for instance, from a list in the front matter of a book:

: 12 ill.

: ill., 2 ports.

: ill., 3 charts (some col.), 4 maps

Predominantly illustrations. If a publication consists wholly of illustrations of either a general or particular type, indicate this with the term "all" before the appropriate type. If an item is predominantly illustrated with illustrations of either a general or specific type, use the term "chiefly."

: all ill.
Publication consists solely of illustrations.

:   all maps

:   chiefly ports.

Notes regarding illustrative matter. If some or all of the illustrative matter is on the lining papers, or if illustrative matter is in a pocket inside the cover of an item, put this information in the note area:

: ill., col. map
The note might say: "Map on lining papers."

: ill., maps
The note might say: "4 maps on 2 folded leaves in pocket."

Specify the number of items before the location.

NON-BOOK ITEMS

In this physical detail element, each medium requires different details in order for the item to be fully described. The lists below show the possible details for various media and the order in which they are to be transcribed if some or all are applicable.

Cartographic materials. Possible details—colour; material; mounting:

1 globe : col.
Coloured or partly coloured.

1 relief model : col., wood

1 celestial globe : plastic, mounted on metal stand

Filmstrips and filmslips. Possible details—sound, given as "sd." (if information is needed to understand the filmslip or filmstrip fully); colour, given as "b&w" or "col.":

3 filmstrips (ca. 50 fr. each) : sd., col.

1 filmstrip (30 fr.) : b&w

Microforms. Possible details—negative; illustrated material (see pp. 102 to 103 for wording); colour:

```
1 microfilm reel : negative
```

```
1 microfilm reel : negative, ill.
```

```
1 microfiche : all ill.
```

```
1 microfiche : chiefly music
```

```
1 microfiche : ill., music
```

```
1 microfilm reel : col.
```
Wholly or partly coloured microform without illustrations.

```
1 microfilm reel : col. & ill.
```
Wholly or partly coloured microform with illustrations.

```
1 microfilm reel : col. ill.
```
Microform with coloured illustrations only.

```
1 microfilm reel : col. ill., col. maps
```
Microform totally consisting of coloured illustrations and maps.

Motion pictures and video recordings. Possible details—aspect ratio and special projection characteristics (motion pictures); sound characteristics, given as "sd." (sound), "si." (silent), or "si. at sd. speed"; colour, given as b&w or col. (a sepia print is described as b&w); projection speed (motion pictures), given if it is considered important; playing speed (video discs), given in rpm:

```
8 film reels (84 min.) : Panavision
```

```
1 videoreel (Ampex 7003) (17 min.) : sd.
```

```
1 film loop (3 min., 20 sec.) : si.
```

```
1 film reel (10 min.) : sd., b&w
```

```
   1 videocassette (25 min.) : sd., col. with b&w
sequences
```

```
1 film reel (1 min., 20 sec.) : si., col., 25 fps
```

```
1 videodisc (4 min.) : sd., col., 1500 rpm
```

Music. Possible details—same as for books, pamphlets and printed sheets (see p. 102):

```
1 score : ill.
```

```
1 score : port.
```

Slides. Possible details—sound (if an integral part, i.e., needed to understand slides fully); system, added only if sound is an integral part; colour (b&w, col., etc.):

```
24 slides : sd. (3M Talking Slide), col.
```

Sound recordings. Possible details—type of recording (sound track films); playing speed (given in rpm, ips, or fps); groove characteristics (discs); track configuration (sound track films); number of tracks (tape cartridges, cassettes, and reels—give the number of tracks only if it is non-standard. The standard number for a cartridge is eight, for a cassette, four); number of sound channels, e.g., mono., stereo., or quad., as appropriate:

```
1 sound track film reel (20 min.) : optical

1 sound track film reel (15 min.) : Phillips-Miller

1 sound disc (35 min.) : 33 1/3 rpm

1 sound cassette (90 min.) : 3 3/4 ips   i.e., L-cassette.

1 sound track film reel (15 min.) : magnetic, 24 fps

1 sound disc (8 min.) : 45 rps, microgroove

  1 sound track film reel (9 min.) : magnetic, 24 fps,
centre track

1 sound disc (45 min.) : 33 1/3 rpm, stereo.

  1 sound tape reel (ca. 55 min.) : 1 7/8 ips, 2
track, mono.
```

Note: *AACR2* shows inches per second, the traditional and standard designation of tape speed in North America. With the advent of metrication, a metric equivalent may be preferred by many librarians.

Three-dimensional artifacts and realia. Possible details—material; colour:

```
3 models (various pieces) : polystyrene

  1 diorama (various pieces) : plywood and papier
mâché

1 jigsaw puzzle (20 pieces) : plastic

1 microscope slide : plastic
```
Name the material of a slide only if it is other than glass.

```
1 model : balsa wood and paper, b&w
```

1 microscope slide : stained

1 model : wood, col.
"Col." used for multi-coloured objects.

1 model : wood, green and white
Name one or two colours.

Transparencies. Possible details—colour (b&w or col.):

3 transparencies (5 attached overlays each) : col.

Other graphic materials.

Art originals. Possible details—medium (chalk, pastel, etc.) on base (board, fabric, etc.):

1 art original : oil on canvas

Art prints. Possible details—general process (engraving, lithograph, etc.) or specific process (copper engraving, chromolithograph); colour (b&w, sepia, col., etc.):

2 art prints : engraving, tinted

Art reproductions. Possible details—method of reproduction (photogravure, collotype, etc.); colour (b&w, col., etc.):

1 art reproduction : photogravure, col.

Flash cards. Possible details—colour (b&w or col.):

12 flash cards : col.

Flip charts. Possible details—double sided; colour (b&w or col.):

1 flip chart (6 sheets) : double sides, col.

Photographs. Possible details—transparency or negative; colour (b&w, col., etc.):

1 photo. : tinted

2 photos. : negative, b&w

Pictures. Possible details—colour (b&w, col., etc.):

1 picture : col.

Postcards. Possible details—colour (b&w, col., etc.):

```
6 postcards : sepia
```

Posters. Possible details—colour (b&w, col., etc.):

```
5 posters : red, white, and blue
```

Stereographs. Possible details—colour (b&w, col., etc.):

```
1 stereograph reel (Viewmaster) (7 double fr.) : col.
```

Study prints. Possible details—colour (b&w or col.):

```
2 study prints : col.
```

Technical drawings. Possible details—method of reproduction if any (blue-print, photocopy, etc.):

```
1 technical drawing : blueprint
```

Wall charts. Possible details—colour (b&w, col., etc.):

```
1 wall chart : col.
```

Dimensions   ②

This element is preceded by *a space, a semi-colon and a space,* usually after the other physical details elements, but it may be after the extent of item element.

The examples in this chapter, unlike those in *AACR2,* treat "cm" and "mm" as symbols, not abbreviations, following the usage of SI; that is, cm and mm are not followed by a period unless they are at the end of a sentence or paragraph.

Always record centimetres with whole numbers. A part of a centimetre should be taken up to the next whole number. For example, 24.2 cm is recorded as 25 cm.

BOOKS, PAMPHLETS, AND PRINTED SHEETS

Volumes 10 cm high and over. Give the height of the volume in centimetres. (If it is bound, this would be the height of the binding.) For example:

```
120 p. ; 24 cm
```

```
34 p. : ill., maps ; 25 cm.
```
Final period indicates end of paragraph, not abbreviation of "centimetres."

Volumes less than 10 cm high. Give the height in millimetres.

```
20 p. : col. ill. ; 85 mm
```
Final period is not shown because a series area is to follow. The same assumption is to be made about all the dimensions elements in the rest of this chapter.

Unusual widths. Give the width of a volume if it is greater than the height or if it is less than one-half the height. Put height first:

```
; 20 x 7 cm   height x width
```
```
; 20 x 31 cm   height x width
```

Multi-volume sets. If the heights of the various volumes differ less than two centimetres, give the largest size. If the heights vary more than two centimetres, give the smallest and largest sizes, separated by a hyphen:

```
; 24-29 cm
```

Sheets. For single sheets give height and width. Add the folded dimensions of an item if it is designed to be folded for circulation:

```
; 48 x 30 cm
```
```
; 48 x 30 cm folded to 24 x 15 cm
```

NON-BOOK ITEMS

Dimensions are recorded differently for the various media. The lists below describe the information required for each medium.

Cartographic materials:

Maps, plans, etc. Two-dimensional: required details—give height x width of the item itself in centimetres:

```
1 map : col. ; 25 x 35 cm
```

Circular: required details—give the diameter of the item itself in centimetres:

```
1 map ; 45 cm in diam.
```

Relief models: required details—give height x width in centimetres:

```
1 relief model : col., plastic ; 45 x 35 cm
```

Optional: Add the depth:

```
1 relief model : col., wood ; 40 x 37 x 2 cm
```

Globes: required details—give the diameter in centimetres:

```
   1 globe : col., plastic, mounted on wooden stand ;
15 cm in diam.
```

Filmstrips and filmslips. Required details—give gauge (width) in millimetres:

```
1 filmstrip (50 fr.) : col. ; 35 mm
```

Microforms. Required details—for aperture cards give height x width of aperture card mount in centimetres; for microfiches give height x width in centimetres; for microfilms give width of microfilm in millimetres; for micro-opaques give height x width in centimetres:

```
15 aperture cards ; 9 x 19 cm

2 microfiches ; 10 x 15 cm

1 microfilm reel ; 16 mm

1 microfilm cartridge ; 35 mm

3 microopaques ; 8 x 13 cm
```

Motion pictures and video recordings:
Motion pictures (16 mm). Required details—give gauge (width) in millimetres:

```
1 film reel (15 min.) : sd., b&w ; 16 mm
```

Motion pictures (8 mm). Required details—give gauge (width) in millimetres, and define it as single, standard, super, or Maurer, etc.:

```
   1 film cassette (18 min.) : sd., col. ;
standard 8 mm
```

Video tapes. Required details—give gauge (width) in inches:

```
1 videoreel (35 min.) ; si., b&w ; 1/2 in.
```

Video discs. Required details—give diameter in inches:

```
1 videodisc (4 min.) ; si., b&w, 1500 rpm ; 8 in.
```

Music. Required details—give dimensions of scores as for books, etc.:

```
1 score (15 p.) ; 28 cm
```

Slides. Possible details—give height x width only if slides are other than 5 x 5 cm (2 x 2 in.):

```
10 slides ; col.
```

```
1 slide ; b&w ; 7 x 7 cm
```

Sound recordings. Where *AACR2* uses inches for the width of tape and the diameter of records, the librarian may follow metric usage if that is standard in the country where the cataloguing is being done.

Sound discs. Required details—give diameter in inches:

```
  1 sound disc (45 min.) : 33 1/3 rpm, stereo.,
; 12 in.
```

Sound track films. Required details—give gauge (width) of film in milli-metres:

```
  1 sound track film reel (20 min.) : magnetic,
25 fps, centre track ; 16 mm
```

Sound cartridges. Possible details—give dimensions for cartridge and tape only if non-standard sizes. Standard dimensions for a cartridge are 5¼ x 7 $\frac{7}{8}$ in., and the standard width of tape is ¼ in.

Sound cassettes. Possible details—given dimensions for cassette and tape only if they are non-standard sizes. Standard dimensions for a cassette are 3 $\frac{7}{8}$ x 2½ in., and the standard width of tape is $\frac{1}{8}$ in.:

```
  1 sound cassette (90 min.) : 3 3/4 ips, mono. ;
7 1/4 x 3 1/2 in., 1/4 in. tape
```

Sound tape reels. Possible details—give diameter of reel in inches; give width of tape if it is other than the standard size of ¼ in.:

```
  1 sound tape reel (60 min.) : 7 1/2 ips,
mono. ; 7 in., 1/2 in. tape
```

Three dimensional artifacts and realia. Required details—give the dimension of the object in centimetres. If necessary, add a word to indicate which dimension is being given:

```
1 doll : plastic ; 45 cm high
```

If three dimensions are given, they should be in this order and format: height x width x depth. If the object is in a box or a container, the box or the container is named and its dimensions given either after the dimensions of the object or as the only dimensions:

```
   1 model (6 pieces) : col. ; 16 x 32 x 3 cm ;
in case, 17 x 34 x 6 cm
```

```
   1 jigsaw puzzle (200 pieces) : plastic, col. ;
in box, 25 x 32 x 5 cm
```

Transparencies. Required details—give height x width of the item in centimetres, excluding the frame or mount:

```
1 transparency (3 overlays) : b&w ; 26 x 22 cm
```

Other graphic materials:

Stereographs. Do not give dimensions.

Art originals, art prints, art reproductions. Required details—give height x width of the item in centimetres, excluding the frame or mount:

```
   1 art reproduction : photogravure ; col. ;
30 x 42 cm
```

Technical drawings and wall charts. Required details—give height x width (in centimetres) when extended and, when appropriate, folded:

```
   1 wall chart : col. ; 244 x 26 cm folded to
30 x 26 cm
```

Other graphics. Possible details—give height x width in centimetres:

```
10 flash cards : col. ; 28 x 10 cm
```

```
1 picture ; b&w ; 15 x 20 cm
```

```
1 flip chart : double sides, b&w ; 23 x 20 cm
```

Items Made Up of Several Types of Material

These include items made up of two or more items which belong to two or more material types, e.g., filmstrip and sound cassette, and miscellaneous packages of print material, e.g., jackdaws.

WITH ONE PREDOMINANT COMPONENT

If the item has one predominant component, describe it in terms of that component. For instance, in the case of a filmstrip with a booklet or a cassette with a libretto, the filmstrip and the cassette would each be considered the predominant component of the item. If the item has no predominant component, see p. 113.

Subsidiary component(s) are treated as accompanying material in one of the following two ways:

Recorded in physical description area—first option. Using this method, the accompanying material is named at the end of the physical description area of the predominant component. *A space, a "plus" sign (+) and a space* separate the last element of the predominant component and the accompanying material being described. This punctuation is followed by the number of pieces of accompanying material, if appropriate, and a term indicative of the medium or format of the accompanying material:

27 p. : ill. ; 21 cm + 20 slides
Before the "plus" sign (+), the predominant component is described; after the "plus" sign the accompanying material is numbered and named.

    1 celestial globe : plastic, mounted on metal
stand + 1 booklet

    1 sound disc (45 min.) : 33 1/3 rpm, stereo. ; 12
mm + 1 teacher's guide

    2 filmstrips (75 fr. each) : sd., col. ; 35 mm +
2 teacher's guides

    1 hand puppet : red and blue ; 20 cm long + 1
instruction sheet

1 microfilm reel ; 16 mm + 1 pamphlet

Optional additions: If the accompanying material is very valuable or important, one may add a statement of its extent, other physical details, and dimensions in accordance with pp. 97 to 111, "Physical Description Area," above. This additional information goes in parentheses after the name of the medium or format of the accompanying material. There is a space preceding the opening parenthesis:

    142 p. : col. ill. ; 35 cm + 1 sound disc (25
min. : 33 1/3 rpm, mono. ; 12 in.)

    1 relief model : col. ; wood ; 35 x 25 x 3 cm + 1
booklet (17 p. ; 10 cm)

Recorded in note area—second option. Adopting this option, the librarian would describe the predominant component in the physical description area, and relegate the description of the accompanying material to the note area. The note should give the location of the accompanying material, if a statement of the location would be helpful:

```
30 slides : col.
```
Physical description of predominant component.

```
Set includes booklet (12 p.) : Notes
on the Amazon River.
```
Note describes accompanying material.

```
150 p. : ill ; 20 cm
```
Physical description of predominant component.

```
Slides in pocket.
Teacher's guide (12 p.)  by John Anderson.
```
Two notes describing accompanying material.

ITH NO PREDOMINANT COMPONENTS

Use the GMD kit for a collection of items with a common title in more than one medium, of which none is recognizably predominant, or for an item composed of miscellaneous print material, e.g., a reading lab or a jackdaw.

Again, the librarian has a choice of methods of description. Apply whichever is most appropriate to the item.

Specific listing of extent—first option. Give the extent of each part or group of parts without further description of each part or group, in the "extent of item" element of the physical description area. End this listing with *a space, a semi-colon, a space and the phrase "in container,"* if there is one, followed by the dimensions of the container:

```
200 activity cards, 20 answer-key booklets,
40 student record cards, teacher's handbook,
placement test ; in container 18 x 25 x 19 cm
```

Separate physical descriptions—second option. If physical information for each item is desired, each part or group of parts belonging to each distinct type of material may be described in full. The first description falls in the regular place of the physical description area, i.e., begins a new paragraph at the second indention. Other descriptions begin new paragraphs at the second indention on the lines immediately below the first:

```
45 slides : col.
```
Regular physical description area.

```
6 transparencies (4 attached overlays each) :
col. ; 26 x 22 cm
1 sound cassette (15 min.) : 3 3/4 ips, mono.
```

One kit contains all of the items listed above.

General term of extent—third option. If the item has a large number of heterogeneous materials, give a general term of extent such as "various pieces." Include the number if possible. This term appears as the extent of the item element:

```
various pieces
```

```
58 various pieces
```

SERIES AREA   ②

Introduction

This area does not appear in the first level of description.
For the second level of description, this area includes at least:
Title proper of series
Statement of responsibility relating to series
ISSN of series
Numbering within the series
Title of subseries
ISSN of subseries
Numbering within subseries
Not all elements of this area or the area itself will necessarily be present for every item to be catalogued.

PUNCTUATION AND SPACING

Punctuation and spacing that precede the series area and that are found between the elements are as follows:

> . — (Title proper of series / statement of responsibility relating to series, ISSN of series ; numbering within the series. Title of subseries, ISSN of subseries ; numbering within subseries)   ②

This area is preceded by *a period, a space, a dash (—) and a space.* The period comes *immediately* after the last letter or number in the preceding area.

CAPITALIZATION

The title proper, parallel title, other title information, and statements of responsibility in the series area are capitalized using the same rules as for the title and statement of responsibility area (see p. 83). Terms used in conjunction with numbering, e.g., v., no., are in lower case.

Title Proper of Series

Transcribe the title of the series as it appears on the item. Do not alter wording, order, or spelling. It may be necessary to change punctuation and capitalization.

If variations in the names of the series are found (other than parallel titles), choose the variation that appears in the chief source of information.

Parallel Titles of Series

Add parallel titles of a series in the order given on the item. Each is separated by *a space, an "equals" sign (=) and a space*:

`. -- (Jeux visuels = Visual games)`

Other Title Information of Series

Include this element only if it provides valuable information in identifying the series. It is preceded by *a space, a colon and a space*:

`. -- (Ecology : communities in nature)`

Statements of Responsibility Relating to Series

Include statements of responsibility appearing in conjunction with the series title only if they are considered necessary to identify the series:

`. -- (Map supplement / Association of American Geographers)`

International Standard Serial Number

Record the International Standard Serial Number (ISSN) if it appears on the item in the standard manner, i.e., ISSN followed by a space, and two groups of four digits separated by a hyphen:

`. -- (Western Canada series report, ISSN 0317-3127)`

Numbering Within Series

SINGLE ITEM

Record the numbering of the item within the series in terms given in the item. Use abbreviations and substitute arabic numerals for other numerals or numbers which are spelled out. This element is preceded by *a space, a semicolon and a space*:

`. -- (Beatrix Potter jigsaw puzzles ; no. 1)`

`. -- (Masterpieces in the National Gallery of Canada ; no. 9)`

```
. -- (Dioramas of American history ; 5)

. -- (At-a-flash time line cards ; set 1)
```

MULTI-PART ITEM

Continuous numbering. Record the first and last number within the series if each item is numbered separately and if the numbering is continuous:

```
; v. 5-10)
```

Other numbering. Record all the numbers:

```
; v. 2, 7, 9)
```

Other designations. Record as given. For example:

```
; v. B)
```

```
; 1980)
```

Subseries

A subseries is a series within a series. The subseries may or may not have a title dependent on the title of the main series.

Give all the details about the main series first and then follow with the name and details of the subseries. The elements of the subseries follow the rules for series (pp. 114 to 116). The subseries is preceded by *a period and a space*:

```
. -- (Standard radio super sound effects. Trains)
```

```
    . -- (Department of State publication ; 8583. East
Asian and Pacific series ; 199)
```

```
. -- (Music for today.  Series 2 ; no. 8)
```
Subseries has no title.

More Than One Series Statement

If an item belongs to two or more series and/or a series and subseries, record each as a separate series statement and enclose each in parentheses. The elements of each series statement follow the rules for series (pp. 114 to 116). The two sets of parentheses are separated by *a space*. If there are two series, the one with the more specific name goes first:

```
    . -- (Video marvels ; no. 33) (Educational progress
series ; no. 3)
```

NOTE AREA

Introduction

For both the first and second levels of description this area includes:
Note or notes

PUNCTUATION AND SPACING

This area begins a new paragraph at the second indention, with a blank line between it and the physical description area if space is available. If space is limited, the note may begin on the line below the physical description area. Each succeeding note also begins a new paragraph at the second indention, with no blank lines separating two or more notes. Any note longer than one line continues at the first indention. Any introductory words are separated from the main content of a note by *a colon and a space*. For example:

```
Title on container: Jack and the beanstalk
```

For both the *first* and *second* levels of description, punctuation and spacing of the note area are as follows:

Notes(s).	① ②

Put a period at the end of each note. (See also p. 82, "General Notes on Punctuation.")

CAPITALIZATION

Begin all notes with a capital letter. If a note consists of more than one sentence, capitalize the first word of each subsequent sentence. Other words are capitalized as appropriate to the language involved.

Form of Notes

ORDER OF INFORMATION

If several notes corresponding to various areas are to be made, do them in the order of the areas. For example, a note that provides further information about the edition area comes before one that elaborates on the physical description area. Use the prescribed punctuation between elements as given for the particular area.

A standard word or introductory phrase assists in the recognition of the type of information presented. These words or phrases include:

Continues:

Library has:

Previously published as:

Sequel to:

Translation of:

Adaptation of: Kipps / by H.G. Wells.
Introductory phrase plus example.

Some notes record numbers borne by the item, other than the ISBN or ISSN:

Supt. of Docs. no.: I19.16:818.

Warner Bros.: K56151.
Number found on sound disc label.

Some notes have fairly standard wording and are self-contained:

Includes bibliographies.
Program notes on the container.

CONTENTS NOTE

This is an important type of formal note.

A note about the contents of an item is made to indicate the presence of material not shown anywhere else in the description, to stress an important component item, or to list the contents:

Bibliography: p. 203-205.

Includes bibliography.

Includes index.

    Contents: The playboy of the Western world /
John M. Synge -- Juno and the paycock / Sean O'Casey --
Riders to the sea / John M. Synge -- Spreading the news
/ Lady Gregory -- Shadow and substance / Paul Vincent
Carroll.
This book of plays was entered under its collective title. The contents note analyzes the component titles with their authors.

    Contents: v. 1. Juno and the paycock. The shadow of
a gunman. The plough and the stars. The end of the

beginning.   A pound on demand -- v. 2. The silver tassle.
Within the gates.   The stars turn red.
This book of plays was entered under its author. The contents note analyzes
the component titles.

   Contents: side 1. Phyllis Webb. Earle Birney -- side
2. John Newlove. Alfred Purdy -- side 3. Irving Layton.
Leonard Cohen -- side 4. George Bowering. Gwendolyn
MacEwen.
Sound recording.

   Partial contents: The playboy of the Western
world / John M. Synge -- Juno and the paycock /
Sean O'Casey -- Riders to the sea / John M. Synge.

"WITH" NOTES

If an item lacking a collective title has been described by one of its titled
parts, the "with" note lists the other titled parts in the order in which they
appear. For example:

With: Symphony no. 2 / Beethoven.

INFORMAL NOTES

These notes are composed or quoted by the librarian and should be brief:

Based on a novel by Thomas Hardy.

STANDARD NUMBER AND TERMS OF AVAILABILITY AREA

Introduction

LEVELS OF DESCRIPTION ① ②

For both the first and second levels of description this area includes:
   Standard number

PUNCTUATION AND SPACING

This area begins a new paragraph at the second indention. If there is a note,
the standard number begins on the line below the last note. If there is no note,
leave one blank line between this area and the physical description area. Do
not leave a line if this means having to use an extra card.

Standard number.

① ②

No period if followed by terms of availability.

The letters which form part of the standard number are capitalized. Any qualifiers that are added to the standard number or to the price are in lower case.

Standard Number ① ②

Give either the ISBN or ISSN for the item. If there are two or more numbers on the item, record only the one which applies to the item being described:

ISBN 0-552-6787-3
One space between the letters "ISBN" and the first digit.

ISSN 0002-9769
One space between the letters "ISSN" and the first digit.

A qualification in parentheses is added after the standard number when an item has two or more standard numbers and the library has both:

```
ISBN 0-07-077605-9 (cloth).--ISBN 0-07-
077606-7 (paper).
```

Terms of Availability—Optional Addition

This element consists of the price. If there is no price, it indicates the terms of availability. Many librarians put this information with the accession information on the shelf-list card only. If used as part of the standard number and terms of availability area, this element would appear on all cards in the set. This element is preceded by *a space, a colon and a space*:

```
: $14.50.
```

```
: Free to schools.
```

```
ISBN 0-07-077605-9 (cloth) : $7.50. --
ISBN 0-07-077606-7 (paper) : $4.50.
```

A qualification in parentheses may be added after the terms of availability if necessary:

```
: $14.50 ($8.50 to members)
```

FACSIMILES, PHOTOCOPIES AND OTHER REPRODUCTIONS

If facsimiles, photocopies and other reproductions are catalogued, describe the copy at hand, using the rules for whatever specific type of material the reproduced edition is, in all areas except the note area.

The note area will describe the details of the original only if they are different from the facsimile; i.e., if the title of the facsimile is the same as the original, then the title is not included in the note:

```
Facsimile of: 2nd., rev. London : Routledge,
1877.
```
The original has the same title and statement of responsibility as the facsimile and therefore these are not repeated.

```
Young, Egerton Ryerson.
   Indian wigwams and northern camp-fires /
Egerton Ryerson Young. -- Toronto : Coles Pub.,
c1970.
   293 p. ; 22 cm. -- (Coles Canadian series)
```
②

```
Facsim. of:  London : Charles H. Kelly, 1893.
```

Informal notes may have to be devised in some situations:

```
Reproduction of:
```

FOOTNOTES

[1]*Books in Print* (Bowker: New York).
[2]*Canadian Publishers Directory* (Quill & Quire: Toronto).

Contents V

Subject Headings

Determining the Subject(s) of an Item 124
Expressing the Subject of an Item 124
    Standard Wording of Subject Headings 124
    Lists of Subject Headings Used as Authorities 125
    PREserved Context Index System (PRECIS) 126
Features of *Sears List of Subject Headings* and *Canadian Companion* 127
    Use of Boldface Type 127
    Classification Numbers 127
    Cross-References 127
    Spellings Used in Headings 128
Headings Omitted From *Sears* 129
    Proper Names 129
    Corporate Names 129
    Common Names 129
Subdividing Headings From *Sears* 130
    Added subdivisions 130
    "Key" Headings 131
    Subdivisions With Limitations 131
    Geographical Aspects of a Subject 132
General vs. Specific Subject Headings 133
Subject Headings for Biography 133
    Individual Biographies 133
    Collective Biographies 133
Subject Analytics 133
Recording Additions to and Variations From *Sears* and *Canadian*
Companion 134
    Headings Used 134
    Additions 134
    Cross-References 134
Use of *Sears* and *Canadian Companion* by the Public 135
Adapting to New Editions of *Sears* 135
Footnotes 135

Chapter V

Subject Headings

DETERMINING THE SUBJECT(S) OF AN ITEM

- Where possible, use CIP (see p. 30, "Cataloguing in Publication (CIP)"), selection tools, and catalogues that give subject headings, to verify or simplify your work.
- For a print item, examine the title, the table of contents, the introduction, and, if necessary, parts of the text.
- For a non-book item, read any accompanying print material such as a teachers' guide; view or listen to the item itself, if need be.
- Check the tracings on the cards in the shelf list for the subject tracings of similar books.
- Group uncatalogued items related by subject for the most consistent and speedy determination of subjects and assignment of subject headings.
- In a school library, assign one to three subject headings per item. More than three headings may occasionally be assigned to a very long or important work. (See also p. 133, "Subject Analytics.") Some books with no definite subject, especially fiction, are not assigned any subject headings.

EXPRESSING THE SUBJECT OF AN ITEM

Standard Wording of Subject Headings

Once the subject is determined, it must be expressed in the standard terminology of the library's catalogue. Spelling, grammatical form and choice among synonymous terms should be kept consistent. Whether the subject headings are assigned in the library, arrive on commercial catalogue cards or are derived from published copy like CIP, the librarian follows an authority to reconcile the wording of the headings.

Lists of Subject Headings Used as Authorities

"SEARS LIST OF SUBJECT HEADINGS" AND "CANADIAN COMPANION"

For most school libraries the authorities are *Sears List of Subject Headings* and *Canadian Companion*. Since there are a few inconsistencies of wording between them, when dealing with a Canadian topic, consult the *Canadian Companion* first and follow it instead of *Sears*.

Sears	*Canadian Companion*
ESKIMOS	INUIT
ICE HOCKEY	HOCKEY
CANADA—PRIME MINISTERS	PRIME MINISTERS—CANADA

Canadian libraries use INUIT; HOCKEY; PRIME MINISTERS—CANADA.

"LIBRARY OF CONGRESS SUBJECT HEADINGS"

Many large and highly specialized libraries, but very few school libraries, use *Library of Congress Subject Headings*[1] (*LCSH*) as their authority. A section of the *LCSH* list, *Subject Headings for Children's Literature*,[2] has been incorporated into *Sears* with a few changes and modifications. In most cases, *Sears* follows the form of LC subject headings. LC cards (see p. 25, "Library of Congress") for children's books may therefore be readily adapted to match a subject catalogue based on *Sears*. An experienced subject librarian may consult *LCSH* and use LC copy or subject cards for a special part of a school library collection where *Sears* does not give sufficient breakdown or detail, e.g., a teachers' professional collection; the extra headings are then noted in the library's copy of *Sears*.

"CANADIAN SUBJECT HEADINGS"

Canadian Subject Headings is meant to be used in libraries that need subject headings for Canadian materials additional to and compatible with *LCSH*. Its section, "English-French Index," supplies French equivalents of English subject headings.

"RÉPERTOIRE DE VEDETTES-MATIÈRE"[3]

This is the Canadian authority for French subject headings. It is patterned on *LCSH* and has a companion, *Index anglais-français des termes utilisés dans le répertoire de vedettes-matière*,[4] which is a bilingual table showing English translations of the French subject headings in LC style.

Librarians in special subject areas have developed controlled vocabularies to identify the concepts and subjects of the documents in their areas. The vocabularies are called thesauri, e.g., *Thesaurus of ERIC Descriptors*.[5] They are unlike *Sears* and *LCSH* in that they do not attempt to cover all subjects, but give all possible terms and cross-references in individual subject areas. The terms used are called descriptors.

Thesauri are often found in professional libraries, such as those specializing in education. (See p. 20, "Professional Reference Service.")

PREserved Context Index System (PRECIS)

PRECIS is a method of subject indexing developed during the last decade by the British National Bibliography for production of its computer-generated catalogues. PRECIS replaces traditional subject heading lists such as *Sears*. The PRECIS Project, funded by the Ontario Ministry of Education, has produced prototype computer-generated microfiche catalogues for one high school and three elementary schools in York Region.

In the subject catalogues, each index entry is followed by brief citations sufficient to locate titles on the shelves. The full bibliographic description is carried in the shelf list.

The following is an excerpt from a subject catalogue using PRECIS. The data in the example could all appear on the same catalogue card or computer print-out:

```
OCEANS
  Pollution by oil

      301.31   WIL  The biological aspects of water pollution.
                      Wilber, Charles Grady.  [1969]
      333.9164 MIC  The oceans in tomorrow's world.
                      Michelsohn, David Reuben.  [1972]
      574.52636 SIL The world within the tidepool.
                      Silverberg, Robert.  [1972]
      628.1683 MAR  Oilspill.  Marx, Wesley.  [c1971]
```

The index also contains two other entries generated from the original input "string," each followed by the same citations:

```
POLLUTION.  Oceans          OIL
  By oil                      Pollution of oceans
```

A single input string, "Oceans pollution by oil," appropriately coded for computer manipulation, produces the three entries. There would also be appropriate "see" and "see also" references which are automatically generated by the computer.

FEATURES OF "SEARS LIST OF SUBJECT HEADINGS" AND "CANADIAN COMPANION"

A detailed explanation of the use of *Sears* and *Canadian Companion* is found in the introduction to both books and should be mastered by any school librarian doing subject work. A brief version follows:

Use of Boldface Type

Headings given in boldface are acceptable subject headings to use. Those not in boldface refer the user to the standard heading:

Dairy cattle. See **Cows**

That which appears in boldface type in *Sears* is typed in capital letters when used as a subject heading on a catalogue card. This practice has been adopted in this book.

Classification Numbers

Numbers shown after the subject headings are taken from the *Abridged Dewey Decimal Classification and Relative Index*, 10th ed.[6] No number is given for some very general subjects:

JET PLANES   629.133

SUBTRACTION
No number given.

SUBMARINES   359.3; 623.82
Two numbers stand for the military and the engineering aspects of submarines, respectively. They indicate two contexts to be referred to in DDC in deciding which of the possible classification numbers suits the item with the subject SUBMARINES.

All of these classification numbers must be checked in the context of *DDC* before being assigned because:
- they might have been changed in a new edition of *DDC*
- there might be other options open that *Sears* is not comprehensive enough to show
- they are meant as an aid to classification but are to be approached with the same reservations as the numbers in the relative index of *DDC*. (See p. 139, "Relative Index.")

Cross-References

Hereafter these will be referred to as "references," as in *Sears*.

These direct the librarian from an acceptable subject heading to other related subject headings that may also be used, or from a non-standard term to the right one. The references in *Sears* may also be used as a guide for making reference cards for the catalogue. (See p. 196, "References.")

An x is used to indicate "see" references that direct the user *from* the words after the x, which are not to be used as headings, *to* the approved headings.

POETS, CANADIAN
    x Canada—Poets; Canadian poets

This means Canada—Poets see POETS, CANADIAN; Canadian poets see POETS, CANADIAN.

The symbol xx is used to indicate "see also" references that have been made in *Sears* in order to direct the user *from* another subject heading *to* the subject heading being considered:

COWS   636.2
    See also DAIRYING; MILK
    x Cow; Dairy cattle
    xx CATTLE; DAIRYING; LIVESTOCK

This means, reading the above example from bottom to top: CATTLE see also COWS; DAIRYING see also COWS; LIVESTOCK see also COWS.

Although many possible "see" and "see also" references are shown in *Sears*, make such cross-references only from terms that library users will be likely to look for in the catalogue. "See also" references are made only when there is additional material in the library under the subject heading to which the user is also referred.

Spellings Used in Headings

Consistency in spelling is essential, especially when variations in spelling will affect the filing location of subject cards in the catalogue. If changes are made in the spellings of the subject headings in *Sears*, the librarian should indicate this in the library's copy.

AMERICAN SPELLINGS VS. CANADIAN SPELLINGS
Webster's Third New International Dictionary of the English Language is the authority followed by *Sears*. The *Canadian Companion* also follows American spelling. The librarian, however, may choose Canadian spelling, for example, THEATRE instead of THEATER.

COPING WITH VARIANT SPELLINGS

By cross-referencing. Variant spellings can be tied together by references, e.g., Innuit see INUIT.

By interfiling. No reference need be made if the words in their two spellings are likely to file next to each other anyway: HUMAN BEHAVIOR; HUMAN BEHAVIOUR. (For information on disregarding small differences in spelling when filing, see p. 186, "Variant Spellings.")

HEADINGS OMITTED FROM "SEARS"

The librarian is authorized to add to *Sears* as necessary with terms from the following categories:

Proper Names

PERSONS AND PLACES

Names of persons and places follow the same rules as for establishing a main entry heading, which are detailed in Chapter III:

ELIZABETH II, QUEEN OF GREAT BRITAIN
LONDON (ONT.)

OTHER

Names of nationalities and ethnic groups, Indian tribes, wars, battles and treaties may be added as required, in a wording that follows the form indicated in *Sears* under the general term:

BATTLES   355.4; 904
　　　　　Names of battles are not included in this
　　　　　　　list but are to be added as needed, e.g.,
　　　　　　　ARDENNES, BATTLE OF THE, 1944-1945; etc.

Sometimes the headings must be devised by analogy; *Sears* shows AMERICANS IN GREECE, so there is a pattern for AMERICANS IN JAPAN, CANADIANS IN GERMANY, etc.

Corporate Names

These may be added as required in the form that they have as main entry headings:

PARTI QUEBECOIS

Common Names

Many common names, including those of specific fruits, games, musical instruments, nuts, tools, trees, vegetables, diseases, organs and regions of the body, chemicals and minerals may be added as needed. Consult *Sears* under an inclusive name of a species or group to find the acceptable form to use for more specific names:
　　• the singular form of the word is used for names of specific
　　　trees, nuts, and fruits:

ELM; PECAN; APPLE

- the plural form of the word is used for names of specific animals, berries, birds, fishes, flowers, tools, and vegetables, except in cases where the word has one form only:

CATS; STRAWBERRIES; CHICKENS; ASTERS; SAWS; POTATOES
but
SALMON *Singular form only.*

- Names of diseases, organs and regions of the body are given in the commonly used form. Use the plural form where the word has a plural and the body has more than one:

KIDNEYS; HANDS; MUMPS
but
ACNE *Plural not in common use.*

NOSE *Body has only one.*

SUBDIVIDING HEADINGS FROM "SEARS"

Added Subdivisions

Subdivisions that may be added to headings to bring out aspects of subjects are shown by *Sears* in the following ways:

LISTED AFTER A TERM

DOGS

DOGS—FICTION

DOGS—PSYCHOLOGY

DOGS—TRAINING

DESCRIBED IN A NOTE

CANADA—POLITICS AND GOVERNMENT   320.971;
        971
    May be subdivided as appropriate by period
        using the subdivisions under CANADA—
    HISTORY

LISTED IN THE FRONT MATTER

Sears includes a table, "List of Subdivisions," from which subdivisions may be taken and used as needed and permitted.

"Key" Headings

A complete breakdown of a few subjects showing all possible subdivisions is given as a sample of format and a guide to the subdivision of similar terms. These examples are called "key" headings and include SHAKESPEARE, WILLIAM, as an example of an author. Further examples are:

Sears	*Canadian Companion*	
UNITED STATES	CANADA	
OHIO *for a state*	MANITOBA *for a province*	
CHICAGO	VANCOUVER	

Subdivisions With Limitations

COLLECTIONS is used after subject headings such as POETRY or DRAMA, to show that the item is an anthology by several authors rather than the work of one:

ENGLISH LITERATURE—COLLECTIONS.

DESCRIPTION AND TRAVEL is used after the names of countries, provinces, and other large geographical areas:

MANITOBA—DESCRIPTION AND TRAVEL

DESCRIPTION instead of DESCRIPTION AND TRAVEL is used after the names of cities:

OTTAWA—DESCRIPTION

FICTION may be used after the names of persons, historical events, animals, sports, etc., to show the literary form:

BALLET—FICTION

BEARS—FICTION

FRONTIER AND PIONEER LIFE—CANADA—FICTION

Note: Instead of subdividing to show literary form, *Sears* sometimes gives a standard term:

SCIENCE FICTION

MYSTERY AND DETECTIVE STORIES

GEOGRAPHY may be used after names of geographical areas or places, for textbooks and such, as described in *Sears*:

CANADA—GEOGRAPHY

ASIA—GEOGRAPHY

HISTORY may be used after names of countries, provinces, cities, or after subjects such as ART to indicate an historical treatment of those subjects:

INDIANS OF NORTH AMERICA—CANADA—HISTORY

ART, ISLAMIC—HISTORY

Period subdivisions may be added as given in *Sears* and its *Canadian Companion*:

NEW BRUNSWICK—HISTORY—1784-1867

UNITED STATES—HISTORY—REVOLUTION, 1775-1783

In the *Canadian Companion*, appropriate subject subdivisions and dates are given for the history of every province.

HISTORY AND CRITICISM is used as the subdivision after headings such as MUSIC and LITERATURE:

MUSIC, AMERICAN—HISTORY AND CRITICISM

CANADIAN LITERATURE—HISTORY AND CRITICISM

Geographical Aspects of a Subject

Sears gives instructions on when and in what manner to show geographical subject subdivisions. Following the instructions, geographical aspects of a subject may be shown by adding, as a subdivision, the name of the specific country, province, city or region:

AUTOMOBILE RACING—BRITISH COLUMBIA

BIRDS—GASPE PENINSULA

With subject headings in art or music, an inverted adjective is used to show the geographical aspect:

SCULPTURE, AMERICAN

FOLK SONGS, SPANISH

In subject headings from literature, the geographical or linguistic aspect is shown by an adjective:

GAELIC POETRY

ENGLISH DRAMA

GENERAL VS. SPECIFIC SUBJECT HEADINGS

It is usually preferable to assign the general, inclusive heading rather than more than three specific ones:

CITRUS FRUIT *not ORANGES; LEMONS; LIMES; GRAPEFRUIT*

General and specific headings are not normally assigned to the same item; for example, a book about farm animals should be assigned the heading DOMESTIC ANIMALS rather than the names of every animal included in the book.

SUBJECT HEADINGS FOR BIOGRAPHY

Individual Biographies

A subject heading is made for the name of the biographee using the same form of the name as for a main entry heading. The subdivision BIOGRAPHY is not used.

MARY STUART, QUEEN OF THE SCOTS

GAULLE, CHARLES DE

Additional subject headings may be assigned if the biography has other subjects worth bringing out in a particular library, for example, historical period or occupation. A book about Florence Nightingale, for example, would have the subject heading NIGHTINGALE, FLORENCE, but might also include the heading NURSES.

Collective Biographies

Biographies of persons belonging to a specific profession or group are entered under the appropriate subject. The subdivision BIOGRAPHY is added when this is necessary to show the biographical aspect of the topic:

SCIENTISTS

WOMEN—BIOGRAPHY

Subject analytics for the individual biographees in a collection may be made when considered necessary for the users.

SUBJECT ANALYTICS

Subject analytic headings are made for subjects that are written of in a chapter or part of a book, for instance, the individuals in a collective biography. The subject analytic may be made for all the subjects in a collective work, or for only certain subjects especially useful to the library's audience.

RECORDING ADDITIONS TO AND VARIATIONS FROM "SEARS" AND "CANADIAN COMPANION"

Directions for checking and adding headings are given in *Sears*. An adapted version follows:

Headings Used

The first time words or terms are used as subject headings, a check mark is placed beside them in the cataloguer's copies of *Sears* and *Canadian Companion*, and in any copies intended for use by the public.

Additions

Sears and *Canadian Companion* are printed with wide right-hand margins to permit additions and changes to be made in the lists. The first time a subject not given in *Sears* or *Canadian Companion* is used, it should be written in the librarian's copy (and the public's copy) in the correct alphabetical place. For example, under the heading ANIMALS, a note states that the names of individual animals may be added. If the subject headings LIONS and LIONS —STORIES are used, these headings should be written in the "L" part of the alphabet, and beside ANIMALS—FICTION write LIONS— FICTION.

Cross-References

A check mark is made beside each suggested "see" and "see also" entry in *Sears* for which a reference card is actually put into the catalogue.

```
√ANIMALS--FICTION  FIC
    √see also names of animals with the subdivision
        FICTION, e.g.,√DOGS--FICTION; etc.
      x Animal stories; Animals - Stories
     xx ANIMALS IN LITERATURE; FABLES; FICTION
```

If reference cards other than those indicated in *Sears* are made, such references may be written into the list and check-marked:

```
√ANIMALS--FICTION  FIC
    √see also names of animals with the subdivision
        FICTION, e.g.,√DOGS--FICTION; etc.        √ BEARS—FICTION
      x Animal stories; Animals - Stories          √ LIONS-FICTION
     xx ANIMALS IN LITERATURE; FABLES; FICTION
```

This means that there are items in the card catalogue with the following subject headings: ANIMALS—FICTION, DOGS—FICTION, BEARS— FICTION, LIONS—FICTION, as well as a cross-reference, namely:

ANIMALS—FICTION see also names of animals with subdivision FIC-
TION, e.g., DOGS—FICTION; BEARS—FICTION; LIONS—FICTION.

Sears makes optional the addition of all new entries in the subject catalogue
to the "see also" card, e.g., FOXES—FICTION; PANDAS—FICTION. The
library should develop a policy on making such additions, according to the
time available and the usefulness of such an expenditure of effort.

USE OF "SEARS" AND "CANADIAN COMPANION" BY THE PUBLIC

Sears and *Canadian Companion* are quite comprehensible to students and
teachers and may be placed near the card catalogue for public use. The subject
headings in boldface type will guide the user to subject headings that may be
available in the card catalogue. If the headings have been checked off in *Sears*
and *Canadian Companion*, the public's copies will be made more convenient
for the user.

ADAPTING TO NEW EDITIONS OF "SEARS"

Every few years there is a new edition of *Sears* and in 1978 its publishing
history was enriched by the publication of the *Canadian Companion*.

New editions and publications introduce conflicts and new terms into the
catalogue. Where terminology for a concept or item with a heading derived
from an old edition is changed in a new edition of *Sears*, begin using the new
headings on present cataloguing. Recatalogue the old items to correspond in
headings as time permits. Meanwhile, make "see also" references to direct
the users temporarily from the old to the new and preferred subject
headings. Recataloguing may be done selectively with the newer and more
important works being given up-to-date headings, while the less important
ones are left as they are, to be gradually removed from consideration by
attrition. The "see also" reference may be removed when all the old headings
have been updated or withdrawn.

FOOTNOTES

[1]*Library of Congress Subject Headings*, 9th ed. (Library of Congress, 1975: Washington).
[2]*Subject Headings for Children's Literature*, 2nd ed. (Library of Congress, 1975:
Washington).
[3]*Répertoire de vedettes-matière*, 8th éd. (Université Laval, Bibliothèque, Section de
l'analyse documentaire, 1976: Québec).
[4]*Index anglais-français des termes utilisés dans le répertoire de vedettes-matière*, 2e éd.
(Université Laval, Bibliothèque, Section de l'analyse documentaire, 1976: Québec).
[5]*Thesaurus of ERIC Descriptors*, 7th ed. (Macmillan Information, 1977: New York).
[6]*Abridged Dewey Decimal Classification and Relative Index*, 10th ed. (Forest Press,
1971: Lake Placid Club, N.Y.).

Contents VI

Classification

Introduction 138
Dewey Decimal Classification System 138
  Introduction to *DDC* 138
  Schedules 138
  Tables 139
  Relative Index 139
Relationship Between Classification and Subject Headings 140
Relationship Between Classification and Literary Form 140
Classifying an Item by *DDC* 140
Expansion of the Abridged *DDC* 142
Abbreviation of Numbers in *DDC* 142
Call Number 143
  Classification Line 143
  Call Letters Line 144
  Line Indicating Special Collection 147
  Optional Line Below Call Letters 147
  Cuttering 147
Special Subjects and Forms 147
  Fiction 147
  Easy Books 148
  Reference Books 148
  Biography 148
  Canadian Literature 149
  Shakespeare 150
Adapting to a New Edition of *DDC* 150
Library of Congress Classification 151
Footnotes 151

Chapter VI

Classification

INTRODUCTION

In a library, the subject or form of each item is represented by a notation, which in school libraries is usually a number assigned from the Dewey Decimal Classification (*DDC*).

DEWEY DECIMAL CLASSIFICATION SYSTEM

DDC is the most widely used system of classification and is the standard for school and most public libraries. It comes in two editions, the three-volume unabridged and the one-volume abridged. The current edition of the unabridged is *Dewey Decimal Classification and Relative Index*, 19th ed. (Forest Press, 1979: Albany, N.Y.) The current edition of the abridged is *Abridged Dewey Decimal Classification and Relative Index*, 11th ed. (Forest Press, 1979: Albany, N.Y.).

The abridged edition is used by more schools than the unabridged, being sufficiently detailed for elementary school collections and some secondary ones.

Introduction to DDC

Whichever edition is used, the introduction should be studied before the rest of the work is applied.

Schedules

DDC divides all knowledge into 10 main classes, referred to as the First Summary. These 10 classes are divided into 100 divisions known as the Second Summary. The Third Summary shows almost 1000 sections. The schedules, which make up the largest part of *DDC*, amplify these summaries, so that there are terms with corresponding *DDC* numbers that come close to covering all the subjects that make up human knowledge.

From the schedules come the notations that are assigned to each item being classified. They are called class numbers.

Tables

The tables give numbers that are to be added to the basic numbers found in the schedules. Their purpose is to bring out special aspects of a subject, such as *form*, e.g., "—03—Dictionary," or *area*, e.g., "—71—Canada."

Expansion showing subdivisions from Table 1, "Standard subdivisions":

530—Physics
As found in the schedules.

—03—Dictionary
As found in Table 1.

530.03—Dictionary of physics
Combined by the librarian.

Expansion showing number from Table 2, "Areas":

784.49—Folk songs
From the schedule.

—65—Algeria
From the area table.

784.4965—Folk songs of Algeria
Combined by the librarian.

Relative Index

The index is an alphabetical arrangement of terms with matching *DDC* numbers. These numbers are meant to be used only as a guide to classification. They should always be checked against the schedules, where each number may be ratified for use, or where instructions may be given to redirect the librarian or to advise on completing the notation.

Never classify from the index alone because:

- There may be many numbers in the index for each term. Only familiarity with the tables will clearly show what aspect of the term each number denotes.
- The numbers in the index may be incomplete or too general. The schedules show hierarchical divisions, scope notes and other aids to precise classification.
- A term in the index is out of its context. When seen in its place in the hierarchical schedules, it can be matched with the most precise class number.

RELATIONSHIP BETWEEN CLASSIFICATION AND SUBJECT HEADINGS

The librarian assigns a number which becomes part of the call number, the key for locating the item on the shelf. Only one class number can be assigned to an item, even though the item may deal with two or more subjects. For example, *Earth and the Universe* [filmstrip] may have two subject headings, ASTRONOMY and OUTER SPACE—EXPLORATION, which correspond respectively to *DDC* numbers 523 and 629.4. Since only one of these numbers may be assigned, the librarian decides to use 523, because the filmstrip set is deemed to be more an introduction to astronomy than to space flight technology.

RELATIONSHIP BETWEEN CLASSIFICATION AND LITERARY FORM

Works of *belles-lettres* and other works whose form is more important than their subject, or whose subject is impossible to specify, e.g., general encyclopaedias, are classified by form rather than subject. Literary works such as essays, poetry and drama are classed in the 800's by genre, language and nationality, not by subject. Biographies may be classed by form in 921, or by subject. (See p. 148, "Biography.") To bring out both the subject and the form, use form subdivisions:

530—Physics

—092—Form subdivision for biography

530.092—Biography of physicists
May be used in a small library for individual or collective biography.

530.0922—Collective biography of physicists

530.0924—Individual biography of a physicist

970—North America

—016—Bibliography

970.0016—Bibliography of North America
Extra zero added as per instructions in schedules.

CLASSIFYING AN ITEM BY DDC

The subject of a book is determined by examining the title, table of contents, preface or introduction, and the text of the book. For non-book items, especially those that have no accompanying teacher's guide or descriptive material, it may be necessary to view or listen to all or part of the material. After determining the subject, use the schedules to assign the most suitable class numbers, according to the following principles:

Be specific. A book dealing with the geography of several countries in Asia will be given the general number 915 for Asia. A book on Japan will be given the specific number 915.2. There are degrees of specificity appropriate to each library however. Less specific and lengthy numbers are used when the quantity of books on a subject is small. For example, a library with one book on Tokyo would be well advised to class it in 915.2, not its specific number, 915.2135.

Be consistent. When optional and multiple numbers are shown in the schedules, always use the same number for a specific subject. In a small collection, it may be preferable to disregard aspects of a subject in the interest of keeping the materials grouped. For example, with cars, despite the many aspects that may be indicated by classification, a small school might use only "629.2—Motor land vehicles, and cycles," plus "796.7—Driving motor vehicles." A larger school, where there are courses and materials on auto mechanics, might have a policy of subdividing 629.2, using "629.24—Chassis," "629.26—Bodies and bodywork," "629.246—Brakes," and so forth. Keep a record of the classifications.

There comes a point where the quantity and diversity of materials in the collection justify finer classification, or placement in different classes, of items that had previously been kept in one class. Receiving new class numbers into the library through commercial cataloguing will likely influence the proliferation of classes. (See p. 24, "Commercial Cataloguing.")

If subdivisions may be used following a number, be consistent in their use. For instance, "Elementary education, 372," may be subdivided by country. If the library's holdings include and likely will always include few books on elementary education in different countries, use only 372; if there are many such titles, i.e., more than 10, use numbers with geographical subdivisions consistently:

372.971—Elementary education in Canada

372.973—Elementary education in U.S.

Group items to classify. Do not classify items in isolation from each other and from the library catalogue. Grouping items with similar subjects will make for quicker and more accurate work. The shelf list is the record of all the classifications accumulated from the past and is therefore the best guide to the precedents to follow. Since there are always new subjects and subjects which have been reclassified in new editions of *DDC*, the notations in the shelf list should be used in conjunction with the schedules.

Keep records. Record in pencil decisions and modifications of numbers, such as expansions and reductions, in the library's copy of *DDC*:

371.219—School enrollment
Make handwritten note "Includes declining enrolment," if a note will speed up future work—contrast of American and Canadian spelling is deliberate.

DDC may show several possible numbers for a subject:

971.01—Canada. Early history to 1763

971.401—Quebec. French period to 1763

The library may use the first class for items on the exploration and settlement of New France, and for the ramifications and conflicts that ensued, and use the latter number for the historical aspects of institutions and customs of New France which persist in Quebec. Decisions made item by item which cumulatively define the two classes can be recorded in the pages of *DDC*, where they will make for quicker, more consistent classifying. Borderline cases will be classified by arbitrary decisions that do little to differentiate 971.01 from 971.401; these cases therefore need not be recorded.

EXPANSION OF THE ABRIDGED DDC

The abridged edition provides enough subject breakdown for an elementary school library, unless the collection is very highly developed overall, or in certain subject areas. Expanded numbers as provided for in the unabridged edition may be used in whole or in part when expansion is considered necessary, as is more likely to happen in a secondary school library:
   The expansion of the number for television indicates how numbers may be expanded for large or specialized collections:

	Unabridged Dewey	*Abridged Dewey*
Television	621.388	621.388
Black & White	621.388 02	*Class together*
Colour	621.388 04	*in 621.388*

Actually, since very few school libraries use numbers expanded more than four places after the decimal, the abridged number will likely be preferred whether the library is using the complete or the abridged *DDC*.

ABBREVIATION OF NUMBERS IN DDC

In CIP, on commercial catalogue cards, and in published cataloguing copy, such as the copy in *Canadiana*, long numbers are divided into segments by apostrophes (called prime marks), which may be lopped off if a library finds a *DDC* notation excessively long for its purpose. (See also p. 24, "Commercial Cataloguing.") Thus in the class number 621.38802, shown as 621.388'02, the 02 may be dropped if the size of the collection does not warrant making special classes for black and white and colour television, as well as television in general.

A number may be cut off at the places marked by a prime, before a subdivision from the tables, or at the place where it ends in the abridged *DDC*. No library, however small, should reduce a number that is in one segment; for instance, "621.388—Television" could be shortened to "621.38—Electronic and communication engineering," but should not be.

A one-segment number is usually five digits or fewer, although 621.388 is six, because the 620's are unusually crowded. Small libraries usually disregard all but the first segment. A two-segment number is usually no more than seven digits. Medium-sized libraries often use the first and second segments, but not the third.

In reducing the notation, never reduce to less than three places, never show a decimal after a three-digit number, and never leave a zero at the end of a number after the decimal. Do not show the space or the prime in the notation on a book or other item.

CALL NUMBER

There is no standard practice to follow in devising call numbers. Some of the acceptable variants are shown below.

The call number for an item is made up of the class number used to denote the subject or type of material, and the call letters. (See p. 144, "Call Letters Line.") The call number is arranged on two or more lines:

```
398.2
CLE
```

```
617.9681
GIF
```

The call number for a book is placed on the spine label, the book card and pocket, and all catalogue cards for an item. In complex packages, it is also put on the container, instruction sheet, and all major parts, e.g., slides in a set.

Classification Line

This line will be either the *DDC* number, or letters such as "B" for biography (seen in some public libraries in place of 921); "F" for fiction ("FIC" or "Fic" are also used by some libraries); "E" for easy books; occasionally "SC" for story collections (seen in the *Standard Catalog Series*[1] and a few libraries); and "SF" (occasionally used instead of "F" to feature science fiction).

Whenever the spine is too narrow for the number to be seen if it is on one line, or the class number will not fit into the spaces before the first indention, it can be rearranged for visibility:

617.
9681
GIF

Alternatively, on a narrow book, the label can go on the front towards the lower left corner near the spine. If there is only a hinge and no spine on a book, there is nowhere for the call number to go except on the cover.

Call Letters Line

This line helps to differentiate books with the same class number. In schools, it may consist of one or more letters, three being recommended, in upper, or upper and lower case. The letters represent:

PERSON OR CORPORATE BODY

The call letters are usually the first letters of the surname of the person, or the first letters of the name of the corporate body responsible for the work. If the name does not have three connected letters to use, the librarian may add adjacent letters to the short name to bring the number up to three. For example:

XBU
Call letters for X, Bureaucrat.

NGM
Call letters for Ng, Maria.

XHE
Call letters formed from author's name, X, and title, Her Story.

With "Mac," there will be an undifferentiated quantity of items shelved by the three call letters, especially in:

F
MAC

The librarian might well follow the lead of some processors and go to four letters, e.g., MACD. More convenience is gained than lost if Mc is rendered as Mac in the call letters, and if four letters are also used for names starting with Mc.

TITLE MAIN ENTRY HEADING

The call letters may be the first three letters of the title, disregarding any initial articles. Titles starting with numerals or symbols will be given the call letters that correspond to the filing access point:

```
7 plays ...
SEV
```
Call letters from the beginning of the title, 7 plays . . .

The line below the classification number in a biography or criticism is sometimes filled out with call letters derived from the subject's name. This coding serves to keep all identically classified items about a subject together on the shelves regardless of author.

To bring biographies together by the name of the person who is the subject (the biographee), the call letters are made up of the first three letters of the surname of the biographee, with the first three letters of the surname of the person or corporate body responsible for the work on the line below. In a small collection, the addition of a third line, i.e., author letters, may not be warranted:

```
971.034            921
SEC      or        SEC
MACK               MACK
```
Laura Secord *by Ruth McKenzie.*

Same as above without author letters:

```
971.034            921
SEC      or        SEC
```
Laura Secord *by Ruth McKenzie.*

For biographies of persons better known by forename than surname, use the first three letters of the name by which the biographee is known:

```
932.021            921
CLE      or        CLE
GRA                GRA
```
Cleopatra *by Michael Grant.*

Biographies and criticism of an author are most usefully arranged next to the author's own works. If these are mostly of one class, e.g., poetry, the books about the author can go next to them:

819.1 *Canadian poetry.*	819.1 *Canadian poetry.*
COH *Leonard Cohen, author.*	COH *Leonard Cohen, subject.*
	OND *Michael Ondaatje, author.*

Some librarians might use 821, 811, or other numbers here.

Although with most authors it is possible to identify one genre which is their forte and to classify biography and criticism of it so that it will be adjacent, there are authors where the placement may be arbitrary, e.g., Thomas Hardy, equally respected as a poet and a novelist. In this case, poetry

Fig. 6:1   Biographies shelved by subject first, then subfiled by author. (In some cases labels have been accepted from the processor even though the author letters have been omitted. The call letters on *Muhammad Ali: Boxing Superstar* do not reflect the example of *AACR2*.)

having a numerical notation, convenience may dictate that works about Hardy go in "821—English poetry." John Updike has several volumes of verse to his credit, but is pre-eminently a novelist; criticisms and biographies of Updike would therefore go in the 813's. Criticism of fiction is never put in F just so that it will be next to the novel being criticized. Rather, scholarly editions of the novels may be classified as shown on p. 147, "Fiction," so that they will be next to the criticisms.

Whenever it seems desirable to guarantee adjacent shelving of items of similar subjects or interdependent themes, regardless of author or title, use the appropriate call letters:

759.6   *Spanish painting and paintings.*
GOY   *Goya, subject.*

759.6   *Spanish painting and paintings.*
VEL   *Velazquez, subject.*

Line Indicating Special Collection

This indicator is placed above the class number to show that items with this special marking are shelved apart in whatever grouping this superscribed lettering indicates. This line, if needed, must almost always be added to commercial catalogue cards and spine labels by the library staff:

R *Designation of a reference book.*
031
COM

REF *Alternative designation of a reference book.*
912
OXF

ITA *Designation of collection shelved by language, i.e., Italian.*
F
COL

Optional Line Below Call Letters

Large libraries construct a different call number for every item. In a school, wherever there is an undesirable pile-up of items with the same call number, including letters, it is possible to differentiate the numbers further by an extra line showing such details as:

- The volume number of an item in a set (especially useful if the spine does not show it or the spine label obscures it).
- The date of chronologically published items in a series, e.g., year-books.
- The copy number, when multiple copies of the same edition are not identified by accession numbers. This expedient is mainly seen in small libraries.
- A notation of edition, if there are several editions.

Cuttering

Many large libraries and some processors follow an alphanumerical author table devised by C.A. Cutter, or an adaptation of it called the Cutter-Sanborn tables. The term "cuttering" is loosely applied to all call letters. School libraries are advised to adapt cuttering to the simpler call letters discussed above.

SPECIAL SUBJECTS AND FORMS

Fiction

Fiction books are not usually given *DDC* numbers but are marked F with the call letters typed beneath. Novels and stories written by authors with the same surname are brought together on the shelf by the call letters. (See p. 144, "Call Letters Line.")

Scholarly editions of works of fiction containing notes, biographical material, glossaries and other aids to study may be classed using numbers such as "813—American fiction," "819.3—Canadian fiction," "823—British fiction," and "843—French fiction."

Easy Books

The letter E is usually used to denote picture books and story books for beginning readers. A class number may also be given:

E
UDR   *or*

E
582
UDR
Easy book on trees.

This means that the item may be moved to the classified section of the collection if it is of value beyond the primary division, or that the easy books may be arranged by subject.

Reference Books

Reference books are classified by subject or form, e.g., "032—British encyclopedia" (form); "503—Dictionary of science" (subject plus form).

They are distinguished from items in the circulating collection by their call number:

REF
031
WEB
Webster's Dictionary of Proper Names. *To be shelved in the reference collection.*

Biography

COLLECTIVE BIOGRAPHIES

Items that contain biographies of several persons are classified in 920 and follow the usual rule for assigning call letters:

920.02
WHO
Who Did What; The Lives and Achievements of 5000 Men and Women . . .

INDIVIDUAL BIOGRAPHIES

A biography or autobiography of one individual is classified in 921 or, in some libraries, B, when the literary form, biography, is to be brought out. It is more useful, however, to class biographies with the subject when they have a specified one as do biographies of sports heroes, musicians, artists, scientists, and political leaders, e.g., 822.33 for the life of Shakespeare. (See also p. 145, "Subject.")

Canadian Literature

DDC shows different ways to classify the literatures of the world, without going into great detail in the case of Canadian literature. The following are some options that are used; to them may be added notations from *DDC*'s Table 3, "Subdivisions of Individual Literatures," though for most collections one of the numbers below with appropriate call letters is probably sufficient for classifying an item of Canadian literature:

OPTION 1

The following numbers from the "American literature in English" schedule may be used:

811—American and Canadian poetry and poets
812—American and Canadian drama and dramatists
813—American and Canadian fiction and novelists
814—American and Canadian essays and essayists
815—American and Canadian speeches and orators
816—American and Canadian letters
817—American and Canadian satire, humour and humorists
818—American and Canadian miscellaneous writings

OPTION 2

The letter C in front of the classification number for American literature can be used to distinguish Canadian from American literature in the English language:

C811—Canadian poetry and poets
C812—Canadian drama and dramatists
C813—Canadian fiction and novelists
C814—Canadian essays and essayists
C815—Canadian speeches and orators
C816—Canadian letters
C817—Canadian satire, humour and humorists
C818—Canadian miscellaneous writings

OPTION 3

All literature in the English language, including Canadian, may be classified in the numbers for "Literatures of English and Anglo-Saxon languages":

821—English and Canadian poetry and poets
822—English and Canadian drama and dramatists
823—English and Canadian fiction and novelists
824—English and Canadian essays and essayists
825—English and Canadian speeches and orators

826—English and Canadian letters
827—English and Canadian satire, humour and humorists
828—English and Canadian miscellaneous writings

OPTION 4

The class 819 may be assigned to Canadian literature with the standard subdivisions for literature. In a school where there is a strong emphasis on Canadian studies, use this fourth table of classification for the most convenient arrangement of Canadian literature:
819.1—Canadian poetry and poets
819.2—Canadian drama and dramatists
819.3—Canadian fiction and novelists
819.4—Canadian essays and essayists
819.5—Canadian speeches and orators
819.6—Canadian letters
819.7—Canadian satire, humour and humorists
819.8—Canadian miscellaneous writings

Shakespeare

The works by and about Shakespeare being so numerous, the unabridged *DDC* shows a special table for call letters that guarantee adjacent arrangement of his works and of commentaries on them:

822.33	*Shakespeare.*	822.3	
T5	*Call "letters" for*	T6	*Call "letters" for*
	a text of "Macbeth."	JAC	*a critique of "Macbeth."*

ADAPTING TO A NEW EDITION OF DDC

Reclassification is expensive. It should be selectively undertaken on items of permanent value and special importance. Most items may remain in the class they were consigned to from an older edition of *DDC* until attrition removes them from the scene. Meanwhile, the subject cards will serve as a guide to subject-related items shelved by varying numbers.

When reclassifying, remove the old classification number on the book card and the catalogue cards, and type in the new ones. Tape new spine labels over the old ones. Change the numbers on the book pockets with stick-on labels.

Items in circulation may be unavailable for correction of their labels, pockets and book cards. Make a note on the book card in the charging tray as a reminder to detain an item for reprocessing on its return. If it gets carded without correction anyway, it should be noticed at inventory time. To be doubly certain that no copy escapes, make a note that revision is pending beside its accession numbers on the shelf-list card.

LIBRARY OF CONGRESS CLASSIFICATION

The classification scheme developed for the millions of volumes in the Library of Congress has been adopted by many other libraries. Where there is a larger collection, in the hundreds of thousands, or in certain subject areas, the LC classification is preferred to *DDC* because:

- Its notation, which uses letters as well as numbers, allows for many classes and very specific classification, without the long numbers *DDC* would require to achieve the same degree of specificity.
- It has tables that run to some 30 volumes, giving a very detailed guide to the classifier who needs it.

It is not recommended that school libraries consider adopting LC classification or reclassifying from *DDC* to LC. *DDC* is the standard scheme for school libraries because:

- *DDC* allows for all the specificity, through expansion, that a school library will ever need.
- *DDC* is more memorable and understandable than LC, because of its rationale and comparative brevity.
- Use of *DDC* keeps the school library's classification compatible with that of most public libraries.
- Commercial cataloguing for schools tends to cost less with *DDC*, which is usually combined with cataloguing simplifications most suited to school-age users.

FOOTNOTES

[1]*Standard Catalog Series* (H.W. Wilson: New York).

Contents VII

Completing the Card Set

Card Set 154
Main Entry Card 154
  Indentions 154
  Placement of Call Number 155
  Main Entry Under the Heading for a Person or Corporate Body ... 155
  Main Entry Under Title 156
Shelf-List Card 157
  Accession Information 157
  Tracings 158
Added Entry Cards 162
  Subject Heading Card 162
  Name Added Entry Card 162
  Title Added Entry Card 163
  Series Added Entry Card 163
  Analytical Added Entry Card 163
Extension Cards 163
Typewriters and Type Styles 164
Sample Cards 166

Chapter VII

Completing the Card Set

CARD SET

A complete set of catalogue cards includes a main entry card, a shelf-list card, and a card for each subject heading and added entry which is traced on the shelf-list card.

When a librarian does original cataloguing, the typing of the cards in the set should follow a standardized format for the placement of the various types of information. There are minor variations to be seen in the practices followed by different libraries and processors, but none is so great that commercially produced cards, or cards copied from another library, cannot be integrated into the card catalogue.

MAIN ENTRY CARD

The main entry card (or unit card) shows the call number (Chapter VI), the main entry heading (Chapter III), and the description of the work (Chapter IV). Each of the other cards in the set is an exact duplicate of the main entry card, with the addition of appropriate data, e.g., tracings, headings.

Indentions

The spacings from the left-hand edge of the card are known as indentions. While these may vary slightly on cards from different sources, the following is an example of commonly found spacing:

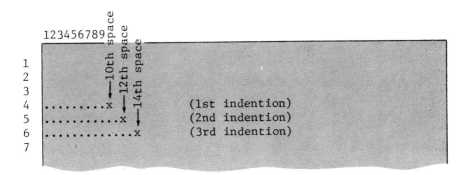

Placement of Call Number

The class number begins on the fourth line down from the top of the card at the left-hand edge. The call letters of the call number begin on the fifth line down at the left edge. If location information, e.g., "Ref.," is given, it is usually placed on the third line of the card, beginning at the left-hand edge just above the class number:

```
1 ┌                   1 ┌
2 │                   2 │
3 │                   3 │ REF
4 │ 423               4 │ 819.009
5 │ MOR               5 │ DIC
```

Main Entry Under the Heading for a Person or Corporate Body

MAIN ENTRY HEADING

The heading begins on the fourth line down from the top of the card at the first indention, i.e., 10th space from the left-hand edge. If the heading is longer than one line, the second and subsequent lines begin at the second indention.

DESCRIPTION OF THE WORK

Chapter IV describes the punctuation, capitalization, and spacing found within and between each area of the description. The following list shows these areas organized into paragraphs. Not every area, however, will appear for each item. It depends on the item itself, and the level of cataloguing chosen by the librarian.

Paragraph one: Title and statement of responsibility area
Edition area
Material (or type of publication) specific details area
Publication, distribution, etc., area

Paragraph two: Physical description area
Series area

Paragraph three: Note area
Paragraph four: Standard number and terms of availability
area

Each paragraph begins at the second indention with the second and subsequent lines in the paragraph coming back to the first indention.

The diagram below shows the card layout for an item with a person or corporate body as main entry heading:

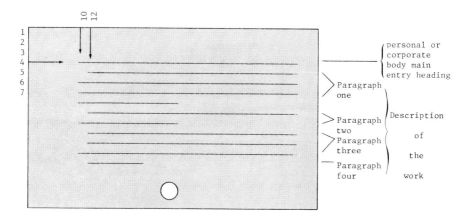

Main Entry Under Title

TITLE MAIN ENTRY HEADING

The title and statement of responsibility area begins on the fourth line down from the top of the card at the first indention, i.e., 10th space from the left-hand edge. It does not, however, stand apart from paragraph one, as does a personal or corporate body main entry. It is, instead, part of the first paragraph of the description.

DESCRIPTION OF THE WORK

Chapter IV includes the punctuation, capitalization, and spacing found within and between each area of description. The following list shows these areas organized into paragraph form. Not every area, however, will appear for each item. It depends on the item itself, and the level of cataloguing chosen by the librarian.

Paragraph one: Title and statement of responsibility area
Edition area
Material (or type of publication) specific
details area
Publication, distribution, etc., area

Paragraph one begins at the first indention with the second and subsequent lines beginning at the second indention. This form of paragraphing is known as a hanging indention.

Paragraph two: Physical description area
                 Series area
Paragraph three: Note area
Paragraph four: Standard number and terms of availability
                 area

Paragraphs two, three, and four begin at the second indention, with the second and subsequent lines in each paragraph coming back to the first indention.

The diagram below shows the card layout, with a hanging indention in the first paragraph:

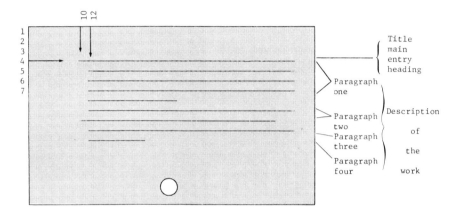

SHELF-LIST CARD

The shelf-list card is a duplicate of the main entry card with the addition of accession information and tracings. Notes are sometimes omitted from the shelf-list card to allow more space for this additional data.

Accession Information

The accession number is either typed or stamped with a sequential numbering machine. Typing saves space if several numbers are to be listed, but the machine is quicker. The machine can be set to repeat the same number on the shelf-list card, the title page or verso of the title page, the pocket and the book card.

On the same line as the accession number, type, in the shortest comprehensible form, any other useful information about the item as desired, such as where it was acquired, when it was acquired, and the net and/or discount price in numbers and/or percent.

For a set of items, the volume number or its equivalent should be placed beside the appropriate accession number.

```
809.       Yesterday's authors of books for children :
89282         facts and pictures about authors and illus-
YES           trators of books for young people, from early
              times to 1960 / Anne Commire, editor ; Adele
              Sarkissian, Agnes Garrett, associate editors.
              -- Detroit : Gale Research, c1977-78
              2 v. : ill. ; 29 cm.                              ②
              ISBN 0-8103-0073-3.
15958  v1  c1  Gale  1977 08    $25.00 net
16383  v2  c1  Gale  1978 04    $25.00 net

  1.  Children's literature--Bio-bibliography.  I. Commire,
Anne.  II. Sarkissian, Adele.  III. Garrett, Agnes Antoi-
nette.
```

Fig. 7:1 Accessioning a multi-part work on a shelf-list card. Use pencil for date and number of volumes to allow for future revisions on this open entry. Allow extra space for pencilled-in digits. Usual spacing of note and accession information is forgone to avoid the use of an extension card.

Tracings

Tracings on the shelf list provide a record of additional cards made to go into the card catalogue as further access points to the item. Since it can always be assumed that there is a main entry card, it does not need to be traced.

The tracings for subject headings and added entries are typed on the shelf-list card below the accession data. If there is not sufficient room on the face of the card, continue the tracing on the back. When typing on the back of the card, insert the card into the typewriter so that the guard hole is at the top, and type any tracings below the hole in order that they may be easily read when the card has been filed in the shelf-list drawer.

Tracings for added entries are capitalized as found in the heading or description of the work on the main entry card.

ORDER OF TRACINGS

> Subject headings
> Name added entries
> Title added entries
> Series added entries
> Analytical added entries

WHEN TO TRACE

Name added entries. These may be made for persons or corporate bodies when one of the following situations exists:
* The users of the library are likely to search the catalogue for the item under these headings.

- Two or three persons and/or bodies are responsible for a particular item. Name added entries may be made for each.
- Four or more persons and/or bodies are responsible for a particular item. A name added entry may be made for the first.
- There are prominently named writers, editors, compilers, corporate bodies, related persons or bodies, but the item is entered under another heading according to the rules in Chapter III.
- There is a translator of a work and the translation is in verse; the translation is important in its own right; the work has been translated into the same language more than once; or the wording of the chief source of information suggests that the translator is the author.
- There is an illustrator and the illustrator's name is given prominence in the chief source of information along with that of the person or corporate body named in the main entry heading; the illustrations occupy more than one-half of the work; or the illustrations are considered an important feature of the work.

Title proper added entry. This is made for every work entered under a personal or corporate body heading unless the title proper is essentially the same as the main entry heading; the title has been made up by the librarian; the title is identical with a subject heading for the same work (optional only when the title would be filed in a dictionary catalogue); or a conventional uniform title has been used in an entry for a musical work.

Series added entry. This is usually made for each separately catalogued title in a series in order to bring all the titles together in the card catalogue under the series access point.

Analytical added entries. These are most often made for works or parts of works contained within a larger work being catalogued. In order to be traced as an added entry, the analyzed part must appear on the main entry card, where it is usually found in the notes area.

- *Title analytics* may be either the title proper or the uniform title, if any, of the parts.
- *Subject analytics* give an analysis of the subjects of different parts of a work:

```
Subject analytics:  Shakespeare, William --
Shaw, George Bernard.
```

```
Subject analytics:  Diamonds -- Emeralds.
```

- *Name-title analytics* are used for the contents of anthologies:

```
Name-title analytics:  Jonson, Ben.  Volpone --
Congreve, William.  The way of the world.
```

- *Title-name analytics,* i.e., name-title analytics reversed, are seldom made.
- *Name analytics,* seldom seen, can be made to analyze a collection of items with non-distinctive titles written by different people:

```
      Name analytics:    Clark, Joe -- Trudeau, Pierre
Elliott.
```

FORMAT OF TRACINGS IN PARAGRAPH FORM

Commercial cards show the tracings listed in one paragraph at the bottom of the shelf list only or on all cards. Tracings may also be listed in a column (see p. 161), but at some expense of space. Some librarians and commercial cataloguing firms begin the tracings near the left edge of the card with second and subsequent lines returning to the left edge. (See Fig. 7:1 in this chapter.) Others begin at the first or second indention with the second and subsequent lines returning to the first indention. (See Fig. 7:3 in this chapter.) The first arrangement, of course, provides the most space.

Two spaces are usually left between tracings so they may be easily scanned.

Subject headings. These are formed according to the instructions in Chapter V. As headings, they appear in upper case but are traced in upper and lower. They are consecutively numbered with arabic numerals. For example:

```
1. Stars.   2. Planets.
```

Some librarians put the subjects in alphabetic order while others list them according to their representation in the work, i.e., from the first subject heading which corresponds to the call number, down to the last one which represents some less inclusive aspect of the work.

Name added entries. These follow the same rules of form as main-entry names (Chapter III). They are numbered with Roman numerals.

```
I. Colwell, Eileen H.   II. Felts, Shirley.
```

In order to be traced as an added entry, the name must appear in the description of the work.

Title proper added entries. These continue in the Roman numeral sequence of numbering. Instead of tracing the actual title proper as found in the description of the work, the librarian uses just the word "Title."

```
... III. Title.
```

If a tracing for a parallel title, title of a related work, or of a form of the title that differs from the title proper is wanted, then this title must be typed in full as it will appear in the added entry heading. Type the word "Title" followed by *a colon and a space* and the desired extra title.

```
...   III.  Title.    IV.  Title: Tom Sawyer
```
Title proper is The Adventures of Tom Sawyer.

Series added entries. These continue in the Roman numeral sequence of numbering. Instead of tracing the actual name of the series and, if applicable, its number, as found in paragraph two of the description of the work, the librarian uses just the word "Series."

```
...   III.  Series.
```

If the tracing for a series differs from that given in the series area, as when the name of the series is altered part way through the purchasing of the series, then the established name of the series must be typed in full as it will appear in the added entry heading. Type the word "Series" followed by *a colon and a space,* and the desired extra name of the series:

```
...   III.   Title.    IV.  Series: PDK fastbacks ; 127.
```
Called "Fastbacks," in No. 127.

Analytics. These may be traced three ways:
- By specifying the type of analytic:

```
Title analytics
```
Meaning that all titles in the contents note have had added entries made for them. This type of tracing is not numbered.

- By giving an explanatory note:

```
Title analytics as per contents note.
```
This type of tracing is not numbered.

- By listing the actual analytics which form the headings. This type of tracing may or may not be numbered.

```
     Title analytics:   I.   As you like it.   II.   Twelfth night.
III.   The tempest.
```

```
     Title analytics:   As you like it  --  Twelfth night  --
The tempest.
```

If analytics are made for partial contents, then each must be specified. Tracings of analytics come after the rest of the tracings.

FORMAT OF TRACINGS, COLUMN FORM

In this format, all the subject headings and the added entries are arranged in the same order as shown on p. 158, "Order of Tracings," but in one column. This column begins at the first indention. No numbers precede the tracings.

If there are many tracings, a double column may be made to avoid having to use the back of the shelf-list card for the overflow.

All tracings will be created in the same way as in the paragraph form. All tracings except the ones for the subject headings will appear the same as in the paragraph form.

Subject headings in the column form are typed in upper case as they will be on the subject heading cards:

```
ROME--CIVILIZATION
ROME--HISTORY
Title
Series
```

This column arrangement is seen only in small libraries.

ADDED ENTRY CARDS

Added entry cards are duplicates of the main entry card with the addition of special headings as indicated on the shelf-list card.

Short added entry headings are typed on the third line down from the top of the main entry card, i.e., one line above the main entry headings, beginning at the second indention.

If the added entry is too long for one line, then it begins on the second line or perhaps even the first line down from the top at the second indention, with the second and any subsequent lines beginning at the third indention.

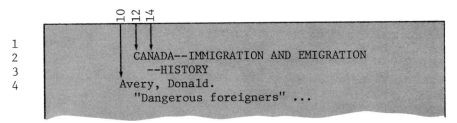

Fig. 7:2 Example of a long subject heading

No periods are added at the end of any subject or added entry headings. Some punctuation may appear, however, as part of the title or name, e.g., *period* after an initial in a name, or *question mark* as part of the title proper. *A period and two spaces* separate the name and the title in name-title and title-name analytics.

Subject Heading Card

Subject headings are typed completely in upper case.

Name Added Entry Card

The name of a person or corporate body is in the same form and has the same capitalization in the heading as if it were a main entry heading.

Title Added Entry Card

The title is capitalized and punctuated in the heading in the same way that it is found in paragraph one of the description or in the tracings.

Series Added Entry Card

The series is capitalized, punctuated, and numbered in the heading in the same way that it is found in paragraph two of the description, except that the parentheses are omitted.

Analytical Added Entry Card

SUBJECT ANALYTIC HEADING

This is typed completely in upper case. As a name-subject analytic, it is in the same form as if it were a main entry heading. (See Chapter III.)

TITLE ANALYTIC HEADING

This is capitalized and punctuated in the same way as in the note from which it comes.

NAME-TITLE ANALYTIC

The title is capitalized and punctuated in the heading as it is found in the "notes" area. The name is in the same form as if it were a main entry heading. The name and the title are separated by *a period and two spaces.*

TITLE-NAME ANALYTIC

The name is in the same form as it is in the "notes" area from which it comes. The title is capitalized and punctuated in the heading as it is in the notes. The title and name are separated by *a period and two spaces.*

NAME ANALYTIC

The name is in the same form as if it were a main entry heading. (See Chapter III).

EXTENSION CARDS

When all the information necessary (particularly notes) cannot be typed on one side of the unit card, an extension card or cards need to be made. On the first card, type "Continued on next card" in parentheses in the lower right-hand corner, on a line even with the guard hole.

On the extension card, type the call number and the main entry heading as they appear on the unit card.

Follow a name main entry heading with *a period, a space, a dash (—) and a space*, the title proper and the GMD if any. The punctuation and capitalization of the title proper are as found on the unit card. If the title proper requires more than one line, it continues at the second indention. After the title proper or GMD, type *an ellipsis* to indicate missing areas and then the date as found on the first card. Two spaces after the date, type the number of the card in parentheses. Leave a blank line and continue with notes. See example on opposite page.

1980. (Card 2)

Leave a blank line and continue with notes.

Follow a title proper main entry heading with *an ellipsis* and then the date as found on the first card. The punctuation and capitalization of the title proper are as found on the unit card. If the title proper requires more than one line, it continues at the second indention. Two spaces after the date, type the number of the card in parentheses. Leave a blank line and continue with notes. See example on opposite page.

TYPEWRITERS AND TYPE STYLES

When buying a typewriter for library use, consider the following accessories and characteristics:

There should be a card-holding platen to keep the cards from slipping in the machine.

Use 12 point type to save both catalogue cards and space in the card files.

The type font, either in the machine or on replaceable elements, should have the characters necessary to make cards in conformity with the cataloguing rules. Many manufacturers offer a special library style of type; this font includes square brackets.

From among all the characters that might occasionally be useful in typing, it is necessary to deliberately choose the small number for which there are spare keys. There will not likely be room for many fractions and symbols of mathematics and business as well as for the special characters and diacritics of French and other languages. If one machine must be used for business functions and correspondence as well as for cataloguing, the choice of font becomes even more difficult. Then, perhaps, a machine with special interchangeable elements should be used. Symbols only occasionally required may be improvised on the keyboard or handwritten, as may characters, frequently needed but not available on a library's present typewriter, e.g., 1/3, [ ], +, ˜ .

```
819.208   Canada's lost plays / edited by Anton Wagner and
CAN           Richard Plant. -- Toronto : CTR Publications,
              1978-
              / v. : ill. ; 24 cm.

              Includes bibliographical references.

              Contents: v. 1. The nineteenth century: -- Can-
          didus, C. The female consistory of Brockville.
          -- Scribble, S. Dolorsolatio, Bush, T. Santiago,
          Davin, N.F. The fair grit, or The advantages of

                            ◯   (Continued on next card)
```

②

```
819.208   Canada's lost plays ... 1978-      (Card 2)
CAN
              coalition. -- Fuller, W.H.  H.M.S. Parliament, or
          The lady who loved a government clerk. -- McIl-
          wraight, J.N.  Ptarmigan, or A Canadian carnival.

              ISBN 0-920644-46-5.

              1. Canadian drama--Collections.  I. Wagner,
          Anton.  II. Plant, Richard.

                            ◯
```

Fig. 7:3 Extension card (More would be needed to record the contents of subsequent volumes.)

SAMPLE CARDS

The following cards have call numbers derived from the unabridged *DDC*, and subject headings from *Sears*, and *Canadian Companion*. Librarians cataloguing at the first level of description might well prefer numbers from the abridged *DDC*.

Most of the examples are shelf-list cards. In a school library, they would be filled out with appropriate accession information.

The samples represent most of the media to be encountered in a school library; the medium of each catalogued item is indicated by the GMD, according to which the cards have been alphabetically arranged.

```
304.871  Avery, Donald.
AVE         "Dangerous foreigners". -- McClelland &
         Stewart, c1979.
          204 p.

          Bibliography:  p. 144-191                    ①
          ISBN  0-7710-0826-0.

18295    M&S  20.11.79  $6.95 pa. - 20%

  1. Canada--Immigration and emigration--History.  2. East
Europeans in Canada.  3. Labor and laboring classes--Can-
ada--History.  4. Radicals      radicalism--History.  I.
Title.
```

Fig. 7:4 Shelf-list card for book, first level of description

167

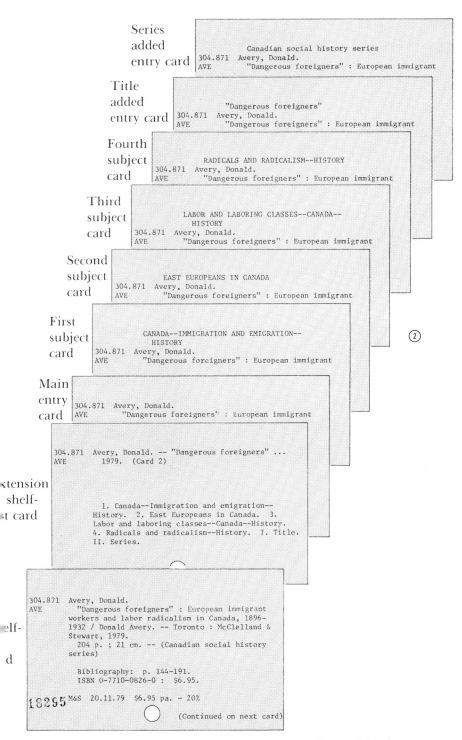

Fig. 7:5 Set of catalogue cards for same book, second level of description

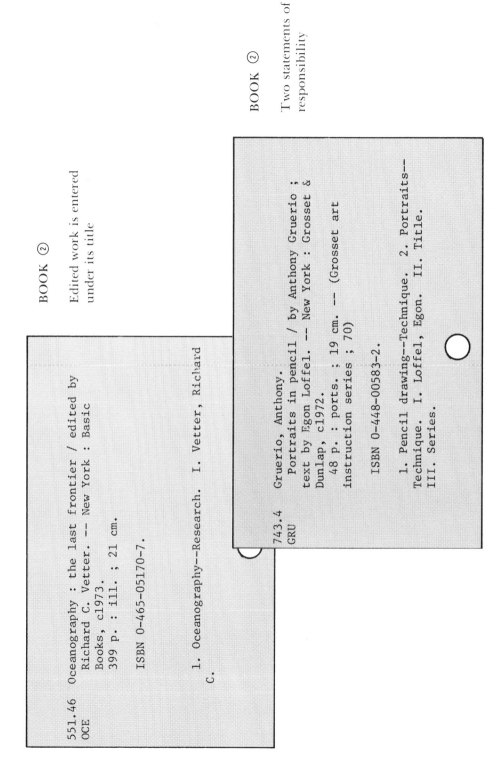

BOOK ②

Edited work is entered under its title

```
551.46   Oceanography : the last frontier / edited by
OCE        Richard C. Vetter. -- New York : Basic
         Books, c1973.
         399 p. : ill. ; 21 cm.

         ISBN 0-465-05170-7.

           1. Oceanography--Research. I. Vetter, Richard
         C.
```

BOOK ②

Two statements of responsibility

```
743.4    Gruerio, Anthony.
GRU        Portraits in pencil / by Anthony Gruerio ;
         text by Egon Loffel. -- New York : Grosset &
         Dunlap, c1972.
           48 p. : ports. ; 19 cm. -- (Grosset art
         instruction series ; 70)

           ISBN 0-448-00583-2.

           1. Pencil drawing--Technique. 2. Portraits--
         Technique. I. Loffel, Egon. II. Title.
         III. Series.
```

FILMSTRIP SET ②

Accompanying material is listed at the end of the physical description area

937.02
MUR

Murray, Warren.
    The history of the Roman republic [filmstrip] / script and photography by Warren Murray. -- New Rochelle, N.Y. : Pathescope Educational Films, [196-?]
    5 filmstrips (ca. 50 fr. each) : col. ; 35 mm + 1 teacher's guide.

    Contents: 1. Rome's beginnings -- 2. Rome and Italy -- 3. The struggle of the orders -- 4. Rome and Carthage -- 5. Rome and the Mediterranean.

(Continued on next card)

937.02   Murray, Warren. -- The history of the Roman
MUR   republic [filmstrip] ... [196-?] (Card 2)

    1. Rome--History--Republic, 510-30 B.C.
I. Title.

FILMSTRIP ①

First level of description
with series area added

Option is used not to repeat
the term "filmstrip" since
GMD is given

Accompanying material is
listed in the note area

GAME ①

First level of description
with series area added

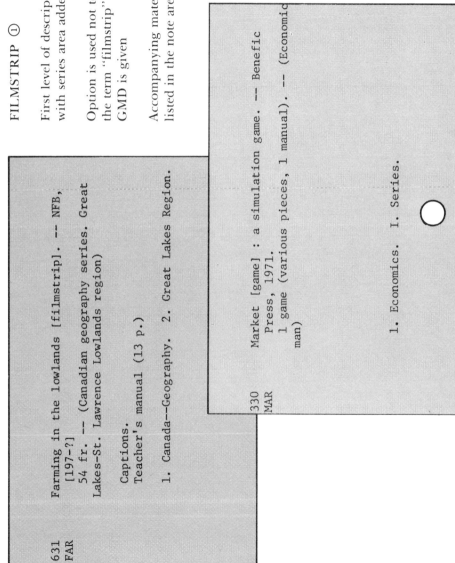

631
FAR
Farming in the lowlands [filmstrip]. -- NFB,
[197-?]
54 fr. -- (Canadian geography series. Great
Lakes-St. Lawrence Lowlands region)

Captions.
Teacher's manual (13 p.)

1. Canada—Geography. 2. Great Lakes Region.

330
MAR
Market [game] : a simulation game. -- Benefic
Press, 1971.
1 game (various pieces, 1 manual). -- (Economic
man)

1. Economics. I. Series.

JACKDAW ②

Components of the kit are
listed alphabetically in
physical description area

```
971.201   Campbell, Marjorie Wilkins.
CAM           The fur trade [kit] / written and compiled
           by Marjorie Wilkins Campbell. -- Toronto :
           Clarke, Irwin, c1968.
              7 broadsheets, 9 fascimiles, 1 map, 1 replica
           of a beaver token. -- (Jackdaw ; no. C5)


              1. Fur trade.  2. Hudson's Bay Co.
           3. The West (Canada)--History. I. Title.
```

SOUND FILMSTRIP ②

Detailed physical description for each component
of the kit is given on a
separate line

Number of frames in each
filmstrip is given in the
note area

```
823      Fromer, Nan.
HAR         The time, life and works of Thomas Hardy
FRO      [kit] / writer, Nan Fromer. -- Pleasantville,
         N.Y. : Educational Audio Visual, c1974.
            2 filmstrips : col. ; 35 mm.
            2 sound discs (ca. 20 min. each) : 33 1/3
         rpm, mono.
            1 teacher's notes (10 p.) ; 22 cm.

            Contents: Pt. 1. Hardy the novelist (78 fr.)
         -- Pt. 2. Hardy the poet (54 fr.)

            1. Hardy, Thomas.  I. Title.
```

MAP ②

Since the publisher's name appears in the statement of responsibility element, it is repeated in a shortened form

```
912.4   Europe [map] / compiled and drawn in the Carto-
EUR        graphic Division of the National Geographic
           Society. -- Scale 1:6,488,000 ; Chamberlin
           trimetric proj. -- Washington, D.C. : The
           Society, c1977.
           1 map : col. ; 57 x 75 cm.

           1. Europe--Maps.
```

LOCALLY PRODUCED ITEM ①

For a locally produced item, the "producer's" name is not repeated in the publication, distribution, etc., area if it appears in the statement of responsibility element

```
567.97  [Tyrannosaurus rex] [model] / [Morning Glory
TYR        Elementary School Grade 5 class]. -- [1980]
           1 model (wire and papier mâché)

           Title supplied by librarian.

           1. Dinosaurs.
```

FILM LOOP ②

531.113 Kinetic energy [motion picture]. -- [Ottawa] :
KIN   NFB, c1968.
          1 film cartridge (4 min.) : si., col. ; super 8
          mm. -- (Physics ; 11)

          Notes on cartridge case by Alfred M. Bork.

          1. Dynamics. 2. Force and energy. I. Bork,
          Alfred M.

MOTION PICTURE ①

First level of description with
added information about sound
and gauge of film so user will
be able to choose proper equipment

Added information about the
distribution

943.086 The Rise and fall of Nazi Germany [motion
RIS   picture]. -- Time, c1947 : Released by
          Blackhawk Films.
          1 film reel (12 min.) : si., b&w ; standard
          8 mm.

          Newsreel footage.

          1. Germany--History--1933-1945.

ART REPRODUCTION ①

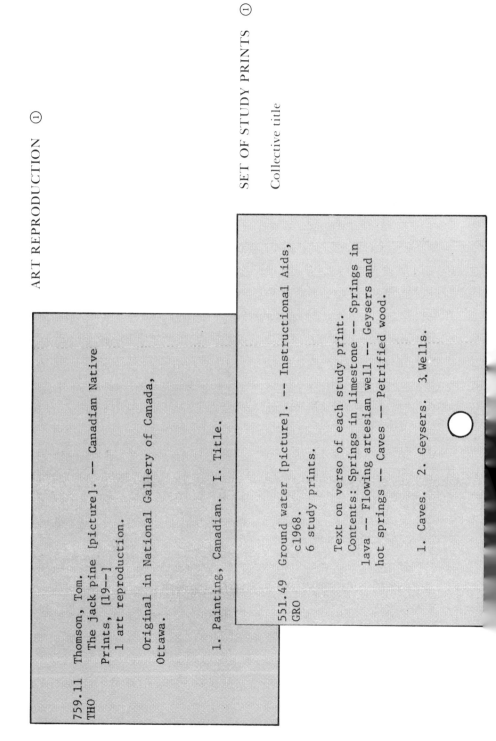

```
759.11   Thomson, Tom.
THO          The jack pine [picture]. -- Canadian Native
         Prints, [19--]
             1 art reproduction.

             Original in National Gallery of Canada,
         Ottawa.

             1. Painting, Canadian.  I. Title.
```

SET OF STUDY PRINTS ①

Collective title

```
551.49   Ground water [picture]. -- Instructional Aids,
GRO          c1968.
             6 study prints.

             Text on verso of each study print.
             Contents: Springs in limestone -- Springs in
         lava -- Flowing artesian well -- Geysers and
         hot springs -- Caves -- Petrified wood.

             1. Caves.  2. Geysers.  3.Wells.
```

SLIDE SET ②

Accompanying material is
listed at the end of the
physical description area

```
581.4   Plant parts [slide]. -- [Chicago] : Society for
PLA       Visual Education, c1969.
          20 slides : col. + 1 set of notes.

          Slides enclosed in plastic sheet.


              1. Botany--Anatomy.  2. Plants.
```

DISC ①

Performer as main entry
heading

```
784.4941 Mouskouri, Nana.
MOU        Songs of the British Isles [sound recording].
           -- Philips, 1976.
           1 sound disc (ca. 36 min.)

           Philips: 9101.024.


               1. Folk songs, British.  I. Title.
```

DISC ②

Collective title

Tracings in optional position
to save making an extension
card

398.21
PIE   The Pied piper and other stories [sound
         recording]. -- New York : Caedmon, c1972.
         1 sound disc (52 min.) : 33 1/3 rpm, stereo. ;
         12 in. -- (Caedmon children's classic. Best
         of all series)

         Told by Keith Baxter.
         Caedmon: TC 1397.
         Contents: The pied piper -- The colony of
         cats -- Thumbelina.

         1. Fairy tales. I. Par   tial title analytics: The
colony of cats -- Thumbe   lina.

CASSETTE ①

First level of description
with series area added

Some librarians in Ontario
may prefer "OECA" for the
producer's name

941.085 Silver jubilee, 1977 [sound recording]. -- Ont.
ELI   Educational Communications Authority, 1977.
SIL   1 sound cassette (30 min.). -- (Victoria
           Day ; pt. 1)

             1. Elizabeth II, Queen of Great Britain.
           I. Series.

177

DISC ①

Uniform title as the main
entry heading. Option is used
not to enclose it in square
brackets.

Accompanying material is
listed at the end of the
physical description area

```
829.3    Beowulf.  Selections.  Sound recording.
BEO          Beowulf. — Spoken Arts, [1966]
             1 sound disc (ca. 32 min.) + 1 text of
         recording (8 p.)

             Read in Old English by Norman Davis and
         Neville Coghill.
             Descriptive notes by Norman Davis on slipcase.
             Spoken Arts: SA 918.

             1. Anglo-Saxon poetry.  I. Davis, Norman.
         II. Coghill, Neville.
```

Contents VIII

Bibliographic Files

Card Catalogue 181
  Dictionary Catalogue 181
  Divided Catalogue 181
Common Qualities of Filing Rules 182
Rules Allowing for Hierarchy and Filer's Decisions 182
  Arrange All Cards Alphabetically 182
  Disregard Initial Articles 182
  Alphabetize Letter by Letter 183
  Initials 183
  Acronyms 184
  Abbreviations 184
  Ampersands 184
  Apostrophes 185
  Numerals 185
  Dates 185
  Compound Words Written as One Word 185
  Hyphenated Words 186
  Variant Spellings 186
  Uniform Titles 186
  "See Also" and "See" Reference Cards 187
  Names 187
  Order of Person, Place, Subject, Title 189
  Works By and About an Author 189
  Subject Arrangement 190
  Series Added Entries 190
Possibilities Allowed in Manual Filing 191
Programmable, Non-Hierarchical Filing Rules 191
  Filing Order of Characters 192
  Initial Articles 193
  Abbreviations, Initials, Initialisms and Acronyms 193
  Names With Prefixes 194
  Numerals 194
  Titles of Honour and Address 194
  Access Points 194
Choosing a Filing Code 196
References 196
  "See" References 196
  "See Also" References 198
  General References 200
  Tracing Reference Cards 200

Other Aids for the User 201
Filing the Shelf List 201
Keeping the Card Catalogue Up to Date 202
Other Library Catalogue Formats 203
  Book Catalogues 203
  Computer Output Catalogues 203
Library Networks and Data Bases 205
Footnotes 205

√

Chapter VIII

Bibliographic Files

CARD CATALOGUE

The user or main catalogue may be set up as:
- A dictionary catalogue with author, title and subject cards interfiled.
- A divided catalogue with separate files for author, title and subject.
- A divided catalogue with author and title interfiled and a separate file for subject.

Dictionary Catalogue

In a dictionary catalogue all cards, author, title, subject, and series, for book and non-book items, are filed in one alphabetical index.

When the title and subject headings for an item would be identical, it is optional to make a title added entry card, because it would file right beside the subject card.

Only one set of cards is filed for an item. If two copies of the same item are received fully processed, the second set of cards will not be needed. The number of copies of that item will be indicated on the shelf-list card.

Divided Catalogue

The divided catalogue may be separated into three sections, i.e., author, title, and subject. Reference cards will file in the appropriate section, e.g., subject reference cards in the subject catalogue. Series added entry cards are filed in the title file.

If preferred, a divided catalogue may be separated into two sections with subject cards for book and non-book items in one alphabetical file, and author, title, and series cards for all items in another alphabetical file. Reference cards will file in the appropriate sections.

In a divided catalogue, title added entry cards will be needed even if title and subject are identical because these will be filed in separate sections of the catalogue.

Only one set of cards is filed for identical copies of an item. The number of copies of an item will be indicated on the shelf-list card.

COMMON QUALITIES OF FILING RULES

All filing is based on the same few principles:
- Sort character by character, i.e., by letter, number, space or symbol.
- Sort character string by character string, that is by groupings of character: words, numbers, acronyms, or symbols.
- Nothing files before something.

The detailed development and interpretation of the above principles can, however, result in great differences in the look of the files.

RULES ALLOWING FOR HIERARCHY AND FILER'S DECISIONS

The following are the most important rules covering cases encountered in filing catalogue cards. These rules have also been applied to the order of entries in book catalogues and bibliographies.

For more complete rules consult the *ALA Rules for Filing Catalog Cards* or the abridged *ALA Rules for Filing Catalog Cards*. With the advent of *AACR2* a few new elements have now to be accounted for, e.g., GMD.

Arrange All Cards Alphabetically

Begin with the top line on the card. The top line is known as the access point or filing heading when cards are being filed in a catalogue. If the access points are the same, and sorting involves subsequent elements, ignore the GMD, if used. Then, sort by whatever follows the GMD.

Disregard Initial Articles

Disregard initial articles in a title and file by the first word following the article. All articles occurring within the filing heading, however, are to be considered when alphabetizing:

A boy at the Leafs' camp
A boy of Taché
Boy of the lost Crusade
Boy on the run
The boy who came with Cartier

Alphabetize Letter by Letter

Begin with the first word (omitting the initial article in a title). The principle involved is nothing before something; therefore a shorter word comes before a longer word beginning with the same letters:

Son of Raven, son of Deer
Songs of the Dream People
Sons of the Arctic

Initials

An initial is regarded as a word and is filed before longer words beginning with the same letter.

Initials standing for names of organizations and commonly used for the full name of the organization are filed as initials, not as if the name were spelled in full:

A. Alekhine vs E.D. Bogolijubow; world's chess championship, 1934
A-B-O blood groups
A.E. Housman
ALA bulletin   *Filed as separate initials.*
A la recherche du temps perdu
Aaron, Henry Lewis

For convenience, some initials may be filed as if written in full; for example, *Sears* renders "United States" as U.S. and files as follows:

United Nations to-day
UNITED STATES—HISTORY
U.S.—HISTORY—REVOLUTION, 1775-1783
United States of America
UNITED STATES—POLITICS AND GOVERNMENT

A reference card will explain the irregularity:

```
U.S.

      This abbreviation is interfiled with United
States.
```

File this notice near the beginning of the "U" drawer, with other abbreviations for that letter, e.g., before U.S.S.R.

Acronyms

An acronym, i.e., a brief form of a corporate name or a term made up of letters commonly written or spoken as one word, is filed as one word unless written as separate initials with a period between each letter. In the latter case it is filed as initials. If the same initialism is sometimes used as an abbreviation and sometimes as an acronym, file as an acronym to be consistent:

U.N.E.S.C.O. see Unesco filed as a word   *"See" reference card.*
Umiaks
Uncle Vanya
Understanding yourself
UNESCO Indian series
Unesco source book
Unicef book of children's legends
The unknown people

Abbreviations

Abbreviations of common words spoken as if spelled in full can be handled in two different ways:

File as if written in full. For example, Dr. is filed as "doctor":

Apache Indians
Apt. 3
Ape in a cave

Doc stops a war
Dr. Cotnoir
The doctor game
Dr. Sadhu's muffins

If preferred, the abbreviations Mr., Mrs., and Ms. may be filed as spelled. A reference card in the catalogue will inform the user of the filing procedure used.

```
    Mister and Mr.

        Both forms of this title of address are
    filed as Mr., not Mister.
```

File this notice where the word "Mister" would be filed.

Ampersands

An ampersand (&) is filed as if written in full in the language in which it is used:

Man alive!
Man dying of pollution
Mandy & the blue box
Mandy and the flying map

Apostrophes

Apostrophes used in elisions or in words in the possessive case are disregarded and the word containing the apostrophe is filed as one word. Do not supply the missing letter or letters:

I saw three ships
I'm moving
Images for a Canadian heritage

Numerals

These are filed as if written in full in the manner in which they are most commonly spoken. For example, *6½* is filed as *six and one-half*; *101* is filed as *one hundred and one*; *12:30 o'clock* is filed as *twelve-thirty*; *4200* King Street is filed as *forty-two hundred*; *1999* is filed as *one thousand, nine hundred and ninety-nine*, unless it is a date or an address.

Dates

Dates are filed as if written in full in the manner in which they are commonly spoken. For example, *1977* is filed as *nineteen seventy-seven*; *1066* is filed as *ten sixty-six*. (See also p. 190, "Subject Arrangement.")

Compound Words Written as One Word

These are usually filed as one word. If such words are also used as hyphenated words in the catalogue, decide on one form and make a reference from the form not used to the form used:

Teen–age		Teenage
see	*or*	see
Teenage		Teen–age

Teen guide to homemaking
Teenage fitness   *Filed as one word.*
Teen-age living   *Filed as one word.*
The teenager and smoking

Teen-age diet book   *Filed as two words.*
Teenage living   *Filed as two words.*
Teen-age suspense stories
Teen theatre

Hyphenated Words

File hyphenated words as two separate words when the part preceding the hyphen is a complete word:

Audio systems handbook
Audio-visual aids
Audio workbook
Audiology

Hyphenated words in which the part preceding the hyphen is a prefix and not a complete word are filed as one word:

Cooper, James Fenimore.
Co-operate with us!
Co-operating : an analysis
Co-operation and conflict
Cooperative management

Variant Spellings

Variant spellings of words are filed under the commonly accepted form regardless of the spelling in the filing heading. Consult a standard Canadian dictionary if in doubt about which spelling to use. Reference cards may be made from the form not used to the form of the word used if confusion could result:

Colour harmony
Color in your life
The colour of Canada

Uniform Titles

Uniform titles are used for sorting as they occur on the card in the entry:

Berlioz, Hector.
   Evenings with the orchestra . . .
Berlioz, Hector.
   [Overtures . . .]
Berlioz, Hector.
   Roméo et Juliette . . .
Berlioz, Hector.
   [Songs . . .]

"See Also" and "See" Reference Cards

"See also" reference cards are filed in their alphabetical place in the card catalogue before other entries beginning with the same word:

WATER BIRDS   see also   names of water birds, e.g., TERNS; etc.
WATER BIRDS
Ripper, Charles, L.

"See" reference cards are filed in their alphabetical place in the card catalogue before other entries beginning with the same word:

Medicine man
Medieval history   see   MIDDLE AGES—HISTORY
Medieval history in the Tudor Age
Meeker, Howie.

Names

Surnames and other proper names are filed alphabetically as spelled; thus similar surnames with slight variations in spelling will not be interfiled even though they may be pronounced the same. A "see also" reference may be made to direct the user to other spellings of a surname if such is considered necessary:

Green, Walter.
Greene, Bruce.

(See also p. 196, "References.")
Proper names with a prefix are filed as one word:

De Brunhoff, Jean.
Dejong, Meidert.
De la Mare, Walter.
De la Roche, Mazo.
Delaware Indians
Del Rey, Lester.

Names beginning with the prefix "Mc" or "Mac" are filed as if written Mac:

MaCaulay, David.
McClung, Nellie.
Macdonald, Anne.
McDonald, Henry.
MacDonald, Margaret.
Macdonald, Zillah.

Note: An alternative method is to file Mc and Mac as spelled. In this case a "see also" reference will direct the user to the other spelling(s).

Single surname entries are filed before compound surnames beginning with the same words. The surname filing heading precedes the first comma:

Hamilton, Virginia.
Hamilton-Merrit, Jane.

Surnames that are the same are subarranged alphabetically by forenames or initials. The principle of nothing before something applies, i.e., a surname followed by an initial precedes the same surname followed by a forename beginning with that initial:

Brown, M.
Brown, M.L.
Brown, MacKenzie.
Brown, Marcia.
Brown, Margaret W.

If an author's surname sometimes appears with initials and sometimes with the forenames in full, disregard the variations in form and interfile cards according to the appropriate subarrangement:

Shaw, George Bernard.
   Arms and the man . . .
Shaw, G.B.
   Caesar and Cleopatra . . .
Shaw, George Bernard.
   Pygmalion . . .

Forenames and surnames with the same access point are filed so that all names that include a surname go first, subfiled by forename. Then all fornames are filed as a group, subfiled by the following word:

George, Gladys.
George, Duke of York. *File by second word, "Duke."*
George I, King of Gt. Brit. *File by "King," not the numeral.*
GEORGE I, KING OF GT. BRIT. *Subject.*
George II, King of Gt. Brit. *File by the numeral within a related group.*
George I, King of Greece.
George, St. *George, Saint, would interfile with George, St.*
George Bernard Shaw vegetarian cookbook *Title.*

Titles of honour and address are ignored unless they are the only other element in the name:

Jones, Mrs. John. *Title of address ignored.*
Jones, Mrs. *Title of address counts.*
Moses, Grandma. *Title of address counts.*
Roberts, Sir Charles G.D. *Title of honour ignored. Subfile by "C."*

Order of Person, Place, Subject, Title

A name entry is filed before other entries beginning with the same word or access point. All other entries, e.g., subject heading entries and added entries for title and series, are arranged alphabetically word by word. If terms are identical in wording but different in function the order in which they are filed is place before subject before title:

London, D.R.
London, Jack.
LONDON, JACK—BIBLIOGRAPHY
LONDON (ENGLAND)—DESCRIPTION *Subject.*
London in spring *Title.*
LONDON (ONT.)—MAPS *Subject.*
London, Ontario, maps *Title.*

Works By and About an Author

Works *by* an author are subarranged alphabetically by title. Disregard designations showing relationship to the work, e.g., comp., illus., joint author, ed., birth and death dates, and other information in apposition.

Cook, Lyn.
    The bells on Finland Street . . .
Cook, Lyn.
    Jody and the general . . .
Cook, Lyn.
    Rebel on the trail . . .

Works *by* precede works *about* an author. Works *about* the author are subarranged alphabetically by main entry heading. Works about the author with a subdivision following the author's name as subject are subarranged alphabetically by subdivision, and then within each subdivision by main entry heading:

Potter, Beatrix.
    The tale of Squirrel Nutkin . . .
Potter, Beatrix.
    The tale of Tom Kitten . . .

    POTTER, BEATRIX
Aldis, D.
    Nothing is impossible . . .

    POTTER, BEATRIX
Lane, Margaret.
    The tale of Beatrix Potter . . .

    POTTER, BEATRIX—BIBLIOGRAPHY
Potter, Beatrix.
    Beatrix Potter centenary catalogue . . .

Subject Arrangement

A subject *without* subdivisions is filed before the same subject with subdivisions.

Subject cards *with* subdivisions are filed alphabetically by the subject subdivision:

FOOD—ANALYSIS
FOOD, ARTIFICIAL
FOOD, FROZEN
FOOD—LAW AND LEGISLATION
FOOD ADDITIVES

Cards with identical subject headings are subarranged alphabetically by the main entry. When main entries are the same, further subarrangement is by title:

BIRDS
Selsam, M.E.
    A first look at birds . . .

BIRDS
Selsam, M.E.
    Tony's birds . . .

BIRDS
Zim, H.S.
    Birds . . .

Subjects with date or period subdivision are arranged chronologically, not alphabetically. The more inclusive period precedes specific period subdivisions. A subdivision that shows two dates is filed by the first one. Where the first dates are the same in two or more headings, file a single date before a double one and file the one with the later second date first. For example:

CANADA—HISTORY—TO 1763 (NEW FRANCE)
CANADA—HISTORY—1763-1867 (NEW FRANCE)
CANADA—HISTORY—1763-1791 (NEW FRANCE)
CANADA—HISTORY—1791-1841
CANADA—HISTORY—19TH CENTURY
CANADA—HISTORY—1841-1867
CANADA—HISTORY—CONFEDERATION, 1867
CANADA—HISTORY—1867-1911

Series Added Entries

These are subarranged alphabetically by the main entry heading unless the series is numbered or dated, in which case the entries are subarranged numerically or chronologically by date:

The Canadians   *Series added entry.*
Gardner, Alison. *Author.*
James Douglas . . . *Title.*

The Canadians   *Series added entry.*
Mayles, Stephen. *Author.*
William Van Horne . . . *Title.*

POSSIBILITIES ALLOWED IN MANUAL FILING

To a large extent, the filing rules described above follow an order of letter by letter and word by word. They deviate, however, when rigorous adherence to an alphanumeric filing order would make for illogical splits in the file, or oppose librarians' concepts of the searching habits of the users. Since filing by these rules is done by human hands, many of the rules can call for the application of some human thought as well:

- Words not spelled alike can be treated as if they were. For instance, McDonald as Macdonald; De la Roche as Delaroche; even, if so desired, color as colour.

- Numbers and dates can be translated into filing words. For example, 1001 nuits as *mille et une nuits.*

- Initials can be treated as whole words. For instance, U.S. as United States; or, as one-letter words, G.B.S.

The 1968 rules co-exist today with a new set of filing rules which are more computer adapatable.

PROGRAMMABLE, NON-HIERARCHICAL FILING RULES

Since the computer observes a collating sequence which is at odds with the rules for manual filing, such rules can only be adhered to in bibliographic files by means of special, expensive programming or by human intervention after a print-out is made. To the eye of a traditional librarian, some computerized files have appeared with entries severely disarranged; for example, numerals have been filed in the order 0, 1, 10, 100, 11, 111, 12, and so on. A confusing variety of expedients and codifications have appeared.

Currently, there is a new reference being developed—the *ALA Filing Rules* (draft edition: 1979). These rules require that a character string (a grouping of characters, most often a word or number) be filed as written, by its appearance, not its sound or its meaning. For example, eight and 8 are not filed together but are filed by their appearance, i.e., filed separately. Filing by the new rules is more mechanical than traditional filing, even if done manually in a card catalogue. Locating a heading is easier by machine, and may be manually, as long as the searcher knows the printed form (words, numbers, punctuation and spacing) of the title or whatever is being searched for in the file. Where there is doubt about the characters in the access point, the searcher may have to try more than one place, e.g., 8, eight.

An arrangement by the new rules will not logically group related items together. A heading as person, place, thing or title will file by its appearance, not its function. Punctuation will have a much-reduced effect on order.

The most important of the draft 1979 ALA rules are:

Filing Order of Characters

Spaces, dashes, hyphens, diagonal slashes and full stops are equal, and count as one space. Multiples of these marks also count as only one space; e.g., *a space, a dash (—) and a space* count as one space.

Stop-gap
Stop school failure
Stop! Shark zone!

If one of these characters precedes the rest of the heading, it is ignored, i.e., only the next character in the filing term is considered:

—to you
To youth

Numerals 0, 1, 2, etc., are filed in numerical order before headings beginning with an alphabetic symbol:

7 plays and how to produce them
8 histoires d'amour
1001 nights
Eight more Canadian poets
One flew over the cuckoo's nest

Letters A to Z follow numerals, upper and lower case being interfiled. Diacritical marks are ignored:

A Paris (à Paris)
A to Z
D-day
A doll's house   *See also "Initial Articles," p. 193.*
Dolls in danger
Dolment, Marcelle.

Punctuation and symbols not mentioned immediately above are ignored, e.g., apostrophe, parentheses, percent sign, dollar sign, asterisk, ampersand and comma. If they are followed by a space, the space counts as a space:

O Canada!
O.J. Simpson
On city streets
#!¢* on you, Mrs. Jones
One Canada
O'Neil, Paul.   *See also "Names with Prefixes," p. 194.*

Optional: The ampersand (&) may be treated as if spelled out in the
language of its context, e.g., and, et, or whatever, instead of being ignored.

Ampersand ignored	*Ampersand spelled out*
Black Americans	Black Americans
Black and blue	Black and blue
Black Beauty	Black & brave
Black & brave	Black Beauty

Initial Articles

Initial articles are ignored. As an internal part of a heading, they are treated
like any other word:

The dog and the boat boy
Dog behavior
Dog in the manger
Dog training

If they are an integral part of a name, articles are not ignored, e.g., Las
Vegas. (For guidelines for French proper names, see pp. 240 to 247.)

Abbreviations, Initials, Initialisms and Acronyms

Abbreviations are not spelled out, but file as written, character by character:

A.A. Milne   *Title.*
A B C's of ecology
The Abbess of Crewe
ABC

Initials, initialisms and acronyms are filed character by character as written,
which means that they are treated as a series of one-letter character strings
if separated by spaces or periods, grouped as one word if not spaced, or if
spaced by commas, apostrophes or some character other than a space, dash,
hyphen, diagonal slash or full stop. For example:

U.S.
U.S.S.R.
UNICEF   *Subject heading.*
United States

Names With Prefixes

A prefix and a name are treated as one word if joined together or separated by an apostrophe. They are treated as two words if spaced apart:

Odell, George.
O'Dell, Scott.
Of human bondage
Oh, what a busy day
O'Hara, John.
Ohio guide

De la Mare, Walter.
Del Monaco, Mario.
Delacroix, Eugène.

Numerals

Arabic numerals file in the order 0, 1, 2, etc.

Colons in numbers are treated as spaces, e.g., in ratios and times of the day: 3:100; 3:45 p.m.

Decimals less than 1 precede 1 in their numerical place. Decimals greater than 1 follow 1 in their numerical place.

Fractions are arranged by numerator, then by the line, which is treated as a space, then by the denominator:

1/8
3/8
3/10

Roman numerals are treated as their arabic equivalents:

Louis 13
Louis XIV
Louis 15
Louis the Thirteenth

Dates expressed as numbers are arranged chronologically:

125 B.C.
99 A.D.
1066
1980

If dates are double or inclusive, file by the first date given. If sets of paired dates start with the same date, the one with the earlier second date precedes. If the date is in words, file it like its numerical equivalent:

U.S.—HISTORY—1783-1809
U.S.—HISTORY—1783-1865
U.S.—HISTORY—CIVIL WAR, 1861-1865
U.S.—HISTORY—1898-1919
U.S.—HISTORY—20TH CENTURY

Titles of Honour and Address

With surnames, these are ignored, i.e., Churchill, Sir Winston Leonard Spencer, files as Churchill, Winston Leonard Spencer.

With given names, they are filing terms:

David I, King of Scotland *All numerals precede all letters.*
David and Goliath *Title.*
David, Elizabeth.
David, Saint.
David, St.
David! We're pregnant *Title.*
David Wilmot, free soiler *Title.*

Access Points

Compare similar access points character by character to arrange them in order:

VANCOUVER
Vancouver aquarium seafood recipes *Title.*
VANCOUVER, GEORGE
VANCOUVER ISLAND
Vancouver, Ltd.
VANCOUVER (WASHINGTON)

If the author headings of two bibliographic records are the same, sort by the first element of the next area, i.e., title proper or uniform title; it may sometimes be necessary to go beyond the title and statement of responsibility area to find something distinctive to sort by:

Seuss, Dr.
  The cat in the hat. . .
Seuss, Dr.
  Green eggs and ham. . .

Main and added entries as a type precede subject headings with the same wording. In manual filing, subject headings will be recognized by their typography and sorted out to be filed separately. In a computer file, they can be identified by their MARC field, and filed according to this rule.

"See," "see also" and general reference cards precede other cards with the same heading:

Canadian literature   *Title main entry.*
CANADIAN LITERATURE   see also AUTHORS, CANADIAN
CANADIAN LITERATURE
CANADIAN LITERATURE—DICTIONARIES

CHOOSING A FILING CODE

Library card catalogues already in existence need not be refiled just because new rules are published. School librarians may safely go on filing by the 1968 rules because:
- Refiling is costly.
- Manual filing by either code requires thought, probably more with the old than the new code, but not enough to justify changing codes.
- The traditional rules may well be preferable, especially for a small collection, in that they allow for logical and hierarchical groupings that help the searcher.
- When most of the material is in one language, filing by the sound and meaning makes sense, e.g., 8 with eight. In a large, multi-lingual file, it may well be easier to search by the symbol than by the meaning, e.g., 8, *ocho, acht, huit.*

Libraries which are new, which are considering closing their card catalogues or which may eventually computerize their cataloguing could file by the new rules in the meanwhile. If the filing is done by students and volunteers, the new rules may be preferable because they require fewer decisions on the filer's part.

It is possible to file consistently by models instead of rules. When volunteers are doing the filing, they can follow such authorities as the indexes to the books in the *Standard Catalog Series,*[1] e.g., *Children's Catalog,*[2] and, for a divided catalogue with a subject file, *Sears.*

REFERENCES

"See" References

PURPOSE

"See" references in the library catalogue direct the user from headings that are not used to ones that are. "See" references can be made to refer:
- from real name to pseudonym:

Clemens, Samuel Langhorne see Twain, Mark

- from earlier name to later:

Barrett, Elizabeth see Browning, Elizabeth Barrett

- from different name of same entity:

Common Market see European Economic Community

- from form of name in another language:

Jeanne, d'Arc, Sainte see Joan, of Arc, Saint

- from different romanization:

Evtushenko see Yevtushenko *Or vice versa if LC transliteration is used.*

- from the non-filing element of a compound name:

Rolland, Solange Chaput- see Chaput-Rolland, Solange

- from the part of a surname following a prefix:

De Gaulle, Charles see Gaulle, Charles de

- from epithet or byname:

Aquinas, Thomas, Saint see Thomas Aquinas, Saint

- from family name of a ruler:

Bonaparte, Napoléon see Napoléon I, Emperor of the French

- from direct form of inverted phrase heading:

Dr. Seuss see Seuss, Dr.

- from full name to initials or acronym used as a heading:

United Nations Educational, Scientific and Cultural Organization see Unesco

- from initials with periods to initials without periods and vice versa; this reference is needed when initials with periods are filed in a different place from initials without:

U.N.E.S.C.O. see Unesco

- from initials or acronyms used as headings:

N.A.T.O. see North Atlantic Treaty Organization
NATO see North Atlantic Treaty Organization

- from numbers filed as words:

4-H Clubs see Four H Clubs

- from abbreviations:

St. see Saint

- from different forms of heading:

Canadian Library Association. Canadian School Library Association see Canadian School Library Association

- from non-authorized subject headings that users might search by:

R.C.M.P. see CANADA. ROYAL CANADIAN MOUNTED POLICE

- from titles or parts of a work entered under the title of the whole work:

New Testament see Bible. New Testament

TYPING "SEE" REFERENCES

Type the headings from which you are referring on the fourth line down from the top of the card beginning at the second indention. If the heading is a reference to a subject heading, but not an authorized subject heading itself, do not type it in upper case. (See "Riel Rebellion, 1885" opposite page.) Leave the next line blank. On the sixth line down, begin at the third indention and type the word "see" in lower case. Leave the next line blank. On the next line, beginning at the first indention, type the heading to which the user is to be referred. Names of persons and corporate bodies are capitalized as explained in Chapter III. Subjects as headings are typed in upper case. (See opposite page.)

"See Also" References

PURPOSE

"See also" references direct the user from headings that are being used to other related headings that are also used. They are usually subject headings.

TYPING "SEE ALSO" HEADINGS

The format of a "see also" reference card is the same as that for a "see" reference. When several terms are referred to, they may be listed in column or paragraph form. (See opposite page.)

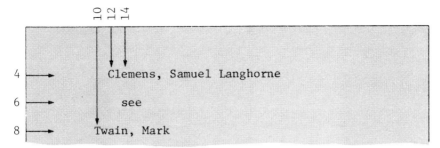

"See" reference. It is the practice of some libraries to insert a period after the names. Periods have not been added in our examples.

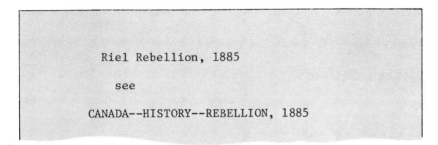

Subject "see" reference

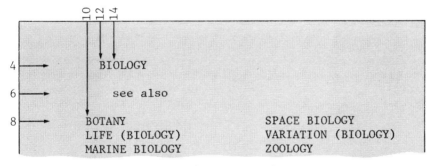

"See also" reference, column form

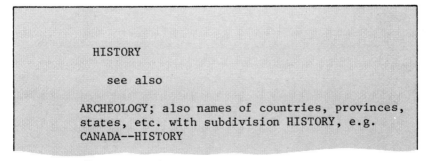

"See also" reference and scope note, paragraph form

General References

Some references are made not to one other heading but to a group of them. Some references are explanatory. General references can be made for reasons like the following:

- To explain the filing. For example:

```
Teen-age

    All titles beginning with this word
are filed as "teenage".
```
This might also be a "see" reference.

```
One hundred

    Other expressions of this number are filed
in this catalogue, e.g. "100" with the numerals
before the "A's", "cent" in the "C's", "a hun-
dred" in the "H's".
```
Useful if 1979 ALA rules are being followed.

- To explain form of entry. For example:

```
De

    French names beginning with this preposition
are filed by the next word, e.g. Gaulle, Charles
de.
```

- To refer to independently catalogued parts. For example:

```
Arabian Nights

    For separately published parts of this col-
lection, see:
Ali Baba
Sindbad the sailor
```
Form of spelling follows AACR2.

Type the heading on the fourth line down at the second indention. Leave the next line blank. Begin the explanation or note on the sixth line down at the third indention, continuing, if necessary, on the seventh line at the first indention.

Tracing Reference Cards

There must be a tracing for every reference card, so that it may be pulled from the catalogue if there is no longer anything for it to refer to:

Warner, Sylvia Ashton- see Ashton-Warner, Sylvia
Wording on reference card.

One day her books, *Teacher, Spearpoint,* and *Spinster* may be withdrawn from the collection. Then the above reference card will also have to be withdrawn.

Trace a reference in one of the following ways:
- Put it last on the shelf-list card after all other tracings, preceding it by an "x", which is the identifier of such a tracing:

x Warner, Sylvia Ashton-.

> If the shelf-list card with the reference on it is withdrawn, trace the reference on another shelf-list card to which it relates; if no relevant items remain, the reference card is disposed of.
- Keep an authority file, a card file of established names with cross-reference indications. Like the shelf list, the authority file is not public, but is meant for the use of the library staff.
- Write the reference in its alphabetical place in *Sears.* (See also p. 134, "Additions.") If it is a subject, add it in capitals. If it is an author or title, add it in upper and lower case.

OTHER AIDS FOR THE USER

A brief guide to the library's filing rules may be posted at the catalogue, or, if the catalogue is in a book or microform, printed as an explanatory page or section. Cards are available with instructions on how to use a card catalogue and may be bought to be filed at the start of each drawer.

Guide cards can be made to show key words, numbers and letters on a tab protruding above the regular cards. These should be filed every few inches in the card catalogue drawers, or at the beginning of new letter groupings (A, B, Mc, Mac) or at places where voluminous or key authors start, or where a much-searched-for subject would benefit from being made conspicuous.

FILING THE SHELF LIST

Cards in the shelf list are filed in the same order as materials are shelved in the library. The shelf list is the tool used for taking inventory of the collection.

Only one shelf-list card is required for identical copies of an item. The shelf-list card will indicate the number of copies held by the library. If additional copies of a title are not identical to Copy 1, for instance, if one is a different edition, a second shelf-list card will be required. (To save time, editions with minor differences *may* be recorded on the same card, with explanatory notes, where justified.)
- Cards for *non-fiction* are filed numerically by the *DDC* number and subarranged by the call letters.

- Cards for *fiction* are filed alphabetically by the call letters, usually from the author's name.

- Cards for picture books and easy reading books are filed alphabetically by call letters. If they have call numbers, they are filed like non-fiction.

- Cards for materials in the *reference collection* are filed in a separate section rather than with the other non-fiction items, as this corresponds to the shelf arrangement and simplifies taking inventory.

- Cards for *non-book items* are filed according to the library's shelving arrangement of such items. If book and non-book items are integrated on the shelves, cards in the shelf list will be interfiled.

KEEPING THE CARD CATALOGUE UP TO DATE

When all copies of an item are withdrawn or missing from the collection, its shelf-list card is withdrawn. All cards for an item must also be withdrawn from the user catalogue files at the same time as the shelf-list card. The tracing on the shelf-list card should indicate all additional cards filed in the user catalogue for an item, except the main entry card. (The main entry card is always made and therefore need not be shown in the tracings on the shelf-list card.) The main entry card will thus be withdrawn, as well as cards for all other added entries and subject headings indicated on the shelf-list card, for example, for title, series and title-name analytics.

Reference cards will not be withdrawn unless there is no longer a need for them. For example, if cards for all material on a particular subject are withdrawn, a "see" or "see also" reference card directing a user to that subject should be withdrawn, or cancelled by pencil on an otherwise still useful card.

```
        BIOLOGY

            see also

        BOTANY                  SPACE BIOLOGY
        LIFE (BIOLOGY)          VARIATION (BIOLOGY)
        MARINE BIOLOGY          ZOOLOGY
```

"See also" reference cancelled because all items on a subject withdrawn

OTHER LIBRARY CATALOGUE FORMATS

Book Catalogues

Although the card catalogue has been the most common form of catalogue until recently, modern technology now enables libraries to develop catalogues in the form of books. A disadvantage of the book catalogue is the greater expense involved to update or amend it. Updating requires either a new edition or manual changes, whereas it is relatively easy to add or pull cards when there is a card catalogue.

The advantages to be considered are that:
- Little space is required compared with a card catalogue.
- Production of multiple copies is cheap once one copy has been made.
- Book catalogues are portable and easy to disseminate to the users, wherever they may be.
- Entries on a page can be more quickly scanned than cards in a file.

A book catalogue can be made by photocopying catalogue cards, by printing data derived from them, or by using the computer.

Computer Output Catalogues

A computer print-out makes a rough-and-ready catalogue; if printed out on several carbons, it more closely resembles a publication. Photo-reduced, reproduced and bound, it becomes a book. Even better, the computer can activate a printing press so that the product no longer looks like a typescript. The computer can also be programmed to produce catalogue cards, if cards are still to be used along with the book catalogue.

SUGGESTIONS FOR DEVELOPING A COMPUTER OUTPUT CATALOGUE

- Experiment in collaboration with a programmer to take advantage of spare computer capacity, or practice on a micro-computer.
- Choose a short bibliography as a first project.
- Allow time to lay a sound foundation for future projects.
- Make a manual mock-up of a page on the typewriter.
- Negotiate with the programmer to see how clearly one can come to reproducing the typed format, considering both the capacity of the machine and the cost.
- Adapt the manual mock-up or prototype to the technical and economic realities.
- Keep a record of all decisions, strategems and agreements.

Quantity of information. Unlike the modular catalogue card that remains 7.5 x 12.5 cm, no matter how much data is on it, an entry in a book catalogue will take a variable amount of space. Data adds bulk to the print-out, and requires computer storage that is charged for by the letter or character. This is one good economic reason to abbreviate and reduce the quantity of information in a computerized book catalogue. Another reason is to keep the size of the print-out and the cost of paper down, if it is made into a book.

Format. Unless the print-out is to be typeset (unlikely in a small library where only a few copies of the book catalogue may be required), consider what can be done to refine the look of the print-out, or "display" as it is called. The simplest display is all capitals in one line of type. Upper and lower case, paragraphing, and underlining can be programmed to enhance readability and preserve some of the features of the card catalogue, but will require deliberate planning and extra expense.

The use of author and subject headings saves space, when, for instance, the author heading prints out once at the beginning of a number of appropriate entries.

Page numbers, guidewords as page headings, "continued on next page" and diacritical marks can be programmed to appear or may be added manually. Cost and ingenuity will determine how completely such details are computerized.

While some microcomputers may not have the capacity to handle many special characters, it is not hard to find a computer with the capacity to make a display varied enough to show upper and lower case and all necessary characters, for example, a print-train that allows all entries in French to be printed out in accordance with the usage of that language.

Photo-reduction. A page from the computer (28 x 38 cm) photo-reduces legibly to a standard metric letter size (21 x 29.5 cm). Even with photo-reduction, the cost of paper and printing may stand in the way of frequent updating of the catalogue. Many libraries are reproducing their catalogues on microfiche; the product is called COM (computer output microform). Once the catalogue is on microfiche, additional microfiche copies may be reproduced at very little cost.

Main entry. Computer programs treat all records as equal, in effect, giving no special prominence to a main entry. The resulting print-out need not show a main entry in every reference to a work.

Filing difficulties. Even assuming that there is no attempt at making a dictionary catalogue, the filing problems in a computer-produced catalogue are great. The programmer has to understand the filing rules that the librarian is following and then aim at implementing them.

LIBRARY NETWORKS AND DATA BASES

The easiest way for a small library to make a computer output catalogue is by tapping the data of a larger library or group of libraries. For example, a number of school boards can pool entries for films into a common computerized data base, from which individual catalogues corresponding to the unique holdings of each member library can be derived. It is most economical if the member libraries establish common standards and authorities, perhaps administered by the largest contributor. Within the network, special accommodation can still be provided, at extra cost; for instance, annotations may be rewritten to suit one library, or more subject headings may be provided for one library than the majority want.

The National Library and the Library of Congress have computerized catalogue records for hundreds of thousands of items in their data bases. Tapes of this information are used by large library networks and by institutions and organizations such as universities, public libraries, library systems, school systems, and commercial processing firms. (See p. 31, "MAchine-Readable Cataloguing (MARC) and (CAN/MARC).")

FOOTNOTES

1Standard Catalog Series (H.W. Wilson: New York).
2Children's Catalog, 13th ed. (H.W. Wilson, 1976: New York).

Contents IX

Processing and Shelving
the Collection

Processing Print Materials 208
    All Print Items 208
    All Books 208
    Classified Books 209
    Unclassified Books 210
    Periodicals and Periodical Indexes 210
    Newspapers 211
    Pamphlets and Clippings 211
Processing Non-Book Materials 212
    All Media 212
    Filmstrips 215
    Sound Recordings 215
    Microforms 216
    Motion Pictures 216
    Pictures 216
    Study Prints, Transparencies and Jackdaws 216
    Posters, Charts and Maps 216
    Globes, Realia and Models 217
    Slides 217
    Toys and Games 217
    Kits 217
    Video Recordings 217
Preparing AV Hardware for Use 217
    Security Measures 217
    Preparation for Circulation 218
Considering Integration vs. Separation 218
    By Medium and Size 218
    By Value, Vulnerability or Purpose 220
Shelving of the Materials 220
    Basic Non-Fiction Sequence 220
    Books Outside the Basic Sequence 220
    Periodicals 222
    Vertical File Material 223
    Non-Book Items 223
Aids to Self-Orientation 225
    Signage 225
    Dummies 226
    Orientation Literature 226
    Colour Coding 226
Footnotes 226

Chapter IX

Processing and Shelving the Collection

PROCESSING PRINT MATERIALS

All Print Items

Ownership marks are put on every item as soon as the invoice is approved for payment (not before, because of the chance the item may have to be returned). Some record of accession is made, varying from a complete shelf-list card for a book to a minimal entry, such as a checkmark, on a periodical record card to indicate arrival of a periodical.

All Books

MARKS OF OWNERSHIP AND PROTECTION

A library assistant should stamp a book in half a dozen places, such as the top and bottom edges, the front and back inside covers (unless they are of dark-toned paper or nicely illustrated, in which case stamp the flyleaves), the verso of the title page and the margin of one or more pages of the text, or the library's chosen "secret" page. One stamp should be on an edge, where it will be visible without the book being opened. More than one size of stamp may be used, including a long, thin one for the edges of picture books and other narrow books, some of which, of course, no stamp will fit.

Sensitive strips or book-plates may be added to complement or anticipate the installation of a magnetic or electronic security system.

Books with dust-jackets. Paper dust-jackets should either be laminated or covered with a transparent book-jacket cover. While the jacket and cover are sometimes glued to the book cover, it is preferable to attach the covered jacket to the cloth cover with tape, especially if the jacket may be removed some time for display, for correction, or for book repair.

Books without dust-jackets. Dust-jackets for hardback books are available commercially, plain, or decorated with motifs representing themes like science fiction or animals. Most librarians simply place a label and label protector directly on the spine, and do not otherwise cover the outside of the book.

Classified paperbacks may be laminated or reinforced. Remove any slip-cases the paperbacks may have come in.

SPECIAL LABELS

Stickers with symbols on them may be added to the spines of some books to make the subject or genre immediately recognizable, e.g., a skull for mysteries. Maple-leaf labels may well be used to make works of Canadian literature recognizable at a glance.

Classified Books

CALL NUMBER

Call numbers are constructed for each item in accordance with the instructions in Chapter VI. The call number is typed on a label for the spine of the book, or book-jacket, if any. It is typed on the book card and pocket, and on all the catalogue cards for the book.

ACCESSION NUMBER

An accession number unique to each volume is put on the title page or verso thereof, on the book card and pocket and on the shelf-list card.

LABEL PROTECTORS

Unless the spine label on the book-jacket is already protected by a transparent book-jacket cover, a transparent seal of durable material such as mylar or acetate should be placed over it, to protect and secure it.

BOOK POCKET

A book pocket is attached to the inside back or front flyleaf of each circulating book. It may be attached with its own adhesive, if any, or with library paste.

Rubber cement is not recommended as its adhesiveness lasts only a few years. The pocket should include the call number, the accession number, the author, if any, and the title.

If a pocket in the usual position would cover a map, picture, or important information like the index, it can be hinged or put on the nearest blank page.

BOOK CARD

The book card shows the same data on it as the pocket in the book so that it will be readily matched with the book it belongs to. (See also p. 228, "Circulation Routines.")

Unclassified Books

EPHEMERAL PAPERBACKS

Paperbacks meant for browsing and for the stimulation of interest in reading need not be classified or given call numbers. Processing can consist of stamping the book, installing a pocket and a book card, and perhaps adding a special label on the spine.

Many librarians choose a book card of a unique colour. To prevent confusion of these paperbacks with other copies of the same title in hardback or paperback, they should also receive a distinctive accession number. The accession number for ephemeral paperbacks could be preceded by "PB." If the librarian uses the same colour book card as that for the catalogued books, the accession number for the ephemeral paperback might be stamped or typed in red, so that the book card will be distinctive.

TEXTBOOKS

Some schools maintain a collection of prescribed textbooks for possible use by students and teachers. They need not be catalogued, but may be grouped on the shelves by subject and grade level. If the librarian has additional copies of some of the texts, it may be worthwhile cataloguing and treating them as part of the circulating collection, but the librarian should not catalogue any that do not qualify as regular library material.

LIBRARY TOOLS

Items such as *DDC*, *Canadian Books in Print*,[1] and telephone directories should be stamped, but need not be catalogued or prepared for circulation in any way. They receive minimal processing unless there is anticipated public interest in or access to them.

Periodicals and Periodical Indexes

Periodicals are not catalogued like books when received. A record of accessions is kept in a visible index file, e.g., Kardex, or in a separate periodical card file.

Protective binders may be obtained for heavily used periodicals; besides reducing wear and tear, these covers lock onto the periodicals and make them hard to walk off with.

For magazines of great appeal and heavy circulation, both pocket and card may justifiably be made and attached. A special colour will identify book cards for circulating periodicals.

Issues of periodicals with a unified theme and historic value may occasionally be singled out for preservation; such issues can be treated as monographs—catalogued, reinforced, and made freely accessible among the circulating books.

Periodical indexes are essential tools for systematically searching out articles in issues of periodicals stored in back files, bound volumes or microforms. There are indexes available for individual periodicals, such as *National Geographic Index*,[2] as well as ones that index articles in a number of periodicals—for instance, *Canadian Periodical Index/Index de périodiques canadiens*,[3] *Abridged Reader's Guide to Periodical Literature*,[4] and *Subject Index to Children's Magazines*.[5]

Since these indexes are themselves serial publications, the record of accession may be maintained in the Kardex, or on a periodical record card, as for any periodical, or they may be catalogued using an open entry. When monthly or semi-monthly indexes have been superseded by cumulative volumes, the former are discarded.

Newspapers

Current issues require no processing, although ownership marks may be stamped on each section. Back issues are usually clipped. (See "Pamphlets and Clippings," immediately below.)

Pamphlets and Clippings

Pamphlets, clippings and pictures from various sources should be stamped with the library's identifying stamp. Clippings and pictures should also be marked with the name, date, or volume and/or number of the source from which they were taken.

Such small items are usually assigned appropriate subject headings from standardized lists like *Sears List of Subject Headings*, and *Canadian Companion*. Where these fall short in providing up-to-date headings for current topics, *Reader's Guide to Periodical Literature*[6] and *Canadian Periodical Index* can be used. Reference books on vertical files contain lists of subject headings which may be used as a standard instead of *Sears* or as a supplement to it. Some libraries with large vertical file collections may want to classify them and file them in Dewey order.

For all subject headings used, an authority file or record is kept in a binder, a card file or by checkmarks and notes in some other authority such as *Sears*.

A general reference or information card is entered in the card catalogue to show that there are pamphlets or clippings on a subject.

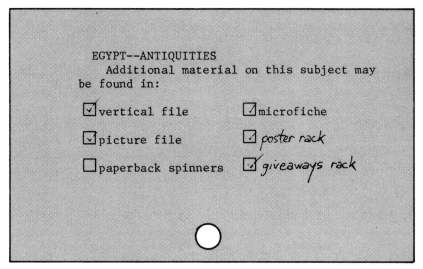

Fig. 9:1 Informal or general information card directing the user to uncatalogued materials. (Note use of pencil for afterthoughts and possibly temporary directions.)

Clippings of lasting or special value may be laminated or mounted before being put into the vertical file. Some of them may be photocopied to make more durable copies, or multiple copies, in anticipation of heavy use. Some subject files may be microfilmed.

PROCESSING NON-BOOK MATERIALS

All Media

MARKS OF OWNERSHIP

Stamp, write, emboss or engrave marks of ownership on all items.

CATALOGUING

Catalogue and classify all media.

CALL NUMBERS

Put a call number and an accession number on all major items in an AV package, e.g., filmstrip, teachers' guide and filmstrip container; affix call number labels, or, where labels will not fit, scratch or write the numbers. Using a code on the label of each part to indicate the scope of the other parts will aid in keeping the package organized and ready for circulation. Include the codes for all items on the book card and pocket to allow a quick check of the package contents on its return. (See Fig. 9:2 opposite page.)

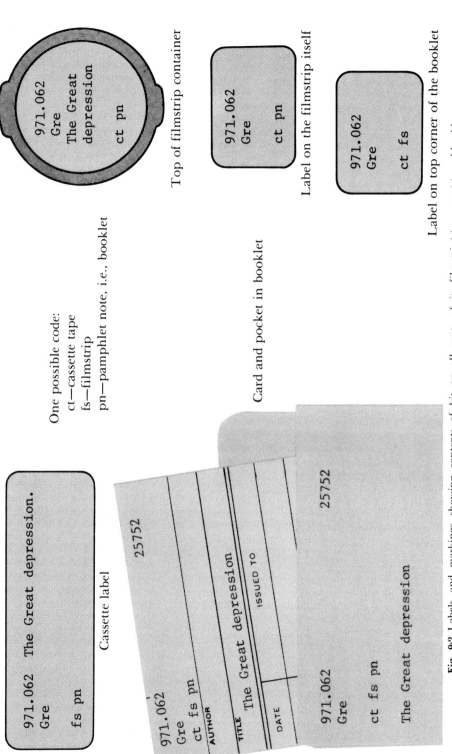

Fig. 9:2 Labels and markings showing contents of kit on all parts of it: filmstrip(s), cassette(s), and booklet

CALL NUMBER LABELS AND PROTECTORS

Use labels which are adapted to the size and shape of the medium being processed, e.g., semi-circular or circular labels for filmstrips, sectors of circles for records. The labels should be protected so that the identification will always stay in place and remain legible. On the market there are acetate or mylar label protectors corresponding in shape to most labels.

MAIN ENTRY AND TITLE LABELS

Add a label with the main entry and title proper when these identifiers are important, yet not clearly visible on the item as received. Use a typed sticker, hand lettering, dymotape, leader tape, or whatever seems best suited to the medium.

Some non-book items have a nature or shape which rules out identification on the face or outward edge. If such is the case, common sense will suggest the most suitable place for the call number and/or main entry and title labels.

ACCOMPANYING LITERATURE

Teachers' guides and pamphlets meant to accompany small AV items but not packaged with them may be arranged in file boxes by call number and brought together with them at the time of circulation.

Flimsy booklets may be mounted in covers purchased or devised in the library. This reinforcement will protect them and serve as a better support for the book pocket than the original cover.

REINFORCEMENT

Many containers need to be reinforced. Where necessary, improvise containers or substitute durable ones, e.g., of strong cardboard or polythene. Single sheets which accompany games, filmstrips or slides may be mounted on Bristol board and laminated for protection. Instructions and other indispensable literature should sometimes be photocopied and the original filed so that a replacement will always be available.

BOOK POCKETS AND CARDS

Whenever possible the book pocket and card should be on the container itself or in any accompanying booklet. If there is no container, or if it is too small or of unsuitable shape for mounting a pocket and there is no accompanying booklet, the appropriate book card should be made out and kept in a special file by medium at the circulation desk. It will be included with the item at the time of circulation.

IMPROMPTU "BOOK CARDS"

Items for which heavy circulation is not foreseen may be left without a pocket and book card. If circulation is requested, a slip or card may be handwritten.

If the item is catalogued, the slip or card will show the call number, title and accession number. Otherwise some identification will have to be improvised, e.g., Zambia (Vertical file) 5 pieces.

Filmstrips

The call number should appear on the filmstrip, its container and any accompanying literature. It is helpful if the container indicates by means of a code what related items there are; for example, it might bear the code "PN," indicating that pamphlet notes are meant to accompany the filmstrip, although they are not necessarily shelved or packaged with it all the time. To ensure that the filmstrip always gets back to its proper container, attach a call number label or scratch the call number on the blank frames at the beginning of the strip, and label the container top with matching identification on a circular or semi-circular label.

Sound Recordings

SOUND DISCS (RECORDS)

Either the pocket is put on the front of the record-jacket to avoid covering the notes that usually appear on the back, or the circulation card is inserted in a specially designed plastic record cover.

SOUND TAPE REELS (OPEN REEL)

The title, call number, accession number, and any other important information, such as act of play or performer of music, should be written on the container, the reel and on leader tape spliced to both ends of the magnetic tape; identification by leader tape is more reliable than by reel because the tape itself may not always be rewound on its original reel. Side 1 and Side 2 of the tape can be differentiated by colours of leader tape. The end of the tape can be secured by a tape clip, and the reel and box by elastics, to prevent accidental spillage. Problems entailed in handling open-reel tape can be bypassed by putting all taped programs for student use on cassettes, reserving the open-reel medium for master tapes where editing and excellent sound may be more important than convenience.

The pocket and circulation card may be attached to the tape box. Plastic boxes may be bought as needed for replacement.

SOUND CASSETTES

The cassette box, the cassette itself and liner notes or accompanying booklets should all bear the same call number and main entry and title information. Side 1 and Side 2 should be clearly marked. For a cassette without a booklet, a loose circulation card can be made and kept in a separate file at the charging desk (to be brought together with the cassette at the time of circulation), a special narrow pocket and book card may be mounted on the container, or it may be circulated in an envelope with a book pocket on it. For a cassette with a booklet or a large, informative box, the pocket and card are put on the accompanying material, which is included with the cassette at the time of circulation.

To prevent accidental erasure, the two tabs found on the edge of the cassette should be punched out; to re-record, the tab holes can be covered with tape.

Microforms

Microforms that are periodicals are not catalogued but are recorded in the periodical record file. Microfiches that are compiled from vertical file materials can be identified by a subject heading at the top of the microfiche itself, and in the card catalogue by an informal or general information card, but otherwise need not be catalogued.

Both microfilm reels and microfiches may take the place of hard-copy books. When they do, they should be fully catalogued like books and filed in shelf-list order. If the microform duplicates a hard-copy item for which the library has catalogue cards, a simple "Library has:" note to that effect may be added to the existing set of cards, to avoid the need for a separate set of cards in the school library. Microforms contained in or accompanying a book may be recorded either as part of the physical description area or in the note area on the cards for the books. (See p. 98, "Extent of Item.")

Motion Pictures

Film loops should have the call number and the main entry, which is usually the title, on the cartridge, the container and any accompanying literature.

8 mm, super-8 and 16 mm films should have the main entry, title and call number written on leader film and their containers.

Pictures

Some original works or valuable reproductions will justify being catalogued. A book pocket and card and identifying information may be mounted on the back. It is possible to buy some reproductions fully catalogued, and mounted, framed, laminated or otherwise processed.

Study Prints, Transparencies and Jackdaws

These are catalogued and have pockets attached to their envelopes. For homemade transparencies and other items without protective covering, supply a reinforced envelope so that a book pocket mounted on it will serve for many circulations.

Posters, Charts and Maps

It is desirable to catalogue these fully, but in many instances, only a general information card need be made for them.

They may be laminated or reinforced at the edges and folds with tape. A book pocket may be mounted where feasible—for instance, on the back of a folded map.

Globes, Realia and Models

It is desirable to catalogue these fully, but sometimes a general information card in the catalogue will suffice. Flimsy items should be reinforced or put in an enclosure for circulation. The book pocket can be mounted on the base, container, or other place most appropriate to the individual item.

Slides

Slides are organized and catalogued as sets. Each slide is labelled with the call number and accession number of its set and given its own number within the set.

Toys and Games

Some games are catalogued, especially educational games which have a definite place in the classification scheme, e.g., a math game, a spelling puzzle, a simulation of the Battle of Waterloo.

To extend the life of the least durable parts, reinforce them. Duplicate and file any instructions in case the originals get lost.

Kits

The label on each part of a kit can serve as a key to the contents of the whole kit if given a suitable code. (See also p. 111, "Items Made Up of Several Types of Materials," and Fig. 9:2.)

Video Recordings

Video cassettes have their call number, main entry and title written on their cartridge, container and any accompanying literature. Open-reel video tapes are prepared for use like open-reel audiotapes (p. 215).

PREPARING AV HARDWARE FOR USE

Security Measures

Fill in, photocopy and return the warranty. The photocopy will include the library's record of the serial number of each machine. File a duplicate copy of the instruction booklets or the original. Engrave ownership identification with a stylus or apply it indelibly in invisible ink, with a security label or with paint and a stencil. Mark the container and detachable parts in the same manner as the basic machine, with the same ownership information and serial number, unless the detachable part is meant to circulate independently, e.g., film reel, lens. The serial number may be the unique one which the manufacturer has put on each machine, or one that indicates what "copy" the machine is, e.g., VCR 1, VCR 2 for video cassette machines.

Preparation for Circulation

Attach a pocket and book card to each item or its container. The pocket and book card have an identifying number and title matching the machine's. Where no pocket may be conveniently glued on, attach it with an elastic or keep the book card in a file to be brought together with the machine at the time of circulation.

Circulation can also be managed by recording borrowings in a binder, by a peg-board matrix with names of borrowers running vertically and names of machines horizontally, or in other ingenious ways.

CONSIDERING INTEGRATION VS. SEPARATION

By Medium and Size

The most far-reaching decision to be made in organizing a multi-media collection is whether all materials, once processed, should be divided by medium, partially integrated, or fully integrated on the shelves by subject classification, regardless of format. Regardless of the choice made on the shelving of the collection, all library cards for all media should be interfiled in the card catalogue.

Integration of media in all formats combines all material by subject, but can present shelving problems. For instance, cassettes and filmstrips do not readily fit together on the same shelves as larger items, such as kits and records. If integration is desired, however, the cassettes and filmstrips may may be housed in media containers or holders, giving them the stability and bulk to be included with the books and larger items.

Another point to consider is the amount of space required when tall items like records and multi-media kits are shelved among the books; the shelves would have to be arranged at wide intervals. While shelving by medium saves space and allows an ideal match between the format of the medium to be housed and the storage unit for it, the user has more than one area to explore to locate material by subject.

Most librarians decide to integrate their collections to varying extents. For instance, the filmstrips, filmloops and microfilms could be in containers on shelves with the book collection, while large-format items such as kits, records and oversize books could be on special shelves in separate locations.

Fig. 9:3 Partially integrated collection showing books, kits, jackdaws and filmstrips inter-shelved. Photo courtesy K. Anthony, L'Amoreaux C.I.

By Value, Vulnerability or Purpose

Even if the collection is fully or partially integrated, some types of materials such as the following are often found outside the usual shelf sequence:

- *Items notoriously theft-prone,* such as automobile repair manuals, cassettes and certain periodicals, may be kept behind the charging desk, in a work-room, or elsewhere, and advertised as available on request.

  If observation, complaints or inventory reveal continual serious loss to the collection, strategies of protection, including installation of security systems, may be researched.

- *Reserve items* intended temporarily or permanently for a particular clientele may be kept out of the main collection.

- *Special collections,* such as reference books, textbooks and paperbacks for browsing, are separated from the basic non-fiction sequence.

- *Exhibit items,* such as historic documents, may be stored in a place of safe-keeping and shown in rotation, perhaps in locked display cases.

- *Librarians' tools,* such as *DDC,* are kept in the library work-room.

SHELVING OF THE MATERIALS

Basic Non-Fiction Sequence

A collection is shelved by call numbers in a sequence which starts from the left of the top shelf of the first section, moves to the second and lower shelves of the first section, then to the second section, and so on.

The call number arrangement begins with 001 and proceeds through to 999. Items with the same classification number are subarranged by call letters. If there is more than one item with the same call number, including call letters, subarrange by title alphabetically.

Books Outside the Basic Sequence

FICTION

Since almost all fiction is unclassified, the letters F and FIC or Fic replace the class number and indicate a separate shelving sequence. The shelf order depends on the call letters and if these are identical, on the authors' names and, within the author grouping, the titles. Few librarians have time for the fastidious shelf-reading needed to maintain this order perfectly.

For treatment of classified, scholarly editions of fiction, see p. 147, "Fiction."

EASY BOOKS

These usually have the letter E in place of the class number. Within the E sequence, they are subarranged as described immediately above. For treatment of classified easy books, if any, see p. 148, "Easy Books."

REFERENCE BOOKS

Reference books are distinguished by an R or REF above the classification number. They are housed in a separate reference area with shelves wider than average. A reference unit two shelves high, topped by a counter, is recommended. Some of the books can be exhibited on the counter, which also makes a convenient surface for consulting the books and taking notes.

Atlases may be separated from the other reference materials and housed in an atlas stand, which allows them to be either laid flat, or sometimes open. Dictionaries may be kept in a special dictionary stand; unabridged dictionaries are best exhibited open on a lectern-type stand.

PAPERBACKS

Ephemeral paperbacks. Paperbacks of an ephemeral sort which are not classified or assigned call numbers are housed on narrow shelving, specially designed racks, or spinners, and become part of an uncatalogued browsing collection.

Quality paperbacks. Quality paperbacks and those needed for research and curriculum support may be classified and housed along with the regular items in the circulating collection.

OVERSIZE BOOKS

Oversize books are often separated from the regular sequence to minimize damage to them and to remove the need for deep and widely spaced shelving everywhere in the library. (See also p. 226, "Dummies.")

BOOKS IN LANGUAGES OTHER THAN ENGLISH

In a bilingual library, books in French and English are classified using the complete range of *DDC* numbers and shelved together regardless of language.

In a unilingually English library, shelving policies may vary for books in French and other languages. The material in a language other than English can be given a suitable identifier above the call numbers, to ensure easy recognition and proper shelving—e.g., ITA for Italian. It can then be shelved as a separate collection subarranged by call number.

Schools wishing to reflect a multi-cultural society may classify materials in languages besides English and French, using the complete range of *DDC* numbers. The librarian then has the option of either integrating them, or keeping them in separate sections for each language, subarranged by call number.

GOVERNMENT PUBLICATIONS

Small collections of government publications can be organized satisfactorily in the following ways:

- *Pamphlets and small paperback booklets* may be kept in the vertical file by subject.
- *Documents in the form of books* may be catalogued like books and shelved in the circulating and reference collections.

Large collections of government publications may be organized by government, subarranged by ministry, department or agency, and shelved in pamphlet boxes.

Periodicals

CURRENT ISSUES

Current issues to which there is public access are often kept on sloping periodical shelving, or, if space must be saved, in tiered racks. They may also be hung on peg-boards. A place may be designated for each title using moveable labels, or the titles may be alphabetically arranged by main entry without labels. Some periodicals meant for browsing may be in random order. Separate groupings by subject or reading level may be made, e.g., teachers' professional journals, primary magazines, science periodicals.

Some popular titles may be best protected by being kept on reserve, replaced on the shelves by a dummy marked "Available on request," and returned to the charging desk after each circulation.

PERIODICAL INDEXES

These are usually kept with the reference collection.

BACK ISSUES

Unless a periodical is likely to be used over a length of time for research purposes, copies are not usually kept more than one or two years. Because storage becomes increasingly difficult as more issues accumulate and more titles are subscribed to, several methods of handling should be investigated:

Storing in back files. Back issues may be kept together in chronological order by title, in appropriate sizes of Princeton files or pamphlet boxes. Although filing is the simplest method of storage, it takes the most space, and leaves the periodicals most vulnerable to loss and damage. Loss can be reduced by keeping especially vulnerable titles behind the charging desk.

Binding into volumes. Research libraries, but not many schools, have periodicals bound into volumes. Binding is costly and limits access to the periodicals, as one bound volume contains many issues.

Buying microforms. Ever-increasing numbers of periodicals may be bought on microfilm or microfiche, formats which take up little storage space compared to hard copy, i.e., paper format.

Clipping. Periodicals not worth keeping intact may be clipped for the vertical file. It may be noted on the record of accession that the clipped issues are eliminated from the library's holdings. (See also p. 211, "Pamphlets and Clippings.")

NEWSPAPERS

Current issues of newspapers may be displayed on newspaper racks or mounted on rods to hold them together with pages in order.

Vertical File Material

Clippings, pamphlets and small pictures are placed in envelopes and folders and alphabetically arranged by subject in filing cabinets. Legal size is a good compromise among the widths available. Order is maintained more easily by the use of hanging files, rather than a system where the files rest on the bottom of the drawers.

Non-book Items

FILMSTRIPS

When not integrated, single filmstrips may be shelved by accession number in a fixed location, but are more usefully arranged by call number on special racks which allow them to move freely and which permit collocation of filmstrips on the same subject.

In an integrated collection, they can be intershelved with books. A filmstrip set's container is usually similar in size to an average book, and single filmstrips can be put in holders or boxes to adapt them to regular shelving.

SOUND RECORDINGS

Sound discs (records). These are best arranged in browser bins, face outward, with the label in the top left or right corner. In libraries, as in stores, as many as possible of the records should have fronts showing rather than spines, which are uninformative, hard to read, and too narrow for labels.

Some libraries do shelve records by subject among the books, spacing the shelves 33 cm apart for the purpose. This is especially true of subject areas like "Music" or "Drama," which may be integrated, while the records in other classifications are shelved by medium.

Cassettes. There is more justification for a closed-access policy on cassettes than for other media; they are particularly vulnerable because of their small size and potential for reuse. Cassettes that are not likely to be stolen may be kept on open shelves.

Cassette shelving may be sloping AV shelving with parallel rods spaced to accommodate cassettes, or narrow shelving, such as that used for paperbacks. If the shelving allows sliding movement and easy intershelving of new items by call number, it will be more economical, convenient and expandable than fixed-position spinners and holders, which are more suited to small collections in domestic settings.

Sound tape reels (open reel). These are the right size for easy integration with books.

MICROFORMS

There are several methods of storage available for microfiches, including loose-leaf pages with pockets, and 12 x 16 cm file drawers. They must be protected from fingerprints and scratches and circulated in envelopes.

Microfiches usually have legible subject or title headings by which they may be alphabetically filed. The headings either come pre-printed or may be assigned in the library.

Some research documents in microfiche are best arranged by document number.

Classified micro-reproductions of books may be filed in order by call number.

Microfilm rolls of periodicals may be arranged on open shelves in their boxes by title and date.

FILMS

16 mm films usually belong to the school board and are generally housed in a centralized film collection from which they are loaned to schools. Access is by title and subject through a printed catalogue, seldom through browsing, since the customers are remote, and the physical films, unlike books, reveal scant information to the browser. Rather than classifying them or shelving them by subject, film librarians usually group them by size and shelve them by accession number.

Films owned within the school (8, super-8 or 16 mm), may be arranged separately by size or intershelved, conspicuously labelled.

PICTURES

Uncatalogued pictures are stored by subject in files. X-ray cabinets are more suitable than letter size or legal size because they make possible the integrated storage of all sizes of pictures up to 47 x 38 cm. Larger pictures may be stored flat in drawers such as those designed for blueprints or maps, or on the shelves of an atlas stand.

Classified pictures are arranged by call number, except when they are being exhibited.

STUDY PRINTS, TRANSPARENCIES IN SETS, AND JACKDAWS

These are fully catalogued and have book pockets and cards attached. They may be stored in various ways depending on the furniture, perhaps with oversize books, in a study-print rack, in the vertical file or a special picture file. Jackdaws may be integrated with books; since they tend to fall off narrow shelves, they may be more neatly, if less accessibly, stored in the vertical file. Single transparencies may be filed like pictures.

POSTERS, CHARTS AND MAPS

Large, shallow drawers such as those mentioned above make suitable shelving. These materials may also be hung vertically by clamps, or kept in large portfolios which can be made from cardboard hinged with bookbinding tape. They may also be rolled in tubes or kept in deep pigeon holes.

GLOBES, REALIA AND MODELS

Some models, etc., may be classified and shelved by subject to add interest to the stacks, e.g., a model of the Globe Theatre. Others may be used decoratively, removed from their proper place in shelf order.

SLIDES

Slides are housed in binders with plastic pockets, in transparent plastic pouches, or in trays.

TOYS AND GAMES

These may be kept partly in a browsing collection. Those which are convenient to shelve and handle and which have educational value may be integrated.

KITS

Unless the library is spacious enough to permit their integration with books, large kits are kept separately on wide shelves.

AIDS TO SELF-ORIENTATION

Since most libraries have less staff and assistants than they would wish, a little time spent in developing aids to self-orientation will eliminate much repetitious personal assistance, and also result in increased self-sufficiency on the part of the library user.

Signage

As an aid to self-service and accessibility, use signs to indicate:
- Materials housed separately, e.g., "Ask for cassettes at desk"
- Rules, e.g., "Quiet reading corner"
- Content of stacks, e.g., "597-599—Birds and animals"
- How to use the library, e.g., "Return books here"

- Reinforcement of library lessons, e.g., "How to write a bibliography," "Dewey Decimal Classification"
- Announcements of materials, e.g., "Summer reading"
- Temporary changes in procedure, e.g., "Books on this cart for Ms. Smith's class"

Dummies

Dummies are blocks, slabs or empty boxes shelved like books or other items and labelled to show the location of materials out of sequence or in broken sequence on the shelves: e.g.,"Michelangelo—See also oversize books"; "Poetry continues on back wall"; "911-912—See also atlas stand."

Orientation Literature

Guidance may be given by leaflets available in the library or by statements included in a student handbook. This literature might include:
- *Floor plans* indicating major areas of the room or stacks.
- *Policy statements* on such matters as circulation, losses and conduct.

Colour Coding

Coloured signs may be used to identify and differentiate functional areas of the library, such as primary area or quiet corner, or parts of the collection, such as fiction.

In a divided card catalogue, the faces of the drawers for subject cards or the labels on them may be specially coloured for quick identification. Colour coding furniture or flooring will make new arrangements of furniture and areas difficult.

FOOTNOTES

[1]*Canadian Books in Print* (University of Toronto Press, 1979: Toronto).

[2]*National Geographic Index* (National Geographic Society: Washington).

[3]*Canadian Periodical Index/Index de périodiques canadiens* (Canadian Library Association: Ottawa).

[4]*Abridged Reader's Guide to Periodical Literature* (H.W. Wilson: New York).

[5]*Subject Index to Children's Magazines* (Subject Index to Children's Magazines: Madison, Wis.).

[6]*Reader's Guide to Periodical Literature* (H.W. Wilson: New York).

Contents X

Circulation and Upkeep

Introduction 228
Date Due Cards 228
Circulation Routines 228
    Items Processed With a Pocket and Book Card 229
    Processed Items Without a Pocket (e.g., single filmstrip, microfiche) 230
    Uncatalogued and Unprocessed Items 230
    Routing of Materials 231
    Periodical Circulation 231
    Reference Books 232
    Non-Book Items 232
    Equipment 232
Renewals 232
Loan Period 232
    Regular Loan Period 232
    Other Loan Periods 233
Retrieval of Library Materials 233
    Overdues 233
    Items on Indefinite Loan 233
Reserved Items 233
    Reserve Collections 233
    Items Reserved for a Customer 234
Machine and Computerized Charging 234
Inventory 235
    Method 235
    Points to Check During Inventory 235
    Benefits of Inventory 236
Weeding 236
Repair and Rebinding 237

Chapter X

Circulation and Upkeep

INTRODUCTION

There are many equally efficient ways of organizing the circulation and upkeep of the collection. The routines outlined in this chapter will serve as a basis from which the creative librarian may develop variations, to suit local needs.

DATE DUE CARDS

Date due cards are stamped before the day's circulation business begins, in quantities sufficient for the transactions of the day. They are dated on the average for two weeks ahead. (See also p. 232, "Loan Period.") Transactions involving other lengths of time may be dealt with as they arise, and special dates due indicated by stamp, handwriting, or colour-coded cards, e.g., "overnight," "48 hours," or "indefinite," for a loan to a staff member. Date cards should be a different colour than book cards. Since they are used over and over, prepare them so that the current date due is plainly distinguishable as the last one on the card or so that the date due is the only one legible after all previous dates have been crossed out.

Some schools use a date slip pasted in the book. This requires the date due to be written or stamped on at the time of circulation and will add to congestion at the charging desk, or will require an attendant to handle circulation.

CIRCULATION ROUTINES

Procedures for charging and returning books should be established during the first month of the school year. Students should know how to borrow and return materials, the time length of loan, and the variety of library services and resources.

Student assistants should be trained to work at the charging desk with a minimum of supervision so that the librarian will be free to give individual help and reading guidance. Students in every class, or library club members, may take turns providing assistance; self-service should be a goal.

The following simple routine is meant to be adapted to local circumstances, i.e., the maturity of the students, the availability of assistance and the degree of self-service desired.

Items Processed With a Pocket and Book Card

CHARGING AN ITEM OUT

A student wishing to borrow an item that has a book pocket and a book card removes the card from the pocket and signs it with his or her name, and room, grade or class number. The assistant (who may not be necessary once the students have mastered the routine) tending the desk sees that the book card is properly filled in and puts it aside to be filed in the charging tray as a record of the transaction. A date card is placed in the book pocket.

At the end of the school day, the date due is stamped on all the cards for items circulated that day so that no stamping need be done during the act of circulation.

The book cards are filed by date and subfiled by call number. If the students are young and do most of their borrowing in class groups during library periods, their cards may be filed by class, then subfiled by call number. Difficult-to-read signatures of young children may be easier to identify if the cards they are on are filed class by class.

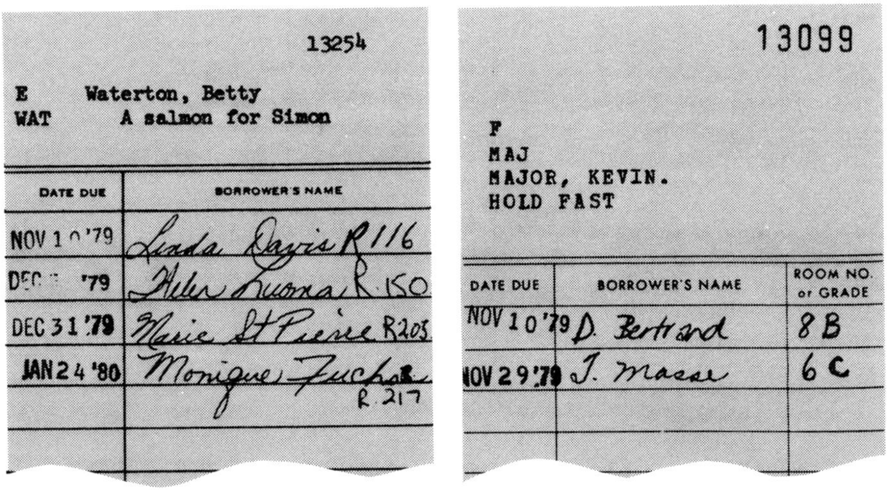

Fig. 10:1 Book cards

When an item is returned, remove the date card; note the date on the card in order to locate the book card in the charging tray, where it has been filed by date and call number, or by class and call number. Check very carefully that the information on the book card matches the information on the book pocket exactly. (A mismatch of an item and its card often has a serious negative effect on library/student relations, because the card for the discharged item will be left in the charging tray where it will be picked up later to have an unjustified overdue notice issued.) The best check on the agreement of the card and the pocket is the accession number, the unique number of each item in the library.

Replace the book card in the book pocket and put the item on a book truck for reshelving. If the book card is marked "Reserved," do not shelve, but go through another routine. (See p. 233, "Reserved Items.") Although the charging-out can be done by the borrowers themselves, most librarians prefer that a librarian, technician or volunteer check the item in.

Processed Items Without a Pocket (e.g., single filmstrip, microfiche)

CHARGING AN ITEM OUT

When there is no room for a pocket, keep the book card in a file at the charging desk. This file is arranged medium by medium and subfiled by call number.

If a student wishes to take out an item, the card is removed from the file by a library assistant. After the student has signed this card, the book card is put in the charging tray. The item and the date card are put into a general-purpose container such as a manila envelope, book bag or carton. In some cases, the date card may be inserted into a book pocket on the container.

Sometimes a book card is attached to an item with an elastic. Treat it like an item whose card is in the book pocket (see p. 229), but attach a date due card with an elastic instead of inserting it in a book pocket.

DISCHARGING AN ITEM

Since the returned item does not have a pocket, the book card must be checked for agreement with the information on the item itself, and the book card must be filed back into the appropriate file at the charging desk.

Uncatalogued and Unprocessed Items

These include items with neither a book pocket nor a book card, e.g., vertical file items.

CHARGING AN ITEM OUT

For uncatalogued items in the library, an improvised slip or card (12.5 x 7.5 cm) must be made out at the time of circulation. The heading on this slip should record an identifier. If the item is complex, then additional features should be added, such as number of pieces, size, material:

Globe Theatre
Model.

CAMBODIA—Map, 4 clippings
Vertical file.

Canadian Books in Print
Uncatalogued library tool identified by its title.

Library table, 3 x 5, cream arborite

The borrower signs this improvised slip or card.
   If the item has a regular loan period and may be enclosed in a container, e.g., an envelope, then a date card is either inserted into the envelope or put in a pocket on the envelope.
   If the item has a regular loan period but a date card cannot be attached in any way, give the borrower the date due card and file the improvised slip under the date due. Alternatively, do not bother with the date card but file the slip in a special section of the charging tray which the librarian can review to remind borrowers or to catch overdue items.
   If the item has an indefinite loan period, do not bother with the date card, but keep a slip, with date of borrowing noted, in a special section of the charging tray.

DISCHARGING AN ITEM

When the above items are returned, the improvised slips are checked against the returned item(s), and then are usually disposed of. If the slips are retained and kept with the item for possible reuse, stroke out the last name to prevent confusion.

Routing of Materials

Routing is a form of circulation which bypasses the usual charging in and out of an item; the names of all the likely borrowers are attached to the item, and it passes from one borrower to the next without being charged in and out each time.
   For special customers, presumably teachers, materials such as catalogues, subject periodicals or bibliographies, may be routed. Attach a slip to the item with the request about passing it on and returning it to the library.

Periodical Circulation

The current issues are normally not circulated but are kept on periodical shelves for browsing and library use. Some librarians keep them behind the charging desk and circulate them like items without book cards or pockets, within or outside the library for restricted lengths of time like a school period or overnight. The extent of circulation should be governed by the availability of duplicates, the importance of the periodical for reference, and the reliability of the borrower.

Back issues may be circulated like items without book cards or pockets.

Reference Books

Since these are meant to be always on hand to answer questions, the librarian may decide either to permit no circulation, or very limited circulation, i.e., overnight only. If the latter is chosen, book cards of a unique colour are made, a sticker saying "overnight loan" is placed on the pocket, and an overnight date card is put in the pocket. The reference books are then allowed to be taken out only after school and must be returned before classes begin the next day. The book cards are put in a special overnight section of the charging tray so that late books may be spotted and tracked down quickly.

Non-Book Items

Where space permits, as on records, kits, video cassettes and study prints, pockets are attached containing book cards. The items are then circulated like books.

Items in small or non-rectangular formats can have a book slip made at the time of circulation (see also p. 230, "Uncatalogued and Unprocessed Items"), or book cards can be made and kept separate at the charging desk in a file in shelf-list order. When an item is to be borrowed, find the appropriate card, fill it out and file it in the charging tray with cards for other materials due the same day.

Equipment

AV equipment that circulates regularly can have a pocket mounted on it for the book card and date dard. Impromptu loans of tables or such occasionally loaned items can be made as described on p. 230, "Uncatalogued and Unprocessed Items."

RENEWALS

If an item has not been reserved by the time its date due has arrived, it may be renewed. The book card is pulled from the file, the borrower's signature or "renewed" is written on it, and the book card is put with the rest of the day's cards. A new date card with a corresponding date due is inserted into the pocket, or otherwise attached, in place of the expired date card.

LOAN PERIOD

Regular Loan Period

For older students, two weeks is an average borrowing period. This can be shortened or lengthened for items or parts of the collection according to the demand. For primary classes that do most of their borrowing in regular library periods, a one-week turnaround time is common.

Other Loan Periods

SHORT TERM

Materials in heavy demand or indispensible to the daily needs of the library are often loaned overnight, for 48 hours, or some similiar short period of time. (See also p. 232, "Reference Books," and below, "Reserve Collections.")

INDEFINITE

Materials for teachers' use or for special projects may often be needed for longer than the regular loan period. There may be no fixed due date given, but, rather, "Indefinite loan" or "Staff" can be marked, and the cards kept in a separate part of the charging tray, to be reviewed from time to time.

RETRIEVAL OF LIBRARY MATERIALS

Overdues

A percentage of borrowed items will not be returned on or before the due date. Book cards remaining in the charging tray under a due date which has passed may be used to make reminders to overdue borrowers. Multiple-copy forms of graduated severity can be used in case second and third notices are required. Original letters and personal approaches can be used in addition to form letters.

The cooperation of homeroom teachers is very important in distributing the forms and in emphasizing their message. The school administration should help the library enforce a firm policy on the return of borrowed library materials and support the librarian's system of persuasions and sanctions.

Items on Indefinite Loan

Librarians should review the file of slips and cards that record items out on indefinite loan with a view to selectively reminding borrowers to return things when finished with them. When an item on indefinite loan to one borrower is requested by another, the librarian should try to make an arrangement suitable to both. An indefinite loan should be made on the understanding that the item is subject to recall in case of higher need.

RESERVED ITEMS

Reserve Collections

Just as reference books may be made to circulate on occasion, other items may also be temporarily removed from circulation and made into a reserve collection. This may be done to oblige a teacher or to support a program at the expense of the casual borrower; the requirements of the teacher or program are then favoured over those of the general customer. Some items may be designated for use in the library only, or for lending to certain people or class-rooms. Reserve collections can also be set up when competition to take out certain materials would cause an unmanageable, greedy scramble. Foresight and planning with teachers result in wise decisions on when and what to reserve.

Items Reserved for a Customer

ON ORDER

If a customer who has ordered or shown interest in an item also wants to borrow it, a notice of its availability should be sent when it has been processed.

ON LOAN

If a customer cannot locate a copy of a desired title that is in the library collection, check the charging tray, starting with the most distant date. If the card for a copy is found, mark "Reserved" and the borrower's name on it. If possible, expedite the return of the item to oblige the new customer. If the borrowing takes its normal course and the item is returned, train whoever is at the desk to notice the "Reserved" marking and notify the person requesting it that it is available. A flag or oversize card may be attached to the book card to make it conspicuous.

MACHINE AND COMPUTERIZED CHARGING

When transactions number several hundred per day, a manual system is heavily taxed. A mechanical or electronic system can provide increased capacity and such features as:
- listings of books by borrower, especially useful if a borrower is leaving the school or wants an accounting
- keeping track of reserves
- automatic listing of overdues, or generation of overdue notices
- instant statistics
- elimination of handwriting, illegibility and delays

A machine charging system pairs a book card with a student card or borrower's plastic identification card (similar to a credit card). A computer system may pair a plastic identification card for the borrower and a punch-card book card for the item and process them through a sensor or optical scanner. Alternatively, the desk attendant may enter data about the item, perhaps the accession number, and about the customer, perhaps the name or school identification number, by key punching or optical scanning.

INVENTORY

Periodic inventories are necessary in order to keep the records of library holdings up to date. A library may inventory its holdings at the end of each school year or continuously. The continuous inventory may be intended to cumulate in a complete inventory, or it may have the more limited aim of simply maintaining order in the most active or important parts of the collection.

Method

The shelf list is the librarian's tool for taking inventory. Cards in the shelf list are filed in the order in which print and non-print items are arranged on the shelves or storage units. (See p. 201, "Filing the Shelf List.")

Before a complete inventory, recall and shelve all borrowed items possible, and shelf read to arrange the shelves in perfect shelf-list order. Interfile the book cards for missing items into the shelf list. Take the shelf-list drawers to the shelves and compare the cards and the shelved items. The cards for any missing items are stood on end or flagged, and a notation is made in pencil next to the accession data, e.g., "Missing June 79" or, for utmost brevity, "M 79." If the item reappears after inventory, the pencilled note is erased. If the item does not reappear, the librarian must decide whether or not to take action, reorder, or pull the shelf-list card and the remainder of the card set, if the item is the only one on the shelf-list card and the librarian will not or cannot reorder it.

Points to Check During Inventory

At inventory the librarian should ascertain:
- that each item is accounted for as present, on loan, or missing
- that the book card is in place
- that the accession number on the shelf-list card, the book card and the book pocket all correspond
- whether recataloguing is needed because of observed errors and discrepancies between the cards and the tools in current use
- whether reclassification and relocation are called for to bring together separated copies of titles and translations noticed as inventory progresses
- whether the collection needs bringing into line with the latest edition of *DDC*
- whether the condition of items calls for quick repairs at the shelves
- whether new labels are needed for neatness and legibility
- whether items should be put aside to be considered for major repair and disposal

Benefits of Inventory

Inventory time is the principal occasion when the library does housekeeping, which includes:

- putting the shelves in perfect order
- amending the shelf list
- rectifying and updating the card catalogue
- making the shelf list and user catalogues reflect the library's holdings
- correcting mismatches of book cards and pockets
- discovering missing items, e.g., small items hidden in bigger ones
- revising statistics of holdings
- removing outdated and damaged materials
- noticing gaps and imbalances in the collection

WEEDING

Use standard bibliographies (p. 3, "Selection Tools") and the opinions of subject specialists in deciding what to deaccession from the library. Regretted purchases or materials of intrinsic value but no future relevance to the school may be consigned to class-rooms, given away, sold, or exchanged with another library. Aging materials with superseded content and little historic value should be discarded, especially in subjects like science and political geography, where lack of topicality can mislead naïve students.

All cards for any title that is being deaccessioned should be withdrawn. The shelf-list card has a record of all the cards for the item that are in the user catalogue, except the main entry card. (See also p. 158, "Tracings.")

In order that discarded books will not be returned or that they will be distinguished if returned, they should be stamped with a note such as "Obsolete copy; given away"; "Discarded by _____, (date)"; "Deaccessioned."

If one copy of a title is discarded, perhaps because it is not worth repairing, a note such as "Discarded '80" is put beside the appropriate accession number or data and a pencil line put through the accession number.

A separate file in shelf-list order can be kept for the deaccessions in case of audit. For discards, only one card needs to be kept, presumably the shelf-list card. For an item missing but not replaced, it is advisable to file its whole set of cards with an elastic around it (never a deforming paper clip). In the event that the item reappears, its cards can be retrieved and re-entered in the shelf list and user catalogues, unless it is decided then to dispose of it with all its cards. Withdrawn cards should be torn up, pencil-marked across the face, or stamped "discarded." Otherwise, they might be mistaken for cards that need filing.

REPAIR AND REBINDING

For AV items, replacement boxes of all shapes and sizes may be substituted for deteriorating ones. Spare filmstrip cans, record liners and jackets, and plastic containers for tapes, games, etc., can be brought into use. The leader tape and leader film on tapes, filmstrips and films may be checked and replaced or renewed, and the tapes and films themselves checked, trimmed and spliced. Call labels and identification can be added to all new containers and titles and labels retyped on stickers or renewed by hand printing.

Books requiring minor repairs can be patched up in the library. The supplies for repairing and booklets of instructions are readily available in the library market. A small library should seldom undertake major mending; it is time-consuming and the results are not professional.

Provided the book is worth repairing, it should be considered for rebinding. Check it to ensure that all the pages are present and intact and that the margins, especially the gutters, are wide enough to allow for the trimming that is part of the rebinding operation.

Books that have a heavy circulation are the most worthwhile rebinding, as are valuable items that are out of print. Many books are published with a reinforced binding, known as library binding. The library will reduce the need for later rebinding if picture books, novels and works that seem destined for heavy use are acquired in library binding where available.

Contents XI

French Usage

Introduction 240
Capitalization 240
Hyphenation 243
Abbreviation 243
Names of Publishers, Distributors, Etc. 244
Filing 245
Footnotes 247
General Reference Sources 247

Chapter XI

French Usage

INTRODUCTION

If a library's holdings in the French language are mainly books about that language, in addition to fiction and non-fiction meant to be used as readers for learning French, they may be classified in the 440's or the 840's and catalogued in English, with English subject headings and descriptive cataloguing. When there are some further items in French that are classified and shelved by subject amid a predominantly English collection, English subject headings and descriptive cataloguing may be used. Even so, attention should be paid to French usage as outlined below.

When the library has a large proportion of materials in French, or when it is bilingual, the French books should be catalogued in French, using:

- French subject headings derived from *Répertoire de vedettes-matière*,[1] and *Liste des vedettes matière de Biblio*.[2]
- French subject headings from bilingual translated lists such as *Index anglais-français des termes utilisés dans le répertoire de vedettes-matière*,[3] and the "English-French Index" of *Canadian Subject Headings*.
- Commercial cataloguing, especially as provided by the Centrale des bibliothèques de Québec.
- Published bibliographies and catalogues such as *Canadiana*[4] and *Choix*.

Care should be taken to observe French usage in capitalization, hyphenation, punctuation and abbreviation. Sometimes the French usage is the same as English; e.g., the French, les Français. Sometimes it is not; e.g., the English language, la langue anglaise; I, je.

CAPITALIZATION

Capitalize only the first word in the name of a corporate body, unless the first word is an article (in which case also capitalize the second word), or unless, of course, a proper noun follows the first word:

240

Presses universitaires de France

Action catholique canadienne

La Presse

Bibliothèque nationale du Canada.

Ontario. Ministère de l'éducation

Note: "Ministère de l'Éducation" is also acceptable usage.
   If the first word in a publisher's name is "Édition(s)," also capitalize the next common noun:

Éditions du Jour

   Do not capitalize the following, as English usually does:
   • proper adjectives of nationality:

un Canadien français

la race anglo-saxonne

   • proper adjectives made from personal names:

le drame shakespearien

   • names of languages:

l'anglais

   • names of religions:

le christianisme

   • words designating members of sects, religious orders and
     political parties:

des protestants

un trappiste

le socialiste

Note: The preceding two examples do not preclude the capitalization of proper nouns, especially names of institutions:

les Jésuites

le Socialiste   *Journal.*

√

- names of places used as common nouns:

un terre-neuve   *Dog.*

du champagne   *Wine.*

- words for public works:

rue de la Montagne-Ste-Geneviève

place Royale

le chemin du Roi

pont des Arts

Note: The significant words after the word for street, etc., are capitalized. (See also p. 243, "Hyphenation.")
- days of the week and months. Holidays, however, are capitalized:

lundi

janvier

Noël

- a title of honour, unless it and the name it modifies are used as the name of a place or as part of a larger name:

sainte Anne

le prince Laurent

but

l'église Sainte-Anne

Sainte-Anne-de-Bellevue

- common nouns used as geographical terms in place names, although they may be modified by proper adjectives or other words that are capitalized:

l'océan Atlantique

la mer Morte

l'île des Lapins

les montagnes Rocheuses

le fleuve Saint-Laurent

Some adjectives, although not proper adjectives, are inextricably linked with nouns to make compound proper names, both parts of which are capitalized:

les États-Unis

la Comédie-Française

Charles le Téméraire
Epithet "Téméraire" being a quasi-*surname.*

HYPHENATION

Hyphens are usually used between forenames and abbreviations thereof:

Marie-Claire Blais

J.-J. Rousseau

They are also used between the words designating places, streets, buildings, etc.:

Trois-Rivières

le département du Pas-de-Calais

le musée Victor-Hugo

ABBREVIATION

Abbreviations that include the last letter of the word abbreviated are not followed by a period:

St

Mlle

but

M. *Monsieur.*

No period follows the symbol of a metric unit, e.g., km, unless it falls at the end of a sentence.
Many French abbreviations are the same as or very similar to English ones, for example, éd., ill., p. Some useful ones which are unique to French are:

augm.—augmenté(e)
av.-pr.—avant-propos *preface*
Cie—compagnie

coul.—couleur(é)(s)
couv.—couverture
dép.—département
dépl.—dépliant *folder*
d.l.—dépôt légal *legal deposit*
n&b—noir et blanc
nouv.—nouveau, nouvelle
no—numéro
préf.—préface
ptie, pties—partie, parties *parts*
rec.—recueil(li) *compilation, compiled*
réd.—rédaction, rédigé, *editing, edited*
s.l.—sans lieu *no place (of publication)*
s.n.—sans nom *no name (of publisher)*
sér.—série
t.—tome
1er—premier
1ère—première
2e—deuxième
3e—troisième

NAMES OF PUBLISHERS, DISTRIBUTORS, ETC.

If the publishing house bears the name of a person, abbreviate the forenames to initials, or omit forenames if the publisher is well known. Omit terms like "Compagnie," ". . . et Fils," ". . . Frères," "Limitée," and equivalents, after the name.

Words indicating the type or place of business are suppressed, e.g., "Maison," "Imprimerie," "Société," "Librairie," "Éditeur," "Édition," along with accompanying adjectives, such as "nouveau," "ancien," "classique":

Beauchemin *for Librairie Beauchemin Limitée*

Garneau *for Éditions Garneau Frères*

Nathan *for Fernand Nathan et Cie, Éditeur*

When an abbreviated form of the name would be confusing or where it would be unrecognizable as a publisher, do not follow the rules above:

Éditions de l'Homme

Presses universitaires de France

In French the usage of capitals and punctuation is subtle and somewhat variable; for further guidance see the references at the end of this chapter.

FILING

A library with a basically French catalogue will follow a filing authority such as *Manuel pratique de classement*, by Jean-Louis Rioux and Andrée Martin.

In either a basically English catalogue or a bilingual one, cards for books in French can be entered according to the rules on p. 182, "Common Qualities of Filing Rules," with the following modifications and amplifications:

Disregard the initial definite article before *common* nouns in a heading. The definite articles are le, la, l' and les:

Pierre le Magnifique
La princesse de Clèves
Le problème mondial de l'alimentation

For articles before *proper* nouns, see pp. 246 to 247.

File by an initial definite article contracted with a preposition (namely, au, du, aux, des):

Au pied de la pente douce
L'auberge du Cheval blanc

File word by word using the initial partitive article (namely, de, du, de la, de l', des):

De la politesse, s'il vous plaît
Delaere et l'Église ukrainienne au Canada
Les délices de l'érable

Disregard the initial indefinite article (un, une):

Un, deux, trois *See example below.*
Unamuno, Miguel de
Un univers en marche

File by un and une when they are *equal to the word "one."* When in doubt whether un is a numeral or a definite article, consider it the latter and disregard it:

Une éducation manquée
Une de perdue, deux de trouvées
L'université électronique

File by the indefinite article (des):

Des enfants comme les autres
Descartes, Réné

√

When the above particles are *not* in the initial position, treat them like any other words and file by them:

Les principes de chimie
Principes de la chimie

File words with *apostrophes* within or between them as spelled. Do not supply the missing letter(s). Do not treat the apostrophe as a space:

Ces enfants de ma vie
Ces visages qui sont un pays
C'est quoi l'État?

Disregard *diacritical marks*:

A la plage [à la plage]
A-t-il un couteau?
Athalie

File *numerals* as words—91 as quatre-vingt-onze:

100 ans de ski français
Les cent quatrains de T'ang
104, rue Royale *Cent quatre.*
101 histoires d'animaux *Cent une.*

For proper names of *countries*, disregard the articles:

L'An de Seigneur
L'Angleterre
Anne of Green Gables

File by articles in *names of cities*. Disregard spaces and file article and noun as one word:

Un lapin rose
La Pocatière
Lapointe, Ernest

(Names preceded by articles in languages other than French follow the same rule, e.g., Los Angeles is filed under "L".)

In the names of certain cities of France where all tradition favours suppression of the article, disregard it. Make a "see" reference to the filing word:

Le Havre voir Havre

For *surnames*, the heading to be filed will have been established according to the rules enunciated in Chapter III. With compound surnames consisting of prepositions, articles, and nouns, file by an *initial article* whether joined to the noun or not. Treat article and noun as one word and do not file word by word:

Laffite le Corsaire
La Fontaine, Jean de
Larousse classique
Latin

File by prepositions and other words preceding the noun in the surname phrase if they appear that way in the heading:

Delagrave
De la Roche, Mazo

but

Gaulle, Charles de
La Fontaine, Jean de

Here the preposition is not a filing word according to the cataloguing rules.

FOOTNOTES

[1]*Répertoire de vedettes-matière*, 8e éd. (Université Laval, Bibliothèque, Section de l'analyse documentaire, 1976: Québec).

[2]*Liste de vedettes matière de Biblio*, 4e éd. (Hachette, 1971: Paris).

[3]*Index anglais-français des termes utilisés dans le répertoire de vedettes-matière*, 2e éd. (Université Laval, Bibliothèque, Section de l'analyse documentaire, 1976: Québec).

[4]*Canadiana* (Bibliothèque nationale du Canada: Ottawa).

[5]*Manuel pratique de classement*, 2e éd. rev. (Collèges de Ste-Anne-de-La Pocatière, 1972: La Pocatière).

GENERAL REFERENCE SOURCES

Allen, C.G., *A Manual of European Languages for Librarians* (Bowker, 1975: New York).

Choix: documentation audiovisuelle (Québec, Ministère de l'Éducation: Montréal).

Choix: documentation imprimée (Québec, Ministère de l'Éducation: Montréal).

Choix jeunesse: documentation audiovisuelle (Québec, Ministère de l'Éducation: Montréal).

Choix jeunesse: documentation imprimée (Québec, Ministère de l'Éducation: Montréal).

Grevisse, Maurice, *Le bon usage*, 9e éd. rev. (Duculot, 1969: Gembloux, Belgique).

La bibliothèque scolaire: petit guide à l'usage du bibliothécaire, out of print (Ontario, Ministère de l'Éducation, 1969: Toronto).

Lévesque, Guy, *Manuel pratique de catalogage*, 2e éd. (Fédération des collèges classiques, 1969: Montréal).

Règles de catalogage anglo-américaines, 2e éd. (ASTED, 1980: Montréal).

Règles de catalogage anglo-américaines: version française (ACBLF, 1973: Montréal).

Thomas, Adolphe V., *Dictionnaire des difficultés de la langue française* (Larousse, 1956: Paris).

Glossary

For technical terms not listed below, first see the index in case they are defined in context, then see a more specialized terminological work.

Definitions are original except where quoted source is indicated as:

AACR2—Anglo-American Cataloguing Rules, 2nd ed. (1978)

DDC—Dewey Decimal Classification and Relative Index, 19th ed. (1979)

NBM—Nonbook Materials: The Organization of Integrated Collections, 2nd ed. (1979)

Access point—The first word on a catalogue card, or of a bibliographical citation, after any initial article. See also "Heading."

Accession—1. An acquisition; the act of acquiring.
2. To enter an item into the library, usually by making a shelf-list card and by assigning an accession number.

Accession number—A serial number assigned to each item as it is entered into the library collection.

Acronym—A word made up of the initials or of the initials and further letters of several longer words, e.g., Unesco, MARC.

Added entry—"An entry, additional to the main entry, by which an item is represented in a catalogue; a secondary entry. See also 'Main entry'." *AACR2*

Alphanumeric—Consisting of both letters and numerals.

Alternative title—"The second part of a title proper that consists of two parts, each of which is a title; the parts are joined by the word *or* or its equivalent in another language, e.g. *The tempest, or, The enchanted island*." *AACR2*

Analytic—See "Analytical entry."

Analytical entry—"An entry for a part of an item for which a comprehensive entry has been made." *AACR2*

Area—"A major section of the bibliographic description, comprising data of a particular category or set of categories," e.g., edition area. *AACR2*

Author—The person or corporate body responsible for a work.

Authority file—A reference list of names and terms established by the library and used as an authority to keep its cataloguing consistent.

Back files—Collections of back issues of periodicals.

Bibliographic(al) citation—Information about an item that is listed in a bibliography or footnote, e.g., author, title, publisher, date.

Bibliography—A list of items. In one sense it is a complete list of all the materials on a subject, by an author or from a place, e.g., *The German National Bibliography*. It may also mean a selected list, e.g., a bibliography on the beaver.

Biographee—The person about whom a biography is written.

Book card—A transaction card bearing such information as the call number, accession number, title and statement of responsibility for the item it accompanies, with spaces for each borrower's name and each due date. Such a card for a non-book item is usually still called a book card.

Book catalogue—A catalogue in the form of a book rather than on cards.

Byname—A secondary name for a person, e.g., nickname.

CIP (Cataloguing in Publication)—Cataloguing data supplied *on* an item, usually on the verso of the title page.

Call letters—Letters which are part of the call number, along with the classification number; they are derived from the statement of responsibility, e.g., the author's surname, or the title, in the case of a title main entry, or occasionally from the subject.

Call number—A code made up of the classification number, call letters, and perhaps other codes; it is used to locate an item on the shelves, and sometimes to distinguish one copy of an item from another.

CAN/MARC—Canadian MARC. See also "MARC."

Cartographic materials—Maps, atlases, globes, satellite photographs and similar items.

Character string—A sequence of any or all of the following kinds of characters: letters, numbers, symbols and marks of punctuation, e.g., a word.

Charging desk—The place where circulation transactions are conducted and recorded.

Charging tray—A box where book cards are kept for items in circulation.

Chief source of information—"The source of bibliographic data to be given first preference as the source from which a bibliographic description (or portion thereof) is prepared," e.g., the title page. *AACR2*

Citation—See "Bibliographic(al) citation."

Class number—That part of the call number which stands for the subject or form of a work.

Classification—"1. An arrangement in some logical order of the whole field of knowledge or of some specified portion thereof.
2. The art of arranging books or other objects in conformity with such a scheme." *DDC*

Classification number—See "Class number."

Classification schedule—A table of subject classes and corresponding numbers and codes, notably, the *DDC* schedules.

Collocate—Place together.

Collective title—"A title proper that is an inclusive title for an item containing several works." *AACR2*

COM (Computer output microform)—Data from the computer displayed on microfilm.

Compound surname—A surname composed of two or more names, sometimes including articles, prepositions, conjunctions and hyphens.

Continuation—A supplement or extra part of a monograph.

Corporate body—"An organization or group of persons that is identified by a particular name and that acts, or may act, as an entity. Typical examples of corporate bodies are associations, institutions, business firms, nonprofit enterprises, governments, government agencies, religious bodies, local churches, and conferences." *AACR2*

Cutter number—An alphanumeric code written beneath the classification number as part of a call number. Technically it is a code derived from the Cutter or Cutter-Sanborn tables, but, loosely speaking, it may be any author letters or similar code.

Cuttering—Assigning a Cutter number or equivalent.

Data base—A large, machine-accessible data file.

Date card—A reusable card which accompanies an item being circulated; the last date stamped on it indicates the date of expiry of the loan period.

Deaccession—Remove from the library's holdings and from the catalogue.

Descriptor—A thesaurus entry which is the standard term for a subject.

Desiderata—Desired items that are hard to find, rare or out of print. Libraries enter these in a special file where they can be checked against lists and catalogues newly received. They may also be referred to specialized dealers.

Dictionary catalogue—A catalogue in which the author, title, subject and other entries are all filed in one alphabetical sequence.

Divided catalogue—A catalogue in which the author, title, and subject entries are filed in separate sequences, e.g., authors in one alphabet, titles in another.

Dummy—A box, block or slab similar in shape to a shelved item, carrying information or directions, usually about the location of items that might be hard to find.

Easy book—A book for children consisting of pictures and a line or two of print per page. It is usually classified with an "E".

Edition—All the copies of a title which are identical, being made from the same master.

Element—"A word, phrase, or group of characters representing a distinct unit of bibliographic information and forming part of an area (q.v.) of the description." *AACR2*

Encumbrance—A provisional deduction from the budget to cover items on order.

End paper—A double leaf in the front and the back of a book, one leaf pasted to the cover, the other forming the first and last leaf in the book, i.e., the flyleaves.

Entry—"A record of an item in a catalogue. See also 'Heading'." *AACR2*

Epithet—A noun, adjective or phrase in apposition to a name, e.g., Juana *the Mad.*

Extension card—A second or other card for the continuation of a catalogue entry which overflows beyond the first card.

Facsimile reproduction—A photo-reproduction, usually to scale.

First indention—The distance from the left-hand margin where the most leftward line of typing or print begins, typically about 10 spaces in.

Flyleaf—A blank leaf at the very front or back of a book.

Front matter—The part of a publication preceding the main text, i.e., title page, table of contents, preface, etc.

Galley proof—The earliest trial printing of a publication, before the pages are clearly separated and printed on both sides.

General material designation (GMD)—"A term indicating the broad class of material to which an item belongs; e.g., sound recording. See also 'Specific material designation'." *AACR2*

Generic term—A subject heading on a high level of generality, e.g., BIRDS, in contrast to one of more specificity, e.g., OWLS.

Guide card—A card carrying easily visible location information in a file, often on an upward-protruding tab.

Hanging indention—A paragraph margin with the first line at the first indention and all subsequent lines at the second; used where there is a title main entry.

Hard copy—A copy of a microform enlarged on paper.

Heading—1. The top line or first complete statement on a catalogue card.
2. The caption over a column or page.

Holdings—All the possessions of the library, or only what it has in any one area or medium, e.g., holdings in French poetry.

Indention—The distance from the left-hand edge of a page or card where a line of print begins. See also "First indention"; "Second indention"; "Hanging indention."

ISBD(G) (General International Standard Bibliographic Description)—The framework for description of library materials followed in *AACR2*.

ISBN (International Standard Book Number)—A number unique to each edition of a book.

Inventory—A check of holdings.

✓

Jobber—Wholesaler.

Kit—"A set of material composed of many textual parts, or, two or more media none of which is identifiable as the predominant constituent of the item." *NBM*

LC AC (Library of Congress Annotated Card)—A form of LC card for children's books including an annotation and simplified subject headings.

Leader—A length of blank tape or film patched to the beginning and end of a tape or film program to protect the program and perhaps to carry identifying data.

Leaf—A page plus its verso.

Legal size—A size of stationery, measuring 8½″ x 14″ (21.5 cm x 35.5 cm).

Library binding—A reinforced binding available on some books at the time of purchase.

Library network—Sharing among libraries of cataloguing done to a common standard, or of reference and circulation services, often computer-assisted.

Location symbol—1. A code in a union catalogue showing which libraries hold a certain item.
2. A code as part of the call number, which indicates a separately shelved special collection, e.g., REF, R.

Main entry—"The complete catalogue record of an item, presented in the form by which the entity is to be uniformly identified and cited. The main entry may include the tracings of all other headings under which the record is to be represented in the catalogue. See also 'Added entry'." *AACR2*

MARC (MAchine-Readable Cataloguing) —The computerized cataloguing format and data file developed by the Library of Congress.

Medium of performance—The instrument, voice or group performing a musical work.

Microform—An optically reduced format such as microfiche or reel-to-reel microfilm.

Mixed responsibility—Authorship or creation of an item wherein different persons or bodies are responsible for different tasks, e.g., writing, illustrating.

Monograph—A finite publication; a work which is not a serial.

National bibliography—A record as complete as possible of all the publishing in a country, usually published as a serial, e.g., *Canadiana*.

Network—See "Library network."

Note—Supplementary information in a catalogue entry, recorded in paragraphs below the description, after the series statement, if there is one.

On-order file—Cards or slips from multiple-copy order forms which duplicate the data on orders. Each entry may be annotated as the supplier reports on the order, and removed when the item is received.

Open entry—An entry with blank spaces left for indeterminate information, e.g., date, number of volumes, which may be added when discovered, or when updating is called for. Interim information is often recorded in pencil.

Other title information—"Any title borne by an item other than the title proper or parallel titles; also any phrase appearing in conjunction with the title proper, parallel titles, or other titles, indicative of the character, contents, etc., of the item or the motives for, or occasion of, its production or publication. The term includes subtitles, *avant-titres*, etc., but does not include variations on the title proper (e.g., spine titles, sleeve titles, etc.)." *AACR2*

Out of print—No longer available from the publisher or for sale, except perhaps as a remainder or second hand.

Parallel title—"The title proper in another language and/or script." *AACR2*

Periodical index—A serial publication which is a listing of periodical articles, sometimes related by subject or reading level, sometimes diverse in subject.

Periodical record card—An accession record consisting of dated squares wherein check marks are made to show the arrival of issues of periodicals.

Picture book—An easy-reading children's book consisting of illustrations with a line or two of text on each page. See also "Easy book."

Princeton file—An open metal box with a bottom and two sides joined by a metal band which has space for a label.

Processing—Adding to a library item some or all of the following: A book pocket and card, a call number label and book-jacket cover or other protective cover as appropriate, along with the accession number and library identification stamp. Cataloguing is sometimes considered to be a part of processing.

Realia—Real objects, e.g., specimens, artifacts, as contrasted to representations, e.g., pictures.

Related body—"A corporate body that has a relation to another body other than that of hierarchical subordination, e.g., one that is founded but not controlled by another body; one that only receives financial support from another body; one that provides financial and/or other types of assistance to another body, such as "friends" groups; one whose members have also membership in or an association with another body, such as employees' associations and alumni associations." *AACR2*

Related work—A supplement, sequel, index, libretto or similar work which has an obvious relationship with or dependency upon another work.

Remainder—An item, usually out of print, offered for sale at a considerably reduced price.

Reprint—1. A facsimile republication of an out-of-print book.
2. An inexpensive edition of a work perhaps somewhat past currency.
3. Any unchanged new issue of a work.

Romanization—Changing characters or letters into the letters of the roman alphabet.

Routing—Circulation of an item among users named on an attached list without requiring the item's return to the charging desk until all users have had an opportunity to study the item.

SDI (Selective dissemination of information)—A reference service, usually partly automated, which consists of the regular provision of current data to match a user profile.

Schedule—See "Classification schedule."

Second indention—The distance from the left-hand margin where the second most leftward line of type begins, typically about 12 spaces in.

"See also" reference—A card or other entry referring the user from a heading with entries under it to one or more other entries with related entries under them.

"See" reference—A card or other entry referring the user from a heading with no entries under it to a heading *with* entries under it.

Serial—"A publication in any medium issued in successive parts bearing numerical or chronological designations and intended to be continued indefinitely. Serials include periodicals; newspapers; annuals (reports, yearbooks, etc.); the journals, memoirs, proceedings, transactions, etc., of societies; and numbered monographic series. See also 'Series' . . ." *AACR2*

√

Series—"A group of separate items related to one another by the fact that each item bears, in addition to its own title proper, a collective title applying to the group as a whole. The individual items may or may not be numbered . . ." *AACR2*

Shared responsibility—Joint authorship, or similar joint collaboration on the creation of an item wherein more than one person or body contributes to the same task, e.g., illustrating, composing.

Shelf list—A file of shelf-list cards or records indicating how the materials are arranged on the shelves.

Shelf-list card—A unit card to which the accession number, acquisition data, subsequent history of the item, and the tracings are added.

Shelf reading—Checking the order of items on the shelves and rearranging them by call numbers in perfect shelf-list order.

Shorts—Ordered items not supplied because they are out of stock, out of print, etc.

Specific material designation—"A term indicating the special class of material (usually the class of physical object) to which an item belongs, e.g. sound disc." *AACR2*

Spine—The closed outside edge or hinge of a publication, usually imprinted with the title, author and publisher data.

Stacks—1. All of the library's shelving units.
2. Such units plus their contents.
3. All such units used for storage as opposed to those used for display, reference and tidying up.

Standard number—The unique numerical identifier of an edition, serial or other publication, e.g., ISBN, ISSN.

Statement of responsibility—"A statement, transcribed from the item being described, relating to persons responsible for the intellectual or artistic content of the item, to corporate bodies from which the content emanates, or to persons or corporate bodies responsible for the performance of the content of the item." *AACR2*

Subject heading—A standard term used as a heading to indicate a subject of the work described below it.

Subordinate body—A corporate body which is a part of a larger corporate body, and which stands in lower hierarchical relationship to it.

Thematic index number—A serial catalogue number for certain composers' works.

Thesaurus—A book or list of descriptors.

Title frame—A frame near the beginning of a film, filmstrip or other material for projection which is the chief source of information.

Title of address—A word preceding a name which is used in conventional polite or formal address, e.g., Mr., Mme., Capt.

Title of honour—A word accompanying a name which indicates nobility or similar high status, e.g., Prince.

Title page—A page near the beginning of a print item which is the chief source of information.

Title proper—"The chief name of an item, including any alternative title but excluding parallel titles and other title information." *AACR2*

Tracings—A record on the shelf-list card, or elsewhere, of all the headings under which an item is entered in the catalogue. The filed entries can be *traced* from this list of headings.

Transliteration—Transposing from one alphabet to another.

Uniform title—"1. The particular title by which a work that has appeared under varying titles is to be identified for cataloguing purposes.
2. A conventional collective title used to collocate publications of an author, composer, or corporate body containing several works or extracts, etc., from several works, e.g., complete

works, several works in a particular literary or musical form." *AACR2*

Union catalogue—A catalogue showing the holdings of more than one library.

Unit card—A basic catalogue card for an item. It may be the main entry card, which, if reproduced and given appropriate headings, tracings, or other additions, makes the rest of the cards in a set.

Verso—The back of a page; the left-hand page; if numbered, usually even-numbered.

Vertical file—A library collection of pamphlets, pictures and clippings filed in cabinets.

Abbreviations

Abbreviations in the names of publishers and other corporate bodies, which follow standard English usage, are not included, e.g., Co., Ltd., Bros.

For French abbreviations see Chapter XI.

PUBLISHERS, PUBLICATIONS AND ORGANIZATIONS

AACR—Anglo-American Cataloguing Rules

AAU/BNA—Association of Atlantic Universities/Blackwell North America (Cataloguing Project)

ALA—American Library Association

BNC—Bibliothèque nationale du Canada

CB—Centrale des bibliothèques (Québec)

CLA—Canadian Library Association

DDC—Dewey Decimal Classification

ERIC—Educational Resources Information Center (U.S.)

GPO—Government Printing Office (U.S.)

HMSO—Her Majesty's Stationery Office (U.K.)

LC—Library of Congress (U.S.)

LCSH—Library of Congress Subject Headings

NCTE—National Council of Teachers of English

NICEM—National Information Center for Educational Media

NLC—National Library of Canada

NUC—National Union Catalog (U.S.)

SI—Système international d'unités (International Metric System)

Supt. of Docs.—Superintendent of Documents (U.S.)

UNICAT/TELECAT—Union Catalogue/Télécommunication catalogage (Cataloguing Project)

UTLAS—University of Toronto Library Automation System

CATALOGUING TERMS

acc.—accompaniment (music)
arr.—arranged
b.—born
b&w—black and white
c—copyright
ca.—circa
cm—centimetre
col.—coloured
corr.—corrected
d.—died
diam.—diameter
ed.—edition
enl.—enlarged
et al.—and others (*et alii*)
facsim.—facsimile

fps—frames per second
fr.—frame(s)
hr.—hour(s)
ill.—illustration(s)
in.—inch(es)
introd.—introduction
ips—inches per second
ISBN—International Standard Book Number
ISSN—International Standard Serial Number
min.—minute(s)
misc.—miscellaneous
mm—millimetre
mono.—monophonic

no.—number(s)
N.T.—New Testament
op.—opus
O.T.—Old Testament
p.—page(s)
pbk.—paperback
photo.—photograph
photos.—photographs
port.—portrait
ports.—portraits
pt.—part
pts.—parts
quad.—quadrophonic
repr.—reprinted
rev.—revised
rpm—revolutions per minute

sd.—sound
sec.—second(s)
ser.—series
si.—silent
s.l.—no place (*sine loco*)
s.n.—no name (*sine nomine*)
stereo.—stereophonic
suppl.—supplement
tr.—translator
v.—volume(s)
vol.—volume (used at the beginning of a statement or with a roman numeral)
1st—first
2nd—second
3rd—third

Index

Italicized page numbers refer the reader to illustrations on those pages.

Terms are indexed under their spelling in *AACR2*, even though they may be found in variant spellings in the places to which reference is made. The spelling of a term as found in the index is the one to be followed in cataloguing.

The index term may be found in a different grammatical form in the place referred to, e.g., a plural noun in the index may be in singular or participial form in the text.

ALA Filing Rules (draft edition, 1979), x, 191
ALA Rules for Filing Catalog Cards, x, 182
Abbreviations,
    English library terms, 257-258
    filing, 184, 193
    French, 243
    French library terms, 243-244
    See also Acronyms; Initials
Abridged editions, *See* Edition area; Editions, changed
Access point, 35, 249
    filing when identical, 189, 195
Accession numbers, 157-*158*, *166*, 209, 212, 249
    ephemeral paperbacks, 210
    leader tape, 215
    shelving by, 224
Accessioning,
    on shelf list card, 157-*158*, *166*
    periodicals, *18, 19*, 210
Acquisition, 2-21
Acronyms, 184, 193, 197, 249
Added entry, 249
    cards, 162-163, *167*
Alternative titles, 85, 249
Analytical entry (or analytics), 159-160, 161, 163, 249
    See also Name analytics; Subject analytics; Title analytics
Anglo-American Cataloguing Rules, x, 35, 79
Area, 81, 249
Art works,
    mixed responsibility, 42
    sample catalogue card, *174*
Articles, initial,

capitalization of next word, 84
    filing, 182, 193
    French, 245-247
    LC's use in uniform title, 66
Attribution of authorship,
    fictitious or erroneous, 38
    unknown, uncertain, or unnamed, 38-39
Audiovisual equipment,
    accompanying literature, 217
    circulation, 232
    processing, 217-218
Audiovisual materials, *See* Filmstrips; Pictures; etc.
Author, 249
    See also Authors, personal; Corporate bodies
Authority file, 46, 201, 211, 249
Authors, personal,
    determining what are, 36
    one, 37
    two or three, with shared responsibility, 39
    four or more, with shared responsibility, 39-40
    in statement of responsibility element, 87-88
    See also Attribution of authorship; Mixed responsibility, works of; Names, personal

Back files, 222, 249
Back orders,
    cancellation, 11
    reporting, 7, *8*, 9
Bible, 71-72
Bibliographic files, 181-205
Bibliographic(al) citation, 249

Bibliographies,
  for French usage, 247
  primary sources, x
  See also footnotes at the end of most
    chapters
Binding,
  books, 237
  periodicals, 222
  See also Library binding
Biographee, 249
  call letters for, 145
Biographer,
  as author/critic, 42
  as editor/compiler, 41
  call letters for, 145
Biography, call numbers for, 145-*146*,
  148
Blanket orders, 13
Book cards, 210, *213*, 214, *229*, 249
  date due of items, 229
  filing, 229
  impromptu, 214-215, 230-231
  non-book items, *213*-214
  paperbacks, 210
Book catalogues, 203, 249
Book pockets, 209-210
  non-book items, *213*-214
Bookstores, 4, 5, 16
"Buying around," 9
Bynames, 51, 249

CAN/MARC, 31-32, 250
CIP, *26*, 30-*31*, 249
COM, 204, 250
Call letters, 144-146, 249
Call numbers, 143-150, 250
  books, *146*, 209
  labels, *213*, 214
  non-book items, 212, *213*, 214-217
  placement on card, *155*
*Canadian Companion, See Sears List of
  Subject Headings, Canadian
  Companion*
Canadian literature, classification, 149-
  150
Canadian Publishers Directory, 9, 94
Canadian Subject Headings, x, 125
  French headings in, 240
  use in CIP, 30

Canadiana, 5, 16, 60, 240
  serial number in CIP, 30
Capitalization,
  edition area, 89
  French, 240-242
  material (or type of publication)
    specific details area, 91
  note area, 117
  physical description area, 98
  publication, distribution, etc., area,
    94
  series area, 114
  standard number and terms of
    availability area, 120
  title and statement of responsibility
    area, 83-84
  title main entry heading, 63, 84
  uniform titles, 64
Card catalogue, organizing, 181-182
Cartographic materials, 250
  statement of projection, 92
  statement of scale, 91
  See also Globes; Maps
Cassettes, *See* Sound recordings
Catalogue cards,
  adapting commercial ones, 27-*29*, 30
  developed from CIP, *31*
  sample,
    level one, 79, *166*, *170*, *172*, *173*,
      174, *175*, *176*, *177*
    level two, *80*, *121*, *158*, *165*, *168*,
      169, *171*, *172*, *173*, *175*, *176*
  typing a set, 154-177
Cataloguing,
  aids and services, 24-31
  backlog, 25
  commercial, 24-30
  derived, *31*-32
  French, 27, 240-247
  networks, 27, 205
  standards, ix, xi, 35, 79
Centrale des bibliothèques, 27, 240
Character strings, 191, 250
Charging desk, 250
Charging tray, 250
Charts,
  physical description area, 97-99, 100-
    101, 106, 111
  processing, 212, 214, 216-217
  storage, 225

Chief source of information, 35-36, 80, 250
Circulation, 228-234
Class numbers, 143-144, 250
Classification, 138-151
Classification schedules, 138-139, 250
Clippings, 211-212, 223
Closed access, 220, 223
 reserve collections, 233-234
Collation, 81
 See also Physical description area
Collective titles, 40, 85, 250
 lack of collective title, 40-41, 85
 uniform titles, 68-69
Colour coding, 226
Commercial services, *See* Cataloguing;
 Processing
Compilers, 40
Components of an item, *See* Predominant component
Compound surnames, 48-49, 250
Computers,
 book catalogues, 203-204
 cataloguing, 27, 31-32, 203-205
 circulation control, 234
 computer output microform, 204
 filing, 191-196
 reference searching, 20
Concordances, *See* Related works
Conferences, 56
Confirmation orders, 13, 14
Contents notes, 118-119, *169*
Copyright date, 96-97
Corporate bodies, 250
 determining what are, 36
 one, 37-38
 two or three, with shared responsibility, 39
 four or more, with shared responsibility, 39-40
 statement of responsibility element, 87-88
 See also Attribution of authorship;
 Mixed responsibility, works of
Corporate names,
 direct word order, 54-55
 form, 53-54
 parenthetical distinctions after, 55
 "see" references, 196-198
 See also Conferences; Exhibitions;

Government bodies; Subordinate
 bodies
Cross references, *See* "See" references;
 "See also" references
Cuttering, 147, 250
 changes, *29*

Data bases, 20, 205, 250
Date cards, 228, 250
Dates,
 distinguishing between personal
 names, 47-48
 filing, 185, 190, 194
 See also Copyright date; Publication
 date
Deaccession, 236, 250
Deposit accounts, 15
Descriptors, 126, 250
Desiderata, 17, 250
Dewey Decimal Classification, x, 138-151
Dewey decimal numbers in *Sears*, 127
Dictionary catalogue, 181, 251
Dimension element, 107-114
Discounts, 7
Divided catalogue, 181-182, 251
Dummies, 226, 251
Dust-jacket covers, 209

ERIC, 20
Easy books, 251
 classification, 148
 shelf list, 202
 shelving, 221
Edition area, 81, 89-90, 251
Editions, changed,
 major modifications, 41-42
 minor modifications, 41
Editorial direction, works with, 40-41,
 165, 168
Elements, 80, 81, 251
 edition area, 89
 material (or type of publication)
 specific details area, 91
 note area, 117
 physical description area, 97-98
 publication, distribution, etc., area,
 93
 series area, 114

standard number and terms of availability area, 119
title and statement of responsibility area, 82-83
Encumbrances, 13, 251
End papers, 251
Entry, 251
Epithets, 51, 251
"see" references, 197
Et al., use of, 88
Exhibitions, 56
Extension cards, 163-164, *165, 167, 169,* 251
Extent of item element, 98-101

Facsimile reproductions, 120-*121*, 251
Fiction,
classification, 147-148
shelf list, 202
shelving, 220
Files,
bibliographic, 181-205
items desired, 6
items on order, 12
Filing, 181-204
according to 1968 ALA rules, 182-191
according to draft 1979 ALA rules, 191-196
French terms, 245-247
Films, film loops, *See* Motion pictures
Filmstrips,
accompanying literature, 214
physical description area, 97-99, 100-101, 103, 109, 111-113
processing, 212, *213*, 214
sample catalogue cards, *169, 170*
shelving, *219*, 223
First indention, *See* Indentions
Flyleaves, 209, 251
Foreign languages, *See* Language of
Free materials, 17
French,
commercial catalogue cards, 27, *29*
usage, 240-247
Front matter, 251

Galley proofs, 251
Games,
physical description area, 97-99, 100-101, 105-106, 107, 110-111, 113-114

processing, 212, 214-215, 217
sample catalogue card, *170*
storage, 225
General International Standard Bibliographic Description, *See* ISBD(G)
General material designation, 86, 251
after uniform titles, 67, *177*
filing, 182
list of standard GMD's, 86
General references, *See* References, general
Generic terms, 251
Geographic names, *See* Place names in headings
Given names only as headings, 51
Globes,
physical description area, 97-99, 100-101, 103, 107, 108-109, 111-113
processing, 212, 214-215, 217
storage, 225
Government bodies,
names entered directly, 60
names entered as subheadings, 58-60
parenthetical distinctions after names, 61-62
Government publications,
acquisition, 16
shelving, 222
Guide cards, 201, 251

Hanging indention, 62, *157, 158,* 251
Hard copy, 251
Headings, 35, 251
Holdings, 251
Hyphens,
compound surnames, 48
filing terms, 185, 186, 188, 192
French, 243

ISBD(G), 80, 251
ISBN, 120, 251
use in warehousing, 12
ISSN, 120
Illustrative matter, 101-103
Illustrators, 41, 45
Imprint, 81
See also Publication, distribution, etc., area

Indentions, 154, *155*, *156*, *157*, 251
  first indention, 251
  second indention, 253
  See also Hanging indention
Initials,
  academic degrees, 45-46
  denoting membership, 45-46
  filing, 183, 188, 193
  names, 45, 46, 47, 52, 53-54
International Standard Bibliographic
  Description, General, *See* ISBD(G)
Inventory, 235-236, 251
Invoices, 13-14

Jackdaws,
  physical description area, 97-99, 100-
    101, 113-114
  processing, 212, 214, 216
  sample catalogue card, *171*
  storage, 224-225
Jobbers, 6-9, 15, 252
  "buying around" at, 9
  periodicals, 17
  personal shopping at, 4-5

Kardex, *18*
  See also Periodical record cards
Kings, *See* Sovereigns
Kits, 252
  accompanying literature, *213*, 214
  physical description area, 97-99,
    113-114
  processing, 212, *213*, 214, 217
  sample catalogue card, *171*
  storage, 225
  See also Jackdaws; Multimedia items

LC AC program, 27, 252
  use in CIP, 30
Labels,
  call number, 209, 212, *213*
  non-book items, 212, *213*, 214
  protectors, 209, 214
  showing main entry, 215
  showing subject, 209
  showing title, 214
Lamination, 209, 212, 214
Language letters,
  call numbers, 147
  separate language collections, 221

Language of,
  authors' names, 46-47
  works with uniform titles, 66-67
Laws, uniform titles for, 70-71
Leader, 215, 252
Leaves, 252
Legal size, 252
Legends, cycles of, 70
Levels of description, 79-80, 81
  edition area, 89
  material (or type of publication)
    specific details area, 91
  note area, 117
  physical description area, 97
  publication, distribution, etc., area,
    93
  series area, 114
  standard number and terms of
    availability area, 119
  title and statement of responsibility
    area, 82-83
Library binding, 25, 237, 252
Library networks, 252
  cataloguing, 27
  cataloguing standards, ix, xi, 35
  reference services, 20
Library of Congress,
  CIP service, 30
  catalogue card service, 25-27, *29*
  classification, 151
  MARC program, 31-32, 205
Library of Congress Subject Headings,
  125
  use in CIP, 30
Librettos, 75
Loan periods, 232-233
Location indicator in call number, 147,
  252
Loose-leaf services, 19

MARC, 27, 31-32, 205, 252
"Mac" and "Mc,"
  call letters, 144
  filing, 187
Main entry (card), 154-157, 252
Main entry headings, 35-76
  labels, 214
  personal or corporate, 155-*156*
  placement on card, 155-157
  title, 156-*157*

Manuel pratique de classement, 245
Maps,
  physical description area, 97-98, 100-101, 103, 108-109
  processing, 212, 214, 216-217
  sample catalogue card, *172*
  storage, 225
Married women's names, 48, 51
Material (or type of publication) specific details area, 81, 90-93
Medium of performance (music), 73-74, 252
Metric units,
  dimension elements, 107-111
  vs. Imperial, 105, 107
Microfiches,
  COM, 204
  vertical file material, 212, 216
Microforms, 252
  periodicals, 216
  physical description area, 98-99, 100-101, 103-104, 109
  processing, 212, 214, 216
  storage, 224
  vertical file material, 212, 216
  See also Microfiches
Mixed responsibility, works of, 41-45, 252
Models,
  physical description area, 97-99, 100-101, 105-106, 110-111
  processing, 212, 214, 217
  sample catalogue card, *172*
  storage, 225
Modifications of works, *See* Mixed responsibility, works of
Monographs, 252
Motion pictures,
  physical description area, 97-99, 100-101, 104, 109
  processing, 212, 214, 216
  sample catalogue card, *173*
  shelving, 224
Multimedia items, physical description area for,
  no predominant component (kit), 113-114, *213*
  one predominant component, 111-113
  See also Jackdaws; Kits
Multiple-copy order forms, *11*-12

Music, uniform titles for, 72-76
  keys, 74
  medium of performance, terms for, 73-74
  opus and thematic index numbers, 74
Musical works of mixed responsibility, 43-44

Name added entries, 160, 162
Name analytics, 160, 163
Names, personal,
  dates with, 47-48
  entry element, 47-53
  filing, 187-188, 194-195
  form, 45-47
  French, 49, 245-247
  non-English, 46-47, 49, 52
  parenthetical distinctions after, 47, 53
  "see" references, 196-197, *199*
  unusual, 52-53
  See also Bynames; Compound surnames; Epithets; Given names only as headings; Nicknames; Pseudonyms; Titled names; Popes; Saints; Sovereigns
National bibliographies, 252
  See also Canadiana
National Library of Canada,
  CAN/MARC program, 31-32
  CIP service, 30, 205
  See also Canadiana
Networks, *See* Library networks
Newspapers, 211, 223
Nicknames, 46, 51
Notes (note area), 81, 117-119, 252
Numerals,
  in call numbers, 145, 147
  filing, 185, 194
  See also Dates

On-order files, 12, 252
Open entry, *158, 165*, 252
Ordering of materials,
  AV items, 16-17
  centralized vs. decentralized, 9-10
  files for, 6
  forms for, *11*, 12, *26*
  frequency, 10
  free materials, 17

government publications, 16
out-of-print items, 6
paperbacks, 15
periodicals, 17-19
reference items, 3
remainders, 16
See also Back orders; Blanket orders;
   Confirmation orders; Deposit
   accounts; Purchase orders;
   Standing orders; Subscriptions;
   Year-end procedures
Other physical details element, 101-107
illustrative matter, 101-103
non-book, 103-107
Other title information element, 87,
252
Out-of-print items, 252
acquisition, 6
reporting, 9
service charge, 7
Overdue items, 233
Oversize items, 218, 221
Ownership, marks of, 208, 212, 217-218

PRECIS, 126
Packing slips, 13-14
Pagination, 99-100
Pamphlets accompanying AV items,
   cataloguing, 111-114
processing, 212, *213*
sample catalogue cards, *169, 170, 171*
storage, 214
Pamphlets as monographic items,
   physical description area, 97-100,
      102-103, 107-108
See also Vertical files
Paperbacks,
acquisition, 15
processing, 208, 210
shelving, 221
Parallel title element, 84, 87, 253
Performer as main entry heading, 44
Periodical indexes, 253
processing, 210-211
shelving, 222
Periodical record cards, *18, 19,* 210, 253
Periodicals,
accessioning, *18, 19*
circulation, 231-232

claiming, 19
microform, 222
storage, 222-223
subscriptions, 17-19
See also Serials
Personal names, *See* Names, personal
Petty cash, 10, 15
Physical description area, 81, 97-114
Picture books, 253
Pictures,
physical description area, 97-99, 100-
   101, 106-107, 111
processing, 212, 214, 216
sample catalogue card, *174*
storage, 224-225
See also Illustrative matter
Place names in headings, 58-62
Place of publication element, 94-95
Popes, 51
Posters,
physical description area, 97-98, 100-
   101, 107, 111
processing, 212, 214, 216-217
storage, 225
Predominant component,
none, 113-114
one, 111-113
Previewing AV items, 7, 16-17
Price,
terms of availability element, 120
accession data, 14, 157-*158*
Prime marks (primes), 142-143
Princeton files, 222, 253
Processing, 208-218, 253
commercial, 24-30
Pseudonyms, 49-50
Publication date, 96-97
in call number, 147
Publication, distribution, etc., area, 81,
93-97
Publishers, producers, etc., 95-96
French names, 244
Punctuation,
description of work, general statement, 82
edition area, 89
material (or type of publication)
   specific details area, 91
note area, 117
physical description area, 97-98

publication, distribution, etc., area, 93-94

series area, 114

standard number and terms of availability area, 119

title and statement of responsibility area, 83

Purchase orders, 13-14

Queens, *See* Sovereigns

Quill & Quire, 5, 9

Realia, 253
  physical description area, 97-99, 105-106, 110-111
  processing, 212, 214, 217
  storage, 225
Rebinding, 237
Records (discs), *See* Sound recordings
Reference items,
  acquisition, 3
  call numbers, 147
  circulation, 232
  classification, 148
  shelf list, 202
  shelving, 221
Reference searches by computer, 20
References, general, *183, 184*, 200, *212*
  filing, 183, 184, 196
  tracing, 200-201
  See also "See" references; "See also" references
Related bodies, 56-58, 253
Related works, 45, 253
Remainders, 16, 253
  foreign editions, 9
Renewal of loan period, 232
Repairing materials, 237
Répertoire de vedettes-matières, 125-126, 240
  use in CIP, 30
Reporting on orders, 7, *8*, 9, 11
Reprints, 16, 253
  facsimile, 120-*121*
Reserved items, 230, 233-234
Revised editions, *See* Edition area; Editions, changed
Reviser, 41-42
Romanization, 46-47, 197, 253
Routing, 231, 253

SDI, *See* Selective dissemination of information (SDI)
SI, 107
  See also Metric units
Saints, 51
  filing, 188, 195
Sample catalogue cards, *See* Catalogue cards, sample
Schedules, *See* Classification schedules
School boards,
  centralized film collections, 224
  collating periodical orders, 19
  ordering procedures, 9-10
Scriptures, uniform titles for, 71-72
Sears List of Subject Headings, x, 125, 127-135
  vertical files, 211
Sears List of Subject Headings, Canadian Companion, x, 125, 127-135
  vertical files, 211
Second indention, *See* Indentions
Security of collection, 208, 212, 217-218, 220
"See also" references, 253
  filing, 187, 196
  purpose, 198
  Sears, 127-128
  tracing, 200-201
  typing, 198-*199*
  See also References, general
"See" references, 253
  filing, 187, 196
  purpose, 196-198
  Sears, 127-128
  tracing, 200-201
  typing, 198-*199*
  See also References, general
Selection, *See* Acquisition
Selection tools, 3
"Selections" as uniform title, 68, 69, 76
Selective dissemination of information (SDI), 20, 253
Sequels, *See* Related works
Serials, 253
  numerical, alphabetical and chronological designations, 92-93
  See also Open entry; Periodicals
Series (series area), 81, 114-116, 254

Series added entries, 159
  filing, 190, 195
  tracing, 161, 162, *168*, *170*, *176*
  typing, 162-163, *167*
Shakespeare, classification of, 150
Shared responsibility, works of, 39-40, 254
Shelf list, 254
  filing, 201-202
  shelving order, 220-221
  tool in inventory, 235
Shelf list card, 157-*158*, *166*, 254
  weeding collection, 236
Shelf reading, 254
Shelving the collection, 218-225
  integration of media, 218, *219*, 220
Shorts, 254
  reporting on, 7, *8*, 9
Signage, 225-226
Sine loco, 95
Sine nomine, 96
Slides,
  physical description area, 97-99, 100-101, 105, 110
  processing, 212, 214, 217
  sample catalogue card, *175*
  storage, 225
Sound recordings,
  music, 72-76
  performer as main entry heading, 44
  physical description area, 97-99, 100-101, 105, 110
  processing, 212, *213*, 214, 215-216
  sample catalogue cards, *175*, *176*, *177*
  shelving, 218, 220, 223-224
Sovereigns, 51
  filing names, 188, 194-195
  "see" reference, 197
Specific material designation, 254
  list of typical designations, 98-99
Spelling,
  filing variants, 186
  subject headings, 128
Spine, 254
Square brackets, use, of,
  approximate dates, 97
  description of the work, 80
  GMD, 86
  main entry heading, 36

physical description area, 99-100
publication distribution, etc., area, 94-97
title and statement of responsibility area, 85-88
uniform title, 64
Stacks, 254
Staff,
  loan periods, 233
  routing of materials for, 231
  suggestions for acquisition, 4
Stamping, *See* Accession numbers; Ownership, marks of; Weeding
Standard number and terms of availability area, 81, 119-120, 254
Standing orders, 13
Statement of responsibility element, 254
  relating to edition, 90
  with title, 87-88
Study prints,
  physical description area, 97-99, 100, 107, 111
  processing, 212, 214, 216
  sample catalogue card, *174*
  storage, 224
Subject analytics, 133-134, 159, 163
Subject headings, 124-135, 254
  English-French lists, 240
  filing, 189, 190, 195-196
  French authority, 125-126
  placement on cards, *162*, *167*
  tracing, 160, 162, *167*
  type face, *162*
Subject subdivisions, 130-132
Subordinate bodies, 254
  determining what are, 36-37
  names entered directly, 57-58
  names entered subordinately, 56-57
  subheadings, 58, 61
  See also Government bodies
Subscriptions,
  books, 15
  periodicals, 17, 19
Subseries, 116
Subtitle, 81
  See also Other title information element
Supplements, *See* Related works

Tape recordings, *See* Sound recordings

Teachers' guides, *See* Pamphlets accompanying AV items
Technical services, 1
Terms of availability element, 120
Textbooks, 210
Thematic index numbers, 74, 254
Thesauri, 126, 254
Title added entries, 159
    filing, 189, 195
    tracing, 160-161, 162
    typing, 162-163, *167*
Title analytics, 159, 163, *176*
Title and statement of responsibility area, 81, 82-88
Title as main entry, 62-63
    capitalization of second word, 63, 84
    hanging indention with, 62, *157, 158*
    labels, 214
    when to use, 63
    See also Uniform titles
Title frames, 80, 254
Title of address, 50-51, 254
    See also Titled names
Title of honour, 50-51, 254
    See also Titled names
Title page, 80, 254
Title proper, 84-86, 254
Titled names, 50-51, 87
    filing, 188, 195
Toys,
    physical description area, 97-99, 100-101, 105, 110-111
    processing, 212, 214, 217
    storage, 225
Tracings, 158-162, 200-201, 254
Translations/translators, 41, 65-69

Transliteration, 46-47, 197, 254
Transparencies,
    physical description area, 97-99, 100-101, 106, 111
    processing, 212, 214, 216
    storage, 224-225
Typewriters for libraries, 164

Uncatalogued materials,
    cards for, 211-*212*, 214
    circulation, 230-231
    See also Vertical files
Uniform titles, 63-76, 254
    capitalization, 64
    filing, 186
    form, 64
    language, 66-67, 72
Union catalogues, 255
Unit cards, 154, 255

Verso of title page, 35, 80, 255
Vertical files, 211-212, 255
    circulation, 230-231
    microfiche, 212, 216
    shelving, 223, 224
Videorecordings,
    performer as main entry heading, 44
    physical description area, 97-99, 100-101, 104, 109
    processing, 212, 214, 217

Weeding, 236
Wholesalers, *See* Jobbers
"Works" as uniform title, 68, 69, 76

Year-end procedures, 10-11

About the Authors

Marilyn H. Kogon lives in Toronto and is a teacher-librarian with the North York Board of Education. She is a member of the editorial boards of *Canadian Materials* and *Canadian Library Journal,* and is a trustee on the North York Public Library Board. She has given many workshops for Ontario school librarians, in addition to teaching a summer course.

George Whalen is a librarian and education officer at the Ministry of Education in Sudbury, Ontario. He also teaches summer courses sponsored by the Ministry of Education to elementary school librarians in Ontario and has been the principal of several of them.